Democracy
and Public
Administration

Democracy
and Public
Administration

Edited by Richard C. Box

M.E.Sharpe
Armonk, New York
London, England

Library of Congress Cataloging-in-Publication Data

Democracy and public administration / edited by Richard C. Box.
   p. cm.
 Includes bibliographical references and index.
 ISBN-13: 978-0-7656-1815-3 (cloth: alk. paper); ISBN-13: 978-0-7656-1701-9 (pbk.: alk. paper)
 ISBN-10: 0-7656-1815-X (cloth: alk. paper);   ISBN-10: 0-7656-1701-3 (pbk.: alk. paper)
1. Public administration. 2. Democracy. I. Box, Richard C.

JF1351.D44 2006
351—dc22   2006015455

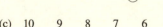

Contents

**Introduction: The Importance of Democracy for
Public Administration**
    Richard C. Box   vii

1. **Democracy and Public Service**
    Mary R. Hamilton   3

2. **Democracy, Public Administrators, and Public Policy**
    Dale Krane   21

3. **A Brief Tour of Public Organization Theory
in the United States**
    Gary S. Marshall   40

4. **Citizens, Citizenship, and Democratic Governance**
    Cheryl Simrell King   64

5. **Democracy, Public Participation, and Budgeting:
Mutually Exclusive or Just Exhausting?**
    Aimee L. Franklin and *Carol Ebdon*   84

6. **Citizen Participation in Performance Measurement**
    Alfred T. Ho   107

7. **Democracy and the "Republican Revival"
in Administrative Law**
    Christine M. Reed   119

8. **En-gendering Democracy: A Feminist Perspective
on the Body Politic**
    Janet R. Hutchinson   131

 9. **Democratic Administration in a Multicultural Environment**
    Mohamad G. Alkadry   150

10. **Nonprofit Organizations, Philanthropy, and Democracy
    in the United States**
    Angela M. Eikenberry   169

11. **The Public Service Practitioner as Agent of Social Change**
    Richard C. Box   194

About the Editor and Contributors   213
Index   217

Introduction

The Importance of Democracy for Public Administration

Richard C. Box

Democracy has always been a central topic in American public affairs. The term can be heard in descriptions of decisions made by local public bodies ("the process used by the city council at the meeting last night wasn't democratic!"), it is often applied to elections ("the result was democratic because the election was conducted fairly"), and it is found in discussion of foreign relations ("we want the people of that region to live in democracy and freedom"). It can be used by people whose intent is to promote greater freedom and self-governance, and by people who use the word democracy as justification for undemocratic actions ("it was necessary to restrict individual freedoms to protect democracy").

Though (or perhaps because) the word democracy is used often and in a wide range of circumstances, what people mean when they use it can be unclear. It literally means "rule by the people," but in practice it may describe a particular way elected leaders are chosen, the way people behave during discussion of public issues, the extent to which people can make certain choices without interference from others, from government, or from corporations, the extent of personal opportunity or well-being, and so on. . . . This lack of definitional clarity has not diminished the relevance of the concept. Instead, conditions such as increasing inequality of wealth and opportunity within and between nations, international war and violence, unsustainable public spending, and environmental degradation make democracy and democratic decision-making especially important. Today, many people feel a heightened sense that democracy is more than an abstraction dealt with in political science courses. It is a valued ideal that can be threatened by forces from without or within; it is a system that can be used for good or bad purposes, and it is a difficult topic to avoid when we think about or discuss government and public affairs.

The practice of public administration in the United States is set within the context of a *liberal-capitalist, representative democracy.* "Liberal" means a society that values individual freedoms; this was the meaning of the term from the beginning of the nation until the middle of the twentieth century, when it came to mean big government and spending on social welfare programs. By "capitalist" we mean a society in which competitive pursuit of economic gain through investment of capital is a central organizing principle, and by "representative" we mean a democracy in which decision-makers are not the people themselves, but those they elect to public office.

The missions, structures, and administrative practices thought to be appropriate in public organizations are significantly influenced by the values held by the people in a society. Public service in a liberal-capitalist society can be particularly challenging, because people want effective and efficient government but they are also skeptical about the public sector and want to control and constrain actions taken by public administrators. There are nations in which the public sector is granted considerable respect and leeway in performing its duties, but in the United States concern for individual freedom places government and its workers in an ambivalent, uncertain situation. This is especially true because government cannot be run only from the top down. The knowledge and expertise of public service practitioners are needed not only to carry out directives from elected governing bodies, but to assist decision-makers in understanding conditions on the ground and the complexities of governmental operations. Practitioners who take an active part in shaping public policy in addition to implementing it may be regarded as violating common understandings of the role of public professionals. This makes it important for them to know about democracy as an ideal and their place in a society that values a particular sort of democracy.

We often tend to think of American founding values as relatively simple, resulting in a straightforward process of creating our form of government, but that is inaccurate. Instead, the period between the American Revolution (1775–1781) and the ratification of the Constitution in 1788 was one of turmoil and heated debate between people with a variety of views. People disagreed about whether to have a stronger national government; there was also tension between those who had wealth and those who did not, disagreements between people in rural and more settled areas and between states, and so on. The governmental system that was created with the ratification of the Constitution was the product of conflict, dialogue, and compromise, not of consensus. Democracy was not a goal in that period; the word suggested social disorder to the founding generation and it was not commonly used until the nineteenth century. Instead, words such as *liberty* and *freedom* were used to describe some of the ideas we now associate with democracy for individuals, and *republic* was used to refer to a governmental unit organized and governed with the consent of the people.

We recognize the ideal of democracy in the Declaration of Independence, and founding-era figures such as Thomas Jefferson were committed to citizen self-determination. However, many government leaders of that era held a somewhat limited view of who should be involved in governance. There were property requirements for voting and it was assumed in many cases, from the local to the national level, that society would be governed by an elite. The nineteenth century was a time of expansion of democracy as property qualifications for voting faded, the national government became more responsive to public will, local governments were restructured to allow greater citizen involvement in policy making, and there was relatively frequent citizen resistance (sometimes violent) to public policies and actions.

Toward the end of the nineteenth century, industrialization and urbanization changed the way many people lived and worked. The Jeffersonian ideal of a rural citizenry consisting of independent farmers and craftspeople—a parallel to the citizenship practices of ancient Athens—was increasingly replaced by work in factories or other private enterprises. For many people, work and private life became separated and work was performed for the profit of others. This change was facilitated by the rise of large companies, making the ideal of democracy more complicated. No longer a matter only of the relationship between citizens and government, democracy was also a matter of the influence of private sector firms on individual lives. Companies controlled transportation costs, causing hardship to farmers, ranchers, and others who shipped their goods by rail, they manipulated the prices of essential goods, they prevented workers from organizing to bargain on wages and working conditions, they worked adults and children long hours in circumstances that were often dirty or dangerous, and they influenced which politicians were elected and the decisions they made while in office.

In the late nineteenth century and especially in the twentieth century, government became active in moderating the effects of the private sector on individuals and the economy through regulation of private firms and by direct assistance to individuals. The professional public service grew at all levels of government, and career practitioners became deeply involved in the processes of creating and implementing public policies. Interest developed in the *politics-administration* relationship because in a democratic society grounded in the concept of individual freedom, the idea of rule by unelected administrators can generate citizen concern.

There are four basic concepts about government and democracy that we should discuss before introducing the chapters of the book. One is the distinction between *procedural democracy*, in which people have equal rights to participate in the economic and public life of society (this is the question of *equality of opportunity*), and *substantive democracy*, in which society considers to what extent it will allow inequalities of wealth, power, and privilege (this is the question of *equality of outcome*, *situation*, or *circumstances*). For many public service practitioners, opportunities to influence procedural or substantive democracy are limited. However, there are times when practitioners are able to help people deal with the complexities of government or participate in decision-making. They may also work to reduce unfairness in the distribution of services or resources and influence policy formulation in ways that fulfill their beliefs about public service.

The second concept is about who makes decisions on public matters. Except in a small governmental unit or a neighborhood, it is difficult for all citizens to decide all issues, so instead a few people are elected for this purpose. This is a *representative democracy* and it may be contrasted with a situation in which it is possible for most citizens to participate in decision-making if they choose. This is a *direct democracy*, found mostly in smaller communities or in citizen organizations in larger communities. The initiative and referendum processes found in some states are another type of direct democracy (all people have an opportunity to vote on a public matter), though they are different in kind from personal participation in debate and decision-making.

The third concept is closely related to the second—it is levels of government. In many local governments, there is an expectation that ordinary citizens can participate in public decision-making by running for office, volunteering to serve on boards and committees, speaking at public meetings, and participating in civic organizations and neighborhood groups. This becomes more difficult at the state level. The national government was not created to facilitate citizen involvement (indeed, the intent of the founders was to insulate the national government from the irrational passions of the masses), and in today's large and complex society most of us could not be direct participants even if we wanted to be. So, democracy can mean different things depending on the level of government. Giving citizens information about and access to public decision-making or acting in the interests of citizens for whom participation is not feasible can be challenging for public service practitioners under any circumstances, but in larger organizations and "higher" levels of government it can be especially difficult.

The fourth concept is the structural form of units of government. In the United States, national and state governments use a *separation of powers* model in which the legislative, executive, and judicial branches are separate and each has prescribed powers. This model is designed to prevent accumulation of excessive power by a single person or branch of government. There are several forms of government at the local level. To simplify, the *mayor-council* model and its variations have separation-of-powers characteristics. The mayor is the chief executive officer and holds powers separate from those of the governing body, the city council (for example, the mayor may appoint certain officials with or without council approval, the mayor may veto acts of the council, and the mayor may have a separate personal staff).

The *council-manager* model and its variations unify policy-making authority in a governing council that oversees implementation through a hired career professional. In this model, the mayor and council are part of a single legislative body in which few powers are separated; the professional manager or administrator is responsible for daily operations rather than the mayor. This model was devised in the early twentieth century to bring businesslike efficiency to government.

A form of local government dating from earliest settlement of the nation is the *town meeting* model, still used in some New England communities. It provides direct democracy in the form of periodic town meetings at which any resident can participate in decision-making. Finally, a form that is used today in relatively few cities is the *commission* model, in which department heads are elected to form the local governing body. These forms of local government have been developed over the history of the nation in response to citizen desires for a public sector that is both democratic, in the sense of responding to public will, and efficient and effective. Sometimes, people think that one form or the other is more responsive or more efficient and effective; for our purposes here, the point is that governmental structure is often used in the search for democracy.

Contents of the Book

This book, *Democracy and Public Administration*, is about the importance of the idea of democracy to public administration. The format of the book is much like that of the typical introductory textbook in public administration, addressing practical administrative topics such as budgeting and finance, policy, and citizen participation. However, each of the topics is approached through the "lens" of democracy, by an author who has conducted research on her or his topic from this perspective. Also, chapters are included that address relatively new or emergent topics in public administration.

Mary R. Hamilton provides an appropriate beginning for the book in Chapter 1, describing the tension between democracy and public service. She writes that "public service in a democracy is a paradox," because public service and democracy are bound together yet have different purposes and values. As a result,

> Public service and democracy are antithetical yet complementary. They
> are antithetical because the existence of a public service in a democracy
> contradicts the notion of government by the people. They are complemen-
> tary because democracies cannot survive without a strong, technically com-
> petent, effective, efficient, and responsive public service.

This passage identifies the central question to be addressed by a book
about democracy and public administration: In a society with a large, multi-
level, complicated governmental system, how can democracy be maintained?
What can public service practitioners do to facilitate access by citizens to the
policy-making process, providing meaningful opportunities for citizens to
make decisions about what government does and how it does it?

The next five chapters each address a key topical area in public administration. These topical areas, and chapter authors, are: policy making (Dale
Krane); administrative theory and behavior (Gary S. Marshall); citizen involvement in governing (Cheryl Simrell King); budgeting (Aimee L. Franklin
and Carol Ebdon); and assessing governmental performance (Alfred T. Ho).
There are other topical areas that might have been included, but each of these
is crucial to the field. These chapters were written by scholars who have
thought deeply about the relationship of these topical areas to democracy. In
each chapter, the reader will find a summary of knowledge about the topic
and also the author's analysis of current issues and trends central to the practice of public administration in a democracy.

The final five chapters discuss focused areas of public administration research and practice, including cutting-edge themes and challenges relevant
for people who work at all levels in public organizations. These themes, and
chapter authors, are: greater democracy in administrative law (Christine M.
Reed); feminist perspectives on democracy (Janet R. Hutchinson); the
multicultural environment of public administration (Mohamad G. Alkadry);
the relationship of the nonprofit sector, government, and democracy (Angela
M. Eikenberry); and the role of the public service practitioner in social change
(Richard C. Box).

All the authors in this volume believe that democracy today is an especially important and pressing matter in the field of public administration. Each
of us has given considerable thought to this question, and a number of us have
also grappled with it as public service practitioners. We hope this book may
contribute to a more democratic society by inspiring readers to think about
and act on the idea that democracy is central to public administration.

Democracy
and Public
Administration

Democracy and Public Service

Mary R. Hamilton

That public service in a democracy is a paradox has been and continues to be a central issue in public administration. Democracies cannot survive without a strong, technically competent, effective, efficient, and responsive public service, but the existence of such a public service contradicts the democratic notion of government by the people. Even in a representative democracy, the contradiction applies since the public service is three steps removed from the people (Mosher, 1982, p. 5). It is fair to say that public service and democracy are both antithetical and complementary (Berkley & Rouse, 2004, p. 99).

There is also no generally accepted theory or model of public administration for American democratic government. Neither the United States Constitution nor other documents related to the founding of the nation provide a model for an administrative component in government. The Constitution specifies a goal of providing for the common defense and producing other public goods, but it says little or nothing about contemporary issues such as providing for the social, economic, and physical well-being of the populace (Ingraham & Rosenbloom, 1990, pp. 211–212).

Scholars have proposed models and/or theories of the appropriate role of public administration in American representative democracy. (Examples include: Ostrom, 1987; Price, 1983; Rohr, 1986; Stillman, 1990.) These proposed theories/models provide very different answers to the question of the role of public administration in the American system, and none has achieved the status of being accepted across the fields of public administration, political science, and/or public policy.

The paradox and lack of a generally accepted administrative model for the public service in our democracy create a set of dilemmas for citizens, elected officials, and public administrators. All have to be concerned with the need for balance between a strong public service and a strong nation based on democratic principles.

Given its centrality as an issue for scholars and practitioners alike, the democracy–public service paradox has been studied extensively. The purpose of this chapter is to introduce the reader to the paradox, briefly explore the resulting body of literature, and summarize suggested approaches to ensuring that public service supports democratic values and principles while also effectively and efficiently administering public organizations and programs.

In the first section of the chapter, I describe the changes in the relationship between public service and democracy in the United States over time and with differing dominant political perspectives. Second, I explore the paradox— the antithetical and complementary aspects of the relationship between public service and democracy—and argue that a strong but circumscribed public service is critical to a healthy, stable democracy. Third, I describe how a public service can be developed that promotes and supports democratic principles and values. Finally, I summarize the roles and responsibilities that American citizens and elected officials have come to expect of public administrators in a democracy.

Differing Perspectives on the Relationship of Public Service and Democracy

The relationship between public service and democracy in the United States has changed since the founding of the nation, and it has differed over the years based on which political perspective was dominant at the time. A brief look at the history of public service in the United States shows how the relationship between democracy and public service has developed and changed. Frederick Mosher, in his classic book, *Democracy and the Public Service*, uses five historical periods to make this point (Mosher, 1982, chap. 3). His categories provide a useful framework for summarizing these historical changes.

Government by Gentlemen, 1789–1829

From the founding of the nation through the early part of the nineteenth century, public service in the United States was dominated by elites—well-educated white men of high social standing. Two categories of personnel made up this first public service: the elites, who were the cabinet members and other high-ranking officials; and the behind-the-scenes workers, who staffed the offices in the capital and across the nation and were largely drawn from the middle and upper-middle classes (Mosher, 1982, pp. 61–64). The elites were highly visible and "exercised significant influence in the making of public policy and had significant responsibility for its execution" (Mosher, 1982, p. 61).

During this period, there was limited citizen participation in politics and ambivalence about the neutrality of public servants. There was also no distinct split between politics and administration. Also during this period, persons in public office were held to high moral standards, and upper-level officials were held in high esteem (Mosher, 1982, pp. 60, 80).

Government by the Common Man, 1829–1883

The second period, from 1829 to 1883, is commonly identified with Jacksonian democracy and the spoils system. The egalitarian ideology that drove the period preached "equal opportunity for public appointment, subject to party loyalty" based on the "doctrine of the simplicity of public work" (Mosher, 1982, p. 65). That doctrine held that government work was simple and could be performed effectively by any person of intelligence (Mosher, 1982, pp. 64–66, 80). The result of applying this doctrine during the nineteenth century was a reduction of the influence of the elites and an increase in the presence of middle- and lower-class people in the public service. However, the ideology also produced a technically less competent public service, widespread corruption, and a decline in the prestige of the public service (Mosher, 1982, pp. 64–66, 81).

Government by the Good, 1883–1906

The late 1800s through the early 1900s was a period when, because of the incompetence, graft, favoritism, and partisanship of the previous period (Stillman, 2000, p. 195), civil service reform was a top priority, so important that some saw it "as a *moral* imperative" (Mosher, 1982, p. 81). The Pendleton Act, passed in 1883, established the first civil service system in the United States. The system was based on merit, employing competitive examinations for entrance into public service, and promoting political neutrality of public employees "and with it the separation of policy and politics from administration" (Mosher, 1982, p. 81). The system was also "open," meaning that entry into the public service was "possible at all levels" (Mosher, 1982, p. 81).

Although the Pendleton Act applied to the federal government, state and local governments soon followed suit and established their own civil service systems to combat graft and corruption at their levels. The Pendleton Act, together with the Progressive and Scientific Management movements during this period, gave rise to a number of innovations in the public service, among them city management (Ingraham & Rosenbloom, 1990, p. 213).

Government by the Efficient, 1906–1937

The period from 1906 to 1937 emphasized efficiency in government operations based on scientific management. During this period, efficiency replaced civil service reform as the moral imperative (Mosher, 1982, p. 81). Cities were the first government entities to use scientific management to combat corruption and improve efficiency in their basic systems and services. Bureaus of municipal research grew up to promote and support this movement. Scientific management was also applied to personnel management at all levels of government and resulted in position classification based on systematic standardization of jobs and proliferation of specializations in government (Mosher, 1982, pp. 79–80, 81).

The marriage of public administration and scientific management created problems. During this period, the leaders of public administration were constantly working to reconcile efficiency with democracy (Mosher, 1982, p. 78). Scientific management also reinforced the "separation of politics and policy from the work of administration" (Mosher, 1982, p. 82).

Government by Managers, 1937-present

In the late 1930s, administrative management replaced efficiency as the ideological emphasis, but efficiency continued to be a goal of government. The Great Depression pushed government to assume a proactive role in managing society and the economy. The New Deal and World War II strengthened this new role of government. With the new role came requirements for different skills and competencies in the public service. Administrators now needed to be "politically sensitive and knowledgeable" as well as technically and managerially competent (Mosher, 1982, pp. 83–84).

The Roosevelt administration saw the public service as "an extension of the chief executive" and "viewed federal employees as having legitimate roles in policy making" because they were extensions of the executive and under executive control (Ingraham & Rosenbloom, 1990, p. 213). As a result, support for separating politics/policy and administration waned during this period (Gawthrop, 1998; Ingraham & Rosenbloom, 1990; Mosher, 1982).

The 1970s brought the Watergate scandal and its ripple effects on government. Mosher (1982) cites the negative impact on the public service of the scandal. He says the events raise serious questions for career public administrators; for example: should a government employee "take and execute instructions from above regardless of their wisdom, their legality, their morality? Should the political and hierarchical ethic take precedence over all other norms—of conscience, or of personal or family or professional or religious allegiancies?" (Mosher, 1982, p. 109). These questions continue to challenge public employees.

Concern about these issues led to a major reform of the federal civil service during the late 1970s. The main thrust of the reforms "was *management:* more flexible management; better motivated management; rewards and penalties for good or bad management; development and selection of better managers; more innovative management" (Mosher, 1982, p. 107).

Since the early 1990s, governments at all levels in the United States have attempted to reduce their workforces and streamline their processes in an effort to reduce costs and improve efficiency. Toward the same objectives governments have also pursued outsourcing and privatization of previously government functions. All of these efforts have shown mixed results, and use of these approaches continues to be controversial. Those who believe in smaller, less intrusive government and government that operates more like business applaud the approaches and find them refreshing and entrepreneurial. Others find the trends produced by these approaches troubling and fear that they are eroding democratic values in the name of efficiency.

The Paradox of a Strong Public Service in a Democracy

In spite of the paradox that public service presents for a democracy and the variety of perspectives on the legitimacy and proper scope of the public service, few would disagree with an observation credited to George Washington, that "the successful administration of government is an object of almost infinite consequence to the present and future happiness of the citizens of the United States." However, in keeping with the paradox, scholars over the years have expressed concern about the dangers that a strong public service poses for a democracy.

Democracy and Public Service Are Antithetical

There have been many arguments over the years that a strong public service is a threat to democracy. In *Democracy in America*, Alexis de Tocqueville cautioned in 1835 that as a democratic people become more equal, government "covers the whole of social life with a network of petty, complicated rules that are both minute and uniform" and by so doing it "hinders, restrains, enervates, stifles, and stultifies so much that in the end each nation is no more than a flock of timid and hardworking animals with the government as its shepherd (Tocqueville, 1969, p. 692). More recently, scholars have echoed Tocqueville and stressed the risk that government expansion (i.e., expansion of the public service) will result in citizens becoming more and

more dependent on government and less and less likely to actively participate in their own governance (Nigro & Richardson, 1987, pp. 102–103).

Mosher (1982) also emphasizes the antithetical nature of public service
and democracy. He writes about the public service being three steps removed
from direct democracy. This leads Mosher to pose several critical questions
for a democracy:

> How does one square a permanent civil service—which neither the people
> by their vote nor their representatives by their appointments can readily
> replace—with the principle of government "by the people"? (p. 7) . . . How
> can a public service so constituted be made to operate in a manner compat-
> ible with democracy? How can we be assured that a highly differentiated
> body of public employees will act in the interests of all the people, will be
> an instrument of all the people? (p. 5)

Because he sees public service as essential to the functioning of a democracy, Mosher spends the balance of his book discussing approaches to address these questions.

Democracy and Public Service Are Complementary

Although the arguments for being wary of a strong public service are compelling, so are the arguments that a strong public service is vital for a strong
democracy.

John Kirlin (2001, p. 142) makes the case in a very inspiring way when he
asserts that "public administration is a central part of the grandest of human
endeavors—shaping a better future for ourselves and those yet unborn." He
argues that the results of public administration have worldwide impact: "The
institutions crafted to achieve human aspirations require administration. . . . The
measure of success is . . . in its enduring value not only to those in a particular
nation, state, or city but worldwide to all who aspire for improved lives."

A different approach to this argument is represented by the comparative
political scientist Ezra Suleiman (2003). Suleiman contends that the public
service "is the instrument by which a democracy can strengthen or weaken
its legitimacy, [therefore] its absence or inefficiency or politicization can
have extraordinary effects on the governance of society" (Suleiman, 2003, p.
24). Because he believes strongly in the importance of a strong public service for a strong democracy, Suleiman is very disturbed by what he terms the
"relentless attacks on and denigration of" the professional public service
over the past two decades in almost all democratic societies (Suleiman, 2003,
p. 2). These attacks have taken the form of de-professionalization of the pub-

lic service (i.e., replacing career professional public employees with political appointees), increasing political control of the public service, questioning the legitimacy of the public service, and denigrating the quality of the people and products of the public service. Suleiman believes that these vicious attacks "have helped to undermine politics, political involvement, and citizenship" (Suleiman, 2003, p. 4).

Making Public Service Safe for Democracy

In spite of the paradox of a public service in a democracy, no democratic nation can function without a public service. Therefore the challenge to citizens, elected officials, the educational system, and the field of public administration is to create conditions that will ensure the public service promotes and supports democracy. A strong public service that supports rather than threatens democracy requires a workforce that is well trained, professional, and firmly grounded in democratic values and principles (Frederickson, 1997; Gawthrop, 1998; Mosher, 1982). This may seem straightforward, but it is fraught with issues of balance between the values of democracy and those of the bureaucracy/public service and between the public interest and personal/private interests.

In this section I will outline the democratic values that should serve as the foundation for public administrators to use as guides for their decisions and behavior. I will also discuss the tensions between democratic and bureaucratic values. Finally, I will briefly describe the kinds of knowledge and skills that public administrators need to prepare them to administer effectively while also promoting democracy.

Democratic Values as the Foundation for Public Service

There is general agreement in the field of public administration that, at minimum, public administrators have a responsibility to administer agencies and programs so that the intent of the Constitution is upheld and citizens can access their basic rights under the Constitution. Dwight Waldo (1980, p. 103) called this an "obligation" of the public administrator. The first obligation, he said, is to the Constitution. That obligation is to uphold democracy and democratic values (which Waldo calls "regime and regime values"), and the Constitution is the foundation of both. Noting the lack of guidance provided by the Constitution for public administration, Waldo writes that the Constitution is "not an unambiguous foundation." Rosenbloom notes that many public administrators in the United States take an oath when they join the public service, committing themselves to support the Constitution. This oath may be interpreted as a commitment to uphold the regime and the regime values (Rosenbloom & Kravchuk, 2005, p. 479).

Waldo (1980, p. 104) also saw an obligation to democracy on the part of public administrators, but acknowledges that the obligation is full of ambiguities such as "Is the will of the people *always* and *only* expressed in law? If in other ways, how? And how legitimated? Is the *will* of the people, however expressed, to be put ahead of the *welfare* of the people as seen by a public official with information not available to the people?" These questions are inherent to the role of public administrators.

Other scholars also discuss the responsibility of public administrators to uphold the "regime values." For example, Frederickson and Hart (1997, p. 196) argue that the Founding Fathers intended that a special relationship "exist between public servants and citizens in a democracy." They write that "it was the Founders' intent that all public servants should view the processes of government as a moral endeavor; theirs is not just to administer but to assist in bringing the ideals of democracy into existence [in the everyday lives of citizens]. . . . Therefore, the primary duty of public servants is to act as guardians and guarantors of the regime values for the American public" (Frederickson & Hart, 1997, pp. 205–206). This duty falls to public administrators because they provide continuity for the citizenry while elected officials come and go.

The notion of public administrators' responsibility for ensuring citizens' access to their basic rights in our democracy is also captured by Janet and Robert Denhardt (2003, p. xi) when they state that "public servants do not deliver customer service; they deliver democracy." The Denhardts mean that public administrators are not only responsible for helping citizens access their rights, but also for "engaging citizens in the work of democracy," i.e., "citizens would do what citizens are supposed to do in a democracy—*they would run the government*" (Denhardt & Denhardt, 2003, pp. 56, 31).

What are the "regime values" cited by Waldo, Frederickson and Hart, Denhardt and Denhardt, and other scholars? They are freedom, equality, justice, and rule of law. These are the values that, if manifested in public institutions, encourage and support "free expression of ideas, free association of persons, representation, . . . due process of law, and the privilege of assuming our soap box and speaking our minds" (Berkley & Rouse, 2004, p. 101).

In addition, the obligation of public administrators in a democracy to work within the rule of law ensures "a governing system in which the highest authority is a body of law that applies equally to all (as opposed to the rule of men, in which the personal whim of those in power can decide any issue)" (Shafritz & Russell, 2005, p. 192). According to Rosenbloom, operating under and promoting the rule of law requires that public administrators understand the Constitution so that they can craft managerial and political approaches based on principles "which have democratic policy very much at heart" (Rosenbloom & Kravchuk, 2005, p. 479).

Conflicts between Democratic and Bureaucratic Values

Public administrators who understand the Constitution and are firmly grounded in democratic values and principles also have to be able to manage administrative organizations effectively and efficiently. Administrative organizations, or bureaucracies, have their own set of values—values that have the potential to conflict with democratic values. When such conflicts occur, it is the public administrator who is commonly tasked with reconciling the competing values.

Examples of democratic and bureaucratic values that have the potential for conflict include: equality (democratic value) and hierarchy (bureaucratic value); citizen participation (democratic value) and participation based on expertise (bureaucratic value); and equity (democratic value) and efficiency (bureaucratic value). (For additional discussion of potential conflicts, see Rosenbloom & Kravchuk, 2005, and Berkley & Rouse, 2004.)

Mosher (1982) expressed concern about the impact of these competing value sets on the public interest. He saw the possibility that when value conflicts occur between democratic and bureaucratic values, decisions could be increasingly made in favor of the "narrower goals of a group, bureau, clientele, or union" (Mosher, 1982, p. 230) instead of the broader goals of the public interest.

Knowledge and Skills Needed by Public Administrators

To meet the expectations of citizens and elected officials, public administrators have to be firmly grounded in democratic values and principles and also have a wide variety of technical skills that will enable them to effectively manage public organizations.

Grounding in Democratic Values and Principles

Public administrators should understand and embrace the Constitution and our nation's basic democratic values. They should also understand and support a commitment to the rule of law. They should use democratic values as the basic guidelines for their own decision-making, behavior, and attitudes. They should hold the public interest as a primary goal and be capable of reconciling the competing interests of the bureaucracy with the public interest, as well as providing the expertise necessary to successfully manage public programs and provide public services.

This is a huge set of requirements for even the most committed and talented public servant. In order to meet these requirements, public administrators need to acquire "a philosophy of public service which is both consistent with and supportive of democracy" (Mosher, 1982, p. 235). This philosophy should include acknowledgment and understanding that

> there is a high ethical content in most significant public decisions. . . . The standards of ethical behavior that are applicable and sufficient to a private citizen in his private social relationships are not in themselves adequate for the public decisions of an administrator. . . . Public decision problems are seldom black or white in relation to their ethical content and consequences. . . . Politics and administrative organization are themselves the best protectors of administrative morality, provided they are open and public. (Mosher, 1982, p. 235)

Public administrators also need to acquire relevant moral qualities and mental attitudes. Moral qualities cannot be easily taught, but can be encouraged and modeled. Mental attitudes are "based upon knowledge and understanding and therefore learnable and teachable" (Mosher, 1982, p. 234).

A set of moral qualities and mental attitudes that I find very relevant to public service today was suggested by Stephen Bailey in 1965. Bailey argued that there are three essential moral qualities: optimism, courage, and "fairness tempered by charity" (Mosher, 1982, p. 234). Mosher outlines the meaning of these three qualities for Bailey:

> Optimism is the confidence and capacity to deal with ambiguous situations constructively and purposively. Courage is the ability to decide and act in the face of difficulties for which withdrawal would be an easier response, and to abide by principle even in unpopular causes. Fairness tempered by charity is demanded by the standards of justice and the necessity that value-laden decisions be governed by the public interest. (Mosher, 1982, p. 234)

Bailey's three mental attitudes "consist of recognition of 1. the moral ambiguity of all persons and all public policies; 2. the contextual forces which condition moral priorities in the public service; and 3. the paradoxes of procedures" (Mosher, 1982, p. 234). Under the first attitude, public administrators need to recognize that most public decisions pit public interests against personal and private interests and may reflect both, and that most public policies have both positive and negative effects. They also need to understand that nothing a public administrator does is value neutral. Every decision, action, program, or policy affects someone, and public administrators who are involved in those decision-making processes are responsible for the effects of their decisions (Gawthrop, 1998, p. 21).

In terms of context, public administrators need to be flexible because different values need priority in different contexts. They also need to understand that as they move up in the bureaucracy their value choices will become increasingly difficult and complex (Mosher, 1982, p. 235). Regarding the paradoxes of procedures, public administrators need to learn that laws, rules, and procedures can be used to promote fairness and openness, or "to prevent action and obscure the public interest" (Mosher, 1982, p. 235).

Technical and Managerial Skills

Today's public administrator needs to be the epitome of Harlan Cleveland's "get-it-all-together" professional (Cleveland, 2002)—conversant with a wide variety of fields of study, able to manage interdisciplinary teams, able to draw on a wide range of knowledge to get her/his job done. In addition, public administrators need to manage increasingly complex networks of individuals and organizations to provide public services. They must be able to do more with fewer resources and still recruit and retain the talent needed. They must lead and collaborate, include with cultural sensitivity, rejuvenate citizenship and participation, revive a focus on the common good, and much more.

While acknowledging that all of these capabilities and skills are desirable (if not realistic) in a well-trained public professional, and that the educational systems are available to train them in most of these areas, I believe the concern that more expertise may mean less focus on the common good is still relevant. Mosher framed this concern as "*the* moral question of the public service in American democracy." He worried that as people in the public service have greatly enhanced their technical and cognitive capacities to perform its tasks, they may have weakened their "concern for, and competence in, reaching social decisions responsibly with the full polity in view" (Mosher, 1982, p. 229).

Mosher writes: "The danger is that developments in the public service may be subtly, gradually, but profoundly moving the weight toward the partial, the corporate, the professional perspective and away from that of the general interest" (Mosher, 1982, p. 230). Mosher also notes Paul Appleby's concern that "the establishment of professional enclaves within public agencies [poses] a very direct threat to both open politics and responsible hierarchy" (Mosher, 1982, p. 232). According to Mosher, Appleby was concerned about "the danger of experts being 'on top rather than on tap'" (Mosher, 1982, pp. 232–

233). Appleby also "feared that functional specialization within agencies would result in 'relative inattention to the large public.' . . . Finally, he feared the effects of . . . career systems of personnel administration—overreliance upon promotions from within, closing the door to outside recruitment, over-emphasis upon security and seniority" (Mosher, 1982, p. 233).

A more recent expression of similar concerns can be found in King and Stivers (1998). These authors argue that public administrators have become so expert and so fixated on efficiency, professionalism, objectivity, and neutrality that they have difficulty respecting the expertise that citizens bring to policy discussions and inadvertently create a gap between citizens and their government. King and Stivers emphasize the need for practicing administrators to develop relationships with citizens that can lead to meaningful collaboration on public policy and implementation issues.

Roles and Responsibilities of Public Administrators in a Democracy

It has been observed above that public service in a democracy is a paradox, public administrators have little guidance from the Constitution, and there is no generally accepted theory or model of administration in a democracy. Despite these conditions, there is guidance from the traditions of the field. There is a range of major roles and responsibilities that have come to be expected of professional public administrators in the United States that can provide guidance for beginning and more seasoned public administrators. Public administrators in a democratic society have a wide range of responsibilities. They are responsible for:

- Upholding democratic values and ensuring that citizens can access their rights, or "delivering democracy."
- Promoting the public interest over individual, private interests.
- Managing and administering public institutions in accordance with democratic values.
- Implementing public policy by executing the laws passed by legislative bodies and in accordance with the instructions provided by executive branch elected officials.
- Being professional, moral, ethical, responsible, and reliable.

"Delivering Democracy"

Public administrators are ultimately responsible to the citizens in a democracy. They are responsible for being fair, just, and equitable in their decisions and dealings, and they are responsible for helping citizens access their rights in keeping with the values of a democracy—liberty, justice, freedom, equality, equity.

In support of this role for public administrators, Gawthrop argues that "our constitutional democracy rests on the basic notion of the inviolability of human dignity" (Gawthrop, 1998, p. 74). He goes on to say that elected officials are certainly responsible for upholding the inviolability of human dignity, but "it is the public administrators for whom this notion of duty has particular importance, since it is the bureaucrats who stand opposite the citizens on a face-to-face, day-to-day basis as the actual implementation of public policy unfolds" (p. 74). Sounding much like Kirlin, Gawthrop exhorts public administrators to move beyond the mundane aspects of their jobs and commit to "the enhancement of the quality of life of the individual citizen [and see themselves as the] agent of the citizen" (p. 74).

Box (1998) and Denhardt and Denhardt (2003) argue that the appropriate role for elected representatives and public administrators in community governance is a supportive role as they help citizens access their right to govern themselves. Box stresses that "community residents are the 'owners' of their communities, so they should be the people to make the necessary decisions about which public services to offer and how to operate them" (Box, 1998, p. 21). Denhardt and Denhardt argue that it is the responsibility of public administrators "to assist citizens in fulfilling their own civic duty to be fully engaged and involved in the work of the polity" (Denhardt & Denhardt, 2003, p. 56). In addition, they write that "public servants, especially including public administrators, have an ethical obligation to extend the boundaries of public participation in the political process in whatever way they can" (Denhardt & Denhardt, 2003, p. 56).

Cooper writes about the "ethical identity of the public administrator" as "that of the citizen who is employed *as* one of us to work *for* us; a kind of professional citizen ordained to do the work which we in a complex large-scale political community are unable to undertake for ourselves" (Cooper, 1991, p. 139). Frederickson and Chandler employ this theme when they propose "an entirely new role for the American public administrator—that of representative citizen" (Frederickson & Chandler, 1997, p. 209). In this role, "frontline public administrators can and ought to act as the agents of citizens bewildered by the complexity of modern government" (Frederickson & Chandler, 1997, p. 210). Also in this role, public administrators are the "primary contact between the citizen and public organizations. When this contact is effectively carried out . . . public administration contributes to an ongoing renewal and reaffirmation of the social contract" (Frederickson & Chandler, 1997, p. 210).

Promoting the Public Interest

Public administrators are also expected to promote the public interest as opposed to promoting individual and private interests. It is not the role of the public administrator to determine or decree the public interest. It is their role to facilitate development of a "collective, shared notion of the public interest" (Denhardt & Denhardt, 2003, p. 65; see also Frederickson, 1997, p. 52; Gawthrop, 1998, pp. 100–101). Denhardt and Denhardt (2003, p. 81) see the public administrator as "a key actor within a larger system of governance including citizens, groups, elected representatives, as well as other institutions." Public administrators in this view are prime actors in ensuring that "the public interest predominates, that both the solutions themselves and the process by which solutions to public problems are developed are consistent with democratic norms of justice, fairness, and equity" (Denhardt & Denhardt, 2003, p. 81).

Managing and Administering Public Institutions

Public administrators are responsible for efficiently, effectively, equitably, and democratically organizing and managing public organizations. In so doing, they are expected to ensure that public institutions are "democratically administered" so as to provide ongoing support for democratic government. According to Levitan, administrative procedures are more important than law in affecting the viability and impact of democratic principles and values. Therefore, administrative procedures should be regularly and frequently reexamined to determine their impacts on such principles and values and changed when necessary to ensure that they consistently support democracy (Gawthrop, 1998, p. 69).

Implementing Public Policy

Public administrators are also responsible for the implementation of public policy. The execution of laws formulated and passed by elected officials is the responsibility of public servants. "Politicians can carry out the will of the electorate only with the help of the [public] service" (Lipset, 1995, p. 235). Gawthrop (1998, p. 124) elaborates on this point: "The responsibility for policy and program implementation must be borne by a diverse array of policy, program, functional, and technical specialists and managers drawn from such professions as accounting, business, law, medicine, engineering, social science, public administration, and so forth."

There is general agreement that public administrators are responsible for *implementing* public policies, but their role in *developing* public policy is more controversial. Although the early notion that politics and administration should be separated has been discarded, there is still reluctance in the field to encourage public administrators to play an active role in the policy process.

Box (1998) provides a useful continuum of roles that public administrators play in the policy process, which he labels *"practitioner intent to influence public policy"* (Box, 1998, p. 139). Box defines three roles: implementers, controllers, and helpers. He defines implementers as "'neutral' practitioners who avoid significant involvement in shaping policy" (Box, 1998, pp. 138–139). He sees the goals of implementers as "to dutifully carry out lawful policy directions in a professional and competent manner and to avoid the potential trouble and risk associated with direct involvement in determining public policy" (Box, 1998, p. 139). They would be at the low, "intent-to-influence-public-policy" end of the continuum.

Controllers, Box writes, include "practitioners who seek to influence the outcomes of the policy process. Implementers and controllers are located at the polar ends of a continuum" (Box, 1998, p. 139). Controllers "seek to guide the policy process and outcomes by influencing the attitudes of their superiors or of elected officials or citizens" (Box, 1998, p. 139).

Helpers "take an active part in policy creation and implementation by serving to interpret public wishes for representatives, presenting professional knowledge of organizational and technical practices to citizens and representatives, and monitoring decision making and implementation to ensure that citizens have opportunities to participate" (Box, 1998, p. 139).

Professional, Moral, Ethical, Responsible, Reliable

Public administrators are also responsible for being well-educated professionals of high moral and ethical character. Gawthrop says this well: "Public-sector managers must be specialists by training and application, and professionals by temperament and commitment" (Gawthrop, 1998, p. 87). Mosher argued that the urgency of public problems and the increasing interconnection of social conditions required interdisciplinary and interprofessional approaches to public issues. He wrote that, "In today's world it is an absolute necessity, for no discipline, no profession, can handle even its own problems by itself" (Mosher, 1982, p. 237). This argument is even more true in today's complex world. Harlan Cleveland's contention that leadership is the "get-it-all-together profession" (Cleveland, 2002) also captures the notion of the public administrator as a skilled professional with the technical and attitudinal abilities to draw on the wide range of disciplines and fields of knowledge that are required to address today's public issues.

In addition to these basic and generally accepted responsibilities, public administrators are also encouraged to "manage public organizations and institutions in such a way as to enhance the prospects for change, responsiveness, and citizen involvement" (Frederickson, 1997, p. 231). Lipset (1995) takes this notion further. He discusses responsiveness, reliability, and responsibility as three desirable characteristics of the public service. A responsive public service, Lipset says, "caters more to the needs of the citizens than to its own tendencies to reproduce and grow" (Lipset, 1995, p. 235). A reliable public service "delivers services that measure up to the standards of international economic competition and diplomacy and to the expectations of the democratic government in power as to the thorough implementation of its policies" (Lipset, 1995, p. 235). Finally, Lipset writes that "a responsible [public] service refrains from discriminating against the [political minority] and against social groups who traditionally possess fewer resources" (Lipset, 1995, p. 235).

Conclusion

As discussed in this chapter, public service in a democracy is a paradox. Public service and democracy are antithetical yet complementary. They are antithetical because the existence of a public service in a democracy contradicts the notion of government by the people. They are complementary because democracies cannot survive without a strong, technically competent, effective, efficient, and responsive public service.

The challenge for a democratic society is to create the conditions that make public service safe for democracy. To do this, citizens, elected officials, and the public administration community need to ensure that the people who enter public service are, in addition to being highly skilled managers, well grounded in democratic values and principles. I have described some approaches to accomplishing these goals.

In addition to the paradox, there is no generally accepted theory or model of public administration for American democratic government. However, there is guidance for public administrators regarding their roles and responsibilities in a democracy. There is a range of major roles and responsibilities that have come to be expected of professional public administrators in the United States. These roles and responsibilities provide the bases for training and educating public administrators and for evaluating their performance.

The paradox of public service in a democracy is not going to go away. It is also unlikely that a general model/theory of public service in American democratic government will be developed and generally embraced in the near future. Therefore, citizens, elected officials, and the public administration community will need to continue to ensure that the public service we create and re-create will consistently promote and support democratic principles and values in all aspects of their administration of public programs and organizations. They will also need to ensure that the proper accountability mechanisms and oversight from legislative, executive, and other external bodies exist and are regularly focused on the need to maintain the balance between a strong public service and a strong democracy.

References

Berkley, G., & Rouse, J. (2004). *The craft of public administration.* New York: McGraw-Hill.

Box, R. C. (1998). *Citizen governance: Leading American communities into the 21st century.* Thousand Oaks, CA: Sage.

Cleveland, H. (2002). Leadership: The get-it-together profession. *Futurist, 36*(5), 42–28.

Cooper, T. L. (1991). *An ethic of citizenship for public administration.* Englewood Cliffs, NJ: Prentice Hall.

Denhardt, J. V., & Denhardt, R. B. (2003). *The new public service: Serving, not steering.* Armonk, NY: M.E. Sharpe.

Frederickson, H. G. (1997). *The spirit of public administration.* San Francisco: Jossey-Bass.

Frederickson, H. G., & Chandler, R. C. (1997). The public administrator as representative citizen. In H. G. Frederickson (Ed.), *The spirit of public administration* (pp. 209–223). San Francisco: Jossey-Bass.

Frederickson, H. G., & Hart, D. K. (1997). Patriotism, benevolence, and public administration. In H. G. Frederickson (Ed.), *The spirit of public administration* (pp. 195–208). San Francisco: Jossey-Bass.

Gawthrop, L. C. (1998). *Public service and democracy: Ethical imperatives for the 21st century.* Chappaqua, NY: Chatham House Publishers.

Ingraham, P. W., & Rosenbloom, D. H. (1990). Political foundations of the American federal service: Rebuilding a crumbling base. *Public Administration Review, 50,* 210–219.

King, C. S., & Stivers, C. (1998). *Government is us: Public administration in an anti-government era.* Thousand Oaks, CA: Sage.

Kirlin, J. J. (2001). Big questions for a significant public administration. *Public Administration Review, 61,* 140–143.

Lipset, S. M. (1995). *The encyclopedia of democracy* (Vol. 1). Washington, DC: Congressional Quarterly.

Mosher, F. C. (1982). *Democracy and the public service* (2nd ed.). New York: Oxford University Press.

Nigro, L. G., & Richardson, W. D. (1987). Public administration and the foundations of the American regime. In R. B. Denhardt & E. T. Jennings, Jr. (Eds.), *The revitalization of the public service* (pp. 99–117). Columbia: University of Missouri-Columbia, Extension Publications.

Ostrom, V. (1987). *The political theory of a compound republic* (2nd ed.). Lincoln: University of Nebraska Press.

Price, D. K. (1983). *America's unwritten constitution: Science, religion, and political responsibility.* Baton Rouge: Louisiana State University Press.

Rohr, J. A. (1986). *To run a constitution: The legitimacy of the administrative state.* Lawrence: University of Kansas Press.

Rosenbloom, D. H., & Kravchuk, R. S. (2005). *Public administration: Understanding management, politics, and law in the public sector.* New York: McGraw-Hill.

Shafritz, Jay M., and Russell, E. W. (2005). *Introducing public administration* (4th ed.). New York: Pearson Longman.

Stillman, R. J. II. (1990). The peculiar "stateless" origins of American public administration and the consequences for government today. *Public Administration Review, 50,* 156–167.

Stillman, R. J. II. (2000). *Public administration: Concepts and cases.* Boston: Houghton Mifflin.

Suleiman, E. (2003). *Dismantling democratic states.* Princeton, NJ: Princeton University Press.

Tocqueville, A. de. (1969). *Democracy in America* (J. P. Mayer, Ed.). Garden City, NY: Doubleday. (Original work published 1835)

Waldo, D. (1980). *The enterprise of public administration: A summary view.* Novato, CA: Chandler & Sharp.

Democracy, Public Administrators, and Public Policy

Dale Krane

Democracy as a form of government rests on procedures and rules by which citizens can exercise significant influence on the shape of public policy. At the same time, democracy itself is a policy choice and depends greatly on the use of public power. Governments by their very nature embody the use of authority and power to facilitate the attainment of collective goals. Public policy refers to a purposive course of action established by public officials that is binding on the residents of a community or nation. Simply put, public policy is what governments choose to do or choose not to do (Dye, 1976). But who makes these policy choices, how these choices are made, and for what ends or objectives are key questions at the heart of any discussion of democracy. Institutions that encourage the expression of popular consent and give citizens tools to ensure public officials respond to public preferences undergird the practices and quality of representative democracy. This connection between democracy as a form of government and as a product of government activity makes the character of a nation's policy-making process critical to the maintenance of popular sovereignty. In effect, the composition and operation of the policy process goes a long way toward determining whether there is "rule by the people."

The Relationship between Democracy and Public Policy

As noted in the Introduction to this volume, debates over the abstract definition of democracy have been long running and carry over to the important issue of which attributes or features of government and the policy process foster "rule by the people." How might one decide that the community or nation one lived in was democratic, while another was less so? The most common and simplest answer to the question of how people exercise popular sovereignty, according to Sartori (1965, p. 73) is "easy—during elections." With the emergence of nation-states, rapid population growth, and urbanization, the Athenian ideal of direct communal democracy became increasingly unworkable, and democracy was redefined as the choice of one's rulers. Instead of the whole adult community actively engaged in making policies, some citizens would be selected to constitute a governing body and these "representatives" would be granted the authority to make choices binding on the whole community.

But elections are only one attribute of democratic government. As Jefferson argued so eloquently, if citizens were to be sovereign, then "certain unalienable rights" had to protected from arbitrary actions by the government. That is, public policy should not abridge an individual's exercise of rights such as those of assembly, belief, representation, speech, and worship. Scholars of democracy have offered numerous lists of fundamental features that must be present for a political system to be considered "democratic." Typically included on these lists are requirements such as: (a) free, fair, and frequent election of public officials; (b) freedom of expression; (c) access to alternative sources of information; (d) associational autonomy (i.e., the right to form groups independent of government control); and (e) inclusive citizenship (Dahl, 1982, pp. 83–99). Other attributes held to be necessary for a functioning democracy include the rule of law, public accessibility to government institutions and officials, equal opportunity, and personal security (Hartmann, 2004; Wayne, 2004). What these various lists imply is democratic government requires more than competitive elections. The ideals of democracy must be "translated and transformed into governing institutions that resolve societal problems and produce policy decisions that reflect the consent of the governed" (Krane & Marshall, 2003, p. 3).

Different societies have organized authority and political power in a variety of ways with the result that several different models of democratic institutions exist. The American diffusion of powers model (i.e., separate institutions of government with powers diffused across these institutions) functions differently from the parliamentary model (fusion of executive and legislative power and concentrated executive power) common in many other nations. Because each model differs institutionally, the process of formulating and implementing public policy also differs, but each model possesses democratic features. Similarly, local government in the United States also exhibits different institutional forms that shape the policy process; for example, municipal government, whether it is mayor-council or manager-council, functions with a unified executive, while many county governments operate with a multiheaded executive (i.e., the board of county supervisors) and diffused executive authority (i.e., multiple elected officials such as sheriff, tax assessor, clerk). It is important to note that the choice of governing institutions is itself a policy choice, albeit one that occurs infrequently in more stable political systems.

Governments, whether democratic or not, exist to achieve certain purposes, among which are social order, conflict resolution, and defense against external attacks. One can find the purposes proclaimed for a nation's government by reading the nation's constitution; for example, think of the goals expressed in the preamble to the U.S. Constitution. Again, as with the lack of agreement on a definition of democracy, there is little consensus on the purposes democratic governments ought to pursue. Perhaps the most widely accepted purpose is the protection of individual rights, defined as freedom from government control. Locke, who held this view, argued that since every exercise of government came at the expense of individual liberty, less public policy was better than more. However, others such as Rousseau argued that government could act positively to increase individual rights, for example to eliminate child labor or protect spouses from abuse. Crucial to democratic purposes are public policies that limit the actions of those in official positions and prevent the emergence of a permanent set of rulers. Turning this idea around, public policy in a democracy strives to open the political process to all citizens and to create opportunities for citizens to participate in the formulation and implementation of public policy.

A second large purpose of public policy in a democracy is the development of the individual to the fullest capabilities possible. The protection of individual rights has long been intertwined with the pursuit of equality. The revolutionary notion that all citizens have "certain unalienable" rights rests on the idea that all persons possess inherent dignity and worth. After all, without equality for all citizens, government by consent of the governed cannot be sustained. Democratic equality refers to more than basic political participation (e.g., equal franchise), it also means equal treatment, for example, one's place in line at the motor vehicle bureau does not depend on one's income or social rank. Equal treatment also entails equality of opportunity—the public provision of basic education, food, health care, and shelter so that all individuals can contribute to their own development as well as participate in the larger community. Jefferson, for example, made the case for free public education because without literate citizens, popular control of the government was impossible. Hungry and ill children cannot learn effectively, so public policy today offers school lunch programs and health care for children from low income families. Increasingly, "the bulk of public policy in a modern democratic nation aims to ensure a minimal quality of life for all and to facilitate, in the words of modern psychology, each person's 'self-actualization'" (Krane & Marshall, 2003, p. 5).

For too many persons, competitive elections serve as *the* defining charac-teristic of democracy, but this solely procedural view is myopic because it ignores the substantive side of public policy and its effects on the conduct and legitimacy of any democratic government. Certainly, procedural poli-cies are necessary to ensure that contests for public office remain open to a broad expanse of individuals and not become the domain of a political class. But legitimacy also depends on the outcomes of public policy. Without poli-cies that protect the security of individuals and their property, a functioning economy is difficult to sustain. Without policies to ensure the "general wel-fare," individuals may not be able to function as citizens. Most fundamen-tally in a democracy, public policy *"responds to the needs and wants of ordinary, everyday citizens"* (Hartman, 2004, p. 16), or government becomes something other than a democracy—it no longer is "We the People."

Democracy and Bureaucracy

In his defense of the House of Representatives, as proposed in the yet to be ratified constitution, Madison in *Federalist 57* states that "The elective mode of obtaining rulers is the characteristic policy of republican government" (Cooke, 1961, p. 384). By a "republican government" Madison meant a government that derived its powers from the great body of the people and in which policy was made by the legislative branch. While it was important for there to be "energy in the executive," as Hamilton argued in *Federalist 70* (Cooke, 1961, p. 471), executive "magistrates" were to serve under the authority and direc-tion of Congress. But, since 1787 Congress has delegated substantial policy-making authority to the executive branch, so much so that most observers of government agree with Carl Friedrich (1950, p. 37) that "bureaucracy is the core of modern government." Yates (1982, p. 1) observes that "democratic decisionmaking takes place more and more in bureaucratic settings," and that American government "has increasingly become a 'bureaucratic democracy.'"

The classical position articulated by Woodrow Wilson, Frank Goodnow, and other "founders" of American public administration held that "adminis-tration lies outside the proper sphere of politics. Administrative questions are not political questions" (Wilson, 1887, p. 210). Many have taken this view to mean administrators were not supposed to engage in politics, and hence there was a sharp line between the politics of policy adoption and the apolitical and technical world of policy administration. It should be noted that the Wilsonian interpretation of politics did not mean that decisions, whether over policy design or implementation, would not lead to "winners and losers"; rather Wilson meant "partisan" politics, as in Democrats versus Republicans (Shafritz & Russell, 2005, p. 33).

More importantly, the argument for viewing administration as an apolitical activity could not stand against the reality of life in public agencies. The congressional-presidential struggles for power over the policy-making process through the first half of the twentieth century undercut the prevailing orthodoxy of separation as did the rapid expansion of national government agencies during the Depression and the two World Wars. Public administration scholars soon determined the politics-administration dichotomy was a fallacy. For example, in 1936 Marshall Dimock noted that "going too far in the formal separation between politics and administration" would be "dangerous" (Dimock, 1936, p. 3). Norton Long (1949, p. 257) declared that the "lifeblood of administration is power," and Paul Appleby (1949, p. 170) stated that "Public administration is policy-making."

But if unelected officials in the bureaucracy make public policy, then the principles of "republican government" are at risk, and the question of effective control over the bureaucracy becomes an issue critical to the maintenance of a democratic government. Debates over how best to constrain the actions of administrative agencies and their staffs have led to a continuing stream of legislation that has imposed control after control on public agencies at all levels of government (Light, 1997). But too many controls can hamstring administrative action and reduce the effectiveness and efficiency of public administrators. The public's demand for cost-effective but responsive government creates a tension over the appropriate role of bureaucrats in a democracy: should public administrators be servants of the people who operate under close legislative supervision or should they be expert professionals who operate with some degree of autonomy? Further compounding this question of the role of bureaucrats in the policy process is the expectation that those who administer particular policies should advocate for those policy areas as well as negotiate with others about the course of public action.

Stillman (1996) has explained in detail that these different value positions on the place of administrators in American democracy can be traced back to viewpoints articulated by Hamilton, Jefferson, and Madison. Since Stillman's exposition is well known, there is no need to repeat it here, but two of his conclusions are important to note. First, the three value traditions remain alive and well, and the "persistent rivalry" between the three value traditions continues to reappear in the constant stream of new controls (under the guise of reform) imposed on agencies. Second, the pursuit of any one of these three values results in a trade-off of benefits and costs with the other two. As a consequence, it is unlikely that the bureaucratic genie will be put back into the "republican" bottle.

Modern governments require large organizations to produce and deliver the diverse array of goods and services demanded by the public. While the necessity and reality of bureaucratic policy making may offend many whose image of democracy is the ballot box, John Markoff (1996, p. 118) pointedly notes that "electoral processes are central to democratic legitimation, but in no state is political life limited to elections." The proper role of bureaucrats in a democracy is an important issue, but it is equally important to understand the various contributions bureaucrats make to the policy process.

Policy Formulation

Decisions to adopt public policies almost always result from a series of actions and decisions made by a number of different individuals who occupy different positions within the larger processes of policy formulation and adoption. That is, prior to the exercise of formal authority by a legislative body, by an executive, or by a court, several phases or types of activity by public and private individuals shape the emergence and development of policy decisions. Different authors have proposed different models of policy formation, but in general all of these models include in the "pre-decision" phase of the policy process the following activities: problem identification, agendasetting, and policy design. The roles public administrators play and their interaction with citizens in each of these three policy formation activities determine whether civil servants support or undermine popular sovereignty.

Problem Identification

Demands for public action commonly arise from the harmful effects or losses caused by some condition or situation in private life. For example, inclement weather, air pollution, and traffic congestion can be irritants, but they also can become sufficiently severe as to impose costs of time and money on individuals and even lead to injuries and death. Other situations, such as financial machinations by corporate executives, drug trafficking, or sex slavery, may be less visible but more insidious in their effects. Whether a societal condition or shift prompts public action depends on the situation being defined as a problem that government ought to solve. That is, some person or group must make the case that a problem exists and that public action is appropriate and necessary to remedy the situation.

The First Amendment grants citizens the rights of free expression, petition, and assembly. These three guarantees provide the foundation for citizens, either individually or in groups, to call to the attention of public officials conditions or situations affecting citizens. A dedicated and tenacious person may succeed in attracting the attention of officials to a harmful economic or social condition—one can think of a Rosa Parks or a Ralph Nader. More typically, interest groups function as the primary means for the identification and articulation of problems to public officials.

Interest groups represent the policy preferences of an extremely varied collection of professional associations, for-profit enterprises, nonprofit organizations, government jurisdictions, ethnic groups, religious denominations, research organizations, and advocacy groups. Because interest groups seek to gain policy benefits for their members at the expense of the larger public, their activity can undermine rule by the majority. However, they play an important democratic role by transmitting the shared concerns of many citizens to public officials. Despite the negative reputation of interest groups, many individuals would not have an impact on policy formulation if their views were not represented by interest groups.

Public administrators also play important roles in problem identification. Associations of professionals who work in the public sector—e.g., firefighters, educators, civil engineers—monitor and report on conditions within their areas of responsibility. These professional associations also establish standards of quality that become benchmarks for the identification of unacceptable situations. The very existence and purpose of some government agencies, particularly at the national level, is to monitor and analyze societal conditions, issue reports on trends, including whether conditions are improving or worsening, make recommendations for action to other parts of the government, and in some cases, take appropriate action. To name a few, one can think of the Federal Reserve Board, the Centers for Disease Control and Prevention, the National Oceanic and Atmospheric Administration, and the Domestic Nuclear Detection Office (Department of Homeland Security).

The technical expertise of the personnel in "monitoring" agencies gives them a degree of legitimacy in describing the nature and severity of problems and in declaring the public's interest in the problem. Many situations that become identified as problems necessitating public action are often "invisible," in that a condition such as homelessness may not be well understood or may be ignored by most citizens (Anderson, 2006, p. 85). Other situations, may be viewed as "private," such as domestic violence, or as the cost of doing business—for example, air pollution. While it often requires a crisis for many citizens to discover a long-standing condition really constitutes a serious problem, the tracking, analysis, and reporting of societal conditions by public agencies not only can educate citizens about the nature and extent of a given situation, but more importantly agencies can also inform citizens as how a situation affects them and the larger public interest.

Agenda-Setting

Typically, a problem gains the attention of public officials when some person or group demands government action to address the problem. The demand can be as simple as a single individual's telephone call asking the local animal control officer to enforce "leash laws," or the demand may be as complex as the public outrage in the aftermath of the 9/11 terrorist attacks over the lax security of America's borders. In many cases, the problem is a routine one (e.g., garbage collection) in that an agency or a jurisdiction has the authority and responsibility to handle the situation. But in other cases, there may be disagreement as to whether the public sector ought to step into the situation (e.g., Internet pornography or real estate commissions), or if it does decide to act, there may be disagreement over the proper type(s) of action. Long ago Schattschneider (1960) observed that conflict over an issue functions as a key factor in whether public officials recognize and act on a societal problem. Persons or groups demanding public action may well encounter opposition from those who benefit from the current situation (e.g., letting one's dog run free or firms that employ illegal aliens) or from those ideologically opposed to public action (e.g., advocates of an absolute position on free expression). In many cases, this political struggle determines whether the problem gets placed on the agenda of a governmental body or whether government officials ignore the issue or deliberately deny the issue a place on their agenda. It is important to remember that just because some person or group calls for a public remedy of a problem or situation, it should not be expected that public officials will respond positively. After all, what some perceive as a "problem" may be a desirable situation for others, and those who benefit from the status quo can be expected to defend the current situation by lobbying public officials not to adopt new policy.

Numerous organizations exist to press for government action in many areas of life; in fact, whole "communities" of specialists work to convince policy makers to enact new or different public policy. The residents of these "policy communities" may work for interest groups, legal firms that lobby, media and public relations companies, professional associations, corporations, nonprofit organizations, universities, private research organizations, and government agencies. To become a member of a given policy community (e.g., economic development) one must develop a reasonable level of knowledge and understanding about the particular area of policy; that is, unless a person or a group possesses a grasp of the problems and issues in a policy area, they are not likely to gain much influence within a given policy community. Members of a policy community do not necessarily agree with each other over ends or means, but they do share the common attribute of extensive specialized knowledge. Mass public opinion can push an issue onto the policy makers' agenda either by raising a chorus of complaints about a current public program or by expressing widespread enthusiasm for some proposed course of public action (Baumgartner & Jones, 1993, pp. 86–90). Although waves of public opinion definitely can prompt policy makers to change public policy, usually "private problems need to be linked to public causes in order to demand governmental attention" (Baumgartner & Jones, 1993, p. 27). One of the critical functions performed by policy communities is the conduct of debate over whether a private problem has a public cause or is amenable to a public solution. Large-scale policy change generally will not occur if members of a policy community are sharply divided on the nature and/or causes of a problem (Hayes, 1992, p. 141).

Public administrators participate actively in policy communities. As previously noted, many bureaucrats monitor, interpret, and report on changes in society. Other civil servants work on the front lines of social and economic problems and acquire "street-level" knowledge of local circumstances. Furthermore, through their interaction with citizens from all sectors of society, public administrators receive feedback from citizens about the current state of affairs. Citizen complaints and compliments offer agency personnel important information about the performance of public programs, and while some bureaucrats may not transmit complaints to their political superiors, many other bureaucrats use feedback to make the case for improvements in public programs.

Agenda-setting entails more than the demand for public action to remedy societal problems; it also includes the search for and supply of feasible solutions to the problems on the government's agenda (Kingdon, 2003, p. 178). Public administrators play an especially important role in the supply of feasible solutions to the public's problems. Because of their professional training, their detailed knowledge of current public programs and policies, and their interaction with the public, agency personnel constitute a major source of policy alternatives. Although many in the public perceive bureaucrats as merely managers of public programs, elected officials fill government agencies with professional and technical experts precisely for the purpose of developing and evaluating possible solutions to policy problems. In some cases, elected officials submit unaltered policy proposals developed by civil servants as bills to be considered by the legislative body. Where policy proposals emanate from interest groups, think tanks, or citizens, elected officials rely on agency personnel to analyze the technical aspects of a proposal, which include adequacy, affordability, effectiveness, implementability, and legality. Obviously, the more complex the societal problem, the more likely any solution will exhibit complex facets that require technical analysis based on specialized knowledge. While elected representatives decide whether to act to solve a public problem, much of the content of how they choose to solve the problem emerges out of the debates among the members of relevant policy communities, and within policy communities, public administrators are critical gatekeepers as to the technical feasibility of alternative proposals.

Policy Design

The creation of a public program usually occurs, as Kingdon (2003, p. 178) observes, when three key processes converge to place the issue on the *decision agenda*: the problem at issue is sufficiently compelling to call for public action, an acceptable solution is found or present, and support by a majority of policy makers exists. While the presence of these three conditions increases the likelihood that a "window of opportunity" to enact the policy is open, the three conditions do not explain the elements that go into the design of a public program. First, a new policy or program's goals and objectives must be specified; for example, the Women's Business Ownership Assistance (WBOA) program (Small Business Act, Sec. 29, 15 U.S.C. 631(h) and 656) proclaims two complementary goals: "to fund private, nonprofit organizations to assist through training and counseling, small business concerns owned and controlled by women, and to remove, in so far as possible, the discriminatory barriers that are encountered by women in accessing capital and promoting their businesses." Second, policy makers must agree on a given instrument of public action, or "policy tool," by which to achieve program goals—in this case, the expenditure of funds via a project grant. Third, the program design will establish an authorized level of annual outlays for the program, if enacted. Fourth, a program's intended beneficiaries or persons eligible for the program's benefits must be specified, or "targeted." The WBOA program identifies certain types of organizations as eligible to apply for the funds, which must be expended to benefit "women entrepreneurs starting their own business or expanding their existing business." Fifth, a program's design typically includes various requirements to be met by eligible organizations or persons, such as details to be reported annually by the nonprofits that receive WBOA grants. Sixth, the design of a program will also identify the agency responsible for administration of the program (Office of Women's Business Ownership, Small Business Administration), delineate the agency's authority, and set out various obligations, such as annual reports. Other program elements may also be included in a program's design.

The ultimate design of a program emerges out of "mark up" sessions in which members of subcommittees and committees in each congressional chamber negotiate over the final language of a bill. While the representatives and senators are the official "architects" of legislation, much of an act's details are produced by various "draftsmen," including congressional staff, administrative agency specialists, interest groups, think tanks, and individual policy entrepreneurs. Each party to the legislative process brings its own preferences and values, and senior managers of administrative agencies will work to advance the interests of their agency (Held, 1991, p. 226). Because lawmakers desire to solve problems and thereby claim credit so as to boost their chances for reelection, they rely on the expertise and information possessed by bureaucrats to assist congressional staff draft an initial design. Agency proposals may not become the final enacted legislation, but they often provide core programmatic elements around which the contending parties bargain. Furthermore, since agency managers participate in a program's design, the legislative drafting process offers an opportunity for agency managers to pursue the interests of the agency. One of the three sides of the well-known triangular "subgovernment model" of policy formulation describes this legislative-administrative interaction as an exchange of expertise and information from the agency in return for additional resources (i.e., appropriations, personnel, tasks) from congressional committees. Consequently, a policy's design will often include elements beneficial to the agency responsible for the policy's implementation. Whether the program's design is beneficial to the program's intended targets depends both on the quality of the design as well as the effectiveness of the program's implementation.

Policy Implementation

The classical model of public administration, as noted earlier in this chapter, holds that administrative matters are not political, but rather technical. According to this view, policy implementation requires the establishment of an appropriate set of routine activities that will bring about the result intended by the choice made in the policy decision. The classic presumption is that partisan and political-interest jockeying ends once a law is enacted or a judicial ruling decreed. However, this orthodox position ignores the reality that the achievement of a program's objectives (or a court order) entails a "process of assembling numerous and diverse program elements" (Bardach, 1977, p. 36), many of which are dispersed across levels of government or held by persons or organizations in the private sector. Converting a law or court ruling into action is not automatic, because the implementation of policy in the American federal union occurs within a matrix of multiple governments and power relationships characterized by fragmented authority and contending political interests. Because many of the government officials and private citizens who must be marshaled to implement a policy are independent of each other and these diverse actors possess their own preferences on a given policy (e.g., favor or oppose), bargaining is required to elicit their cooperation. Choices made by agency managers and staff will often reflect more than their professional judgment about how best to achieve the legislature's or court's intent; their decisions will also reflect compromises or trade-offs among contending interests and values. Consequently, implementation combines the technical tasks of administration with the resolution of political issues.

Citizens are supposed to be sovereign in a constitutional democracy, and democratic theory holds that policy choices made by the people's elected representatives are the authoritative expression of public purposes (Appleby, 1962; Mayo, 1960). Madison, in *The Federalist Papers*, argued that the proposed constitution would place the executive branch under the control and direction of Congress. For Madison this meant the litmus test of accountability in a republican system of legislative supremacy was the adherence by administrators to legislative intent. That is, to the degree policy implementation diverges from the policy enacted by a legislature, then the people's purposes are undercut. However, the ability of administrators to effect the legislature's intent is a function of: (1) the design of the policy itself; (2) the resources provided to and the constraints imposed on administrative agencies; (3) the choices made by agency personnel; and (4) the larger political context surrounding the policy initiative (Mazmanian & Sabatier, 1983, pp. 20–33). These same factors also affect the relationship between bureaucrats and citizens as well as the quality of service to citizens.

Policy Design and Implementation

Successful achievement of a policy's goals depends on the quality of its design as well as its implementation. No matter how well implemented, a poorly crafted or targeted policy will not be effective. Ideally, legislators would possess a clear understanding of what actions will remedy a pressing problem. This situation occurs when the causes of the societal problem are known and consensus exists not just about the causes, but also about the most effective means for ameliorating the problem. However, when the cause(s) of a problem is unclear or little consensus as to a problem's cause(s) prevails, it becomes more difficult to design an effective policy. Similarly, when debate over solutions does not yield consensus, policy is difficult to design. Simply put, if legislators produce poor program designs or choose to sketch policy in generalized terms, these choices affect the actions of administrators as well as the attainment of successful policy performance.

For example, the 2003 Medicare Modernization Act contained a new prescription drug benefit for senior citizens (Medicare Part D). Unfortunately, the implementation of this new policy has revealed several design flaws, such as confusion among seniors caused by the multiplicity of available plans (leading to the low rate at which seniors have signed up for the new benefit), failure to cover low-income seniors whose medications were paid for previously by Medicaid, and confusion between national and state governments as to what prescription drugs are to be included on the formulary of approved medicines (Krane & Koenig, 2005, pp. 17–19; Meyerson, 2006; Weisberg, 2006). The evolution of environmental protection laws is a good example of lawmakers using administrative agencies as problem identifiers and solvers. In this case, legislative policy makers acknowledged they had a poor understanding of a problem and so they enacted a general policy creating a new administrative agency (the Environmental Protection Agency) to investigate the sources of the problem and to propose policy solutions. Another example of how design choices may affect implementation can be seen in the history of the Community Development Block Grant program. Drawing on the experiences with the Model Cities program and responding to the 1960s and 1970s "new politics" demands for citizen participation in policy making and implementation, Congress converted several urban development grant programs into a block grant with two parts: a formula grant to larger cities, and state-administered grants for smaller communities. In both cases, Congress mandated that municipalities must hold public hearings over the content of the plans cities were required to submit as a condition for receipt of funds. Here one can see that it is possible to design policy features that enhance opportunities for citizen participation in program implementation. The recent trend toward the use of tax expenditures (i.e., tax credits, deductions, exemptions) as a policy tool demonstrates that it is possible to design a policy that does not depend on creating a specialized agency to provide the goods or services—the tax break only requires a change in the tax code (Howard, 2002, p. 413).

Resources for and Constraints on Policy Implementation

In addition to a policy's design, the resources provided to and the constraints imposed on an administrative agency directly shape implementation. While many candidates and many in the general public rail against "throwing money" at problems, most understand that without adequate funding public purposes will not be achieved. The large amounts of funds to purchase school desegregation compared to the lack of monies to ensure and protect the franchise for minorities is striking (Krane, 1985). Similarly, the number, diversity, and quality of an agency's personnel (e.g., trained professionals versus patronage appointments) as well as its facilities and equipment (e.g., up-to-date computers) can affect agency performance.

Because public administrators may act only under legal authority granted to their agency, the nature and extent of authority provided by a policy's design is at once a resource and a constraint on performance. The ability of the Internal Revenue Service to collect taxes rests on the extensive investigative authority possessed by the agency as well as the substantial penalties it may levy for noncompliance. Policy decisions on the content of sex education programs ("abstinence only" versus contraceptive information) determine whether public health agencies gain or lose ground against the spread of sexually transmitted diseases (McFarlane & Meier, 2001).

It is important to note briefly that all administrative agencies function under three general sets of rules. First, national and state administrative agencies must follow the procedures established in their respective administrative procedures acts (APAs). These APAs set standards for agency operation, lay out steps to be followed for various agency activities, and establish boundaries over access and information to agency proceedings. Despite the widespread view that the writing of regulations by administrative agencies is a closed process, the federal APA has long permitted substantial public participation, and more recently, Congress has enhanced participation through the adoption of a negotiated rulemaking process. Second, administrators not only must follow "due process" but they also must provide "equal treatment." That is, the work of administrative agencies must abide by the framework of national and state civil rights laws. Third, national and state statutes dictate a long list of management and control requirements that affect agency implementation. These requirements include directives on budgeting and auditing, contracts and procurement, human resources and work conditions, and codes of conduct and ethics (Cooper et al., 1998, pp. 63–66). These three general policy frameworks inject democratic practices and values into the bureaucratic world.

Choices Made by Agency Personnel

Many citizens have little understanding of the chains of implementation activities that extend from Washington, DC, and state capitals to their community, but they do care greatly about the choices made by public servants in their localities and neighborhoods because those choices directly influence their everyday lives. Although bureaucrats function under a considerable set of rules, they do possess varying degrees of discretion. Some civil servants work at highly routine jobs that permit little discretion, while others carry out tasks that require considerable judgment. Obviously, the more discretion the policy or program grants to agency personnel, the more critical for citizens these individualistic decisions become. Police officers at a traffic stop can give you a warning, issue a ticket, or arrest you; a public school teacher may assign "easy" or challenging homework; and a street repair crew may decide the pothole in front of your house is not yet deep enough to fill. In effect, policies do not become "real" for citizens until they encounter bureaucrats at work.

Furthermore, the discretionary choices made by agency personnel can enhance or hinder attainment of the policy's purposes. Ball, Krane, and Lauth (1982, p. 197) explain:

> Administrative discretion is, at once, a virtue and a vice. Through the possession of discretion, a government agency can "fine tune" its implementation activities to specific situations and circumstances. On the other side of the implementation coin, freedom to translate legislative mandates into administrative action can lead to a wide range of interpretations from minor modifications to goal distortion and displacement.

Whether a regulatory agency, for example, adopts a general rule by which to decide whether violations have occurred or adopts a case-by-case approach has significant consequences for how the agency conducts its work as well as for the outcomes of the agency's decisions. Use of a general principle will produce more consistent and uniform decisions compared to a case-by-case approach; on the other hand, a general principle as a decision criterion is less sensitive to individual variation in cases. Here one can see the dilemma discretion poses for public administrators: which of several important democratic values should be served?

Political Context and Implementation

Scholars of policy implementation have long observed the importance of economic, political, cultural, and social change on the success or failure of a public policy (Van Meter & Van Horn, 1975). Certainly, economic, cultural, and social trends impact not just the demand and design of public policy, but also make it easier or harder to achieve a policy's goals. A program to assist displaced workers by retraining them as computer programmers may well fail to achieve its purpose of reducing unemployment because employers decide to "outsource" jobs for basic computer programmers to overseas locations. The unexpected arrival of non-English-speaking refugees may overwhelm an agency's ability to assist other indigent persons in the locality and may prompt the agency to hire interpreters. Police officers may arrest a parent for what appears to be a case of child abuse when, in fact, the spots on the child's back are the result of warm stones, a folk medicine practice common in some cultures.

Political conditions constitute the most immediate and important parameter on policy implementation. Changes in the partisan affiliation of elected executives may lead to new and different orders to career administrators that direct them to enforce the law more or less vigorously. The emergence of a new interest group or social movement (e.g., consumer protection) may alter an agency's established relationship with other interest groups (e.g., manufacturers) such that the agency is caught between contending parties. As a consequence, agency managers may be forced to seek compromises that alter the agency's practices.

Changes in the political context of a policy may also occur because of shifts in public opinion. When the change in public opinion is large and coalesces around a relatively clear position, as noted earlier in this chapter, elected policy makers are likely to respond. However, it is less certain that bureaucrats respond to shifts in public opinion. Stillman (1996, p. 100) claims that "generally public opinion is too transitory and amorphous to have much influence on the typical public agency." But Stillman also says that he is not suggesting that public opinion never influences administrative actions. Agencies may be sensitive to general public opinion because a poor public image can affect the agency's standing with elected officials. Over time, agencies may alter their practices to increase their support from the general public, as the Army Corps of Engineers did in transforming itself from an agency perceived as a detriment to the environment to an agency with a substantial commitment to environmental protection (Mazmanian & Nienaber, 1979). Studies of variation in the political cultures of American states also indicate that citizens in different parts of the country hold different ideological orientations toward government and politics including the roles of public administrators (Flentje, 2000). These different cultural expectations establish parameters of what constitutes acceptable styles of state and local administration. On balance, public opinion does have some effect on policy implementation, and civil servants do not necessarily behave in accordance with the Kafkaesque image some have of bureaucrats.

Policy Design, Bureaucracy, and Democracy

Surprising to some, many democratic theorists do not discuss or go into much detail about the place and role of bureaucracy. Concern over bureaucracy, when the topic is broached, focuses on the question of whether bureaucratic officials will faithfully follow the policy directives of legislatures and elected executives. That administrators will use their resources to alter public policy and thus weaken popular sovereignty is the principal democratic fear. This concern of course, is an important one in public administration. The debates over how best to ensure the accountability of bureaucrats have a long and distinguished history, and numerous means have been proposed by which to control civil servants (Gormley & Balla, 2004, pp. 10–11).

But another question about the use of bureaucracy as an instrument of popular sovereignty also bears on the place and role of bureaucracy in a democratic government—in what ways does the public expect and empower public administrators to act? To be sure, the public does not and will not support a "rogue" bureaucracy, but the public does expect administrative agencies to act and to act in ways preferred by the public, for example, respond to a disaster in an expeditious and effective manner. Considine (2005, pp. 191–192) argues that "policy-making always involves a dual structure." By this he means every policy design has an "instrumental dimension" of decisions, programs, and outcomes as well as a "developmental dimension" of norms and relationships. That is, policy choices not only seek to achieve particular goals and objectives, but the goals and objectives contained in policy decisions communicate expectations about the future condition of the community or nation (e.g., less crime). As Schneider and Ingram instruct (1997, pp. 140–141): "Policy teaches lessons about what groups people belong to, the characteristics of groups with which people identify, what they deserve from government, and what is expected from them . . . whether the problems of the target population are legitimate ones for government attention, what kind of game politics is (public-spirited or the pursuit of private interests), and who usually wins." The developmental dimension of policy design also includes expectations about the behavior of bureaucrats and their relationships with the policy's targets and the general public—for example, the IRS is expected to collect taxes and apprehend tax cheaters, but to do so in a way that is not burdensome or overly intrusive to ordinary citizens.

Smith and Ingram (2002, p. 566) decry the "blind spot" policy studies have for the relationship between policy tool choices and the condition of democracy. But policy design also includes more than just the "instrument of action" by which the policy goal is to be achieved; policy design creates an official role for administrators and among these many and diverse roles are: agent, expert, guardian, leader, mediator, partner, servant, and steward. It is important to understand that the role assigned to administrators establishes more than just a function to be performed, it also includes norms about the interaction between citizens and administrators. The interaction of tool choice with role expectation affects agency performance and policy outcome, and crucially defines the standards of accountability to which the policy and its administrators are held (Posner, 2002). Rule *by* the people can be protected from "unfaithful" actions by imposing controls on unelected officials, but it is important to understand that rule *for* the people can be expanded through the roles and relationships embodied in a policy's design.

References

Anderson, J. E. (2006). *Public policymaking* (6th ed.). Boston: Houghton Mifflin.

Appleby, P. H. (1949). *Policy and administration*. Tuscaloosa: University of Alabama Press.

Appleby, P. H. (1962). *Citizens as sovereigns*. Syracuse, NY: Syracuse University Press.

Ball, H., Krane, D., & Lauth, T. P. (1982). *Compromised compliance: Implementation of the 1965 Voting Rights Act*. Westport, CT: Greenwood.

Bardach, E. (1977). *The implementation game: What happens after a bill becomes a law*. Cambridge, MA: MIT Press.

Baumgartner, F. R., & Jones, B. D. (1993). *Agendas and instability in American politics*. Chicago: University of Chicago Press.

Considine, M. (2005). *Making public policy: Institutions, actors, strategies*. Cambridge, UK: Polity Press.

Cooke, J. E. (Ed.) (1961). *The Federalist*. Cleveland, OH: The World Publishing Company.

Cooper, P. J., Brady, L. P., Hidalgo-Hardeman, O., Hyde, A., Naff, K. Ott, J. S. and White. H. (1998). *Public administration for the twenty-first century*. Fort Worth: Harcourt Brace College Publishers.

Dahl, R. A. (1982). *Dilemmas of pluralist democracy: Autonomy vs. control*. New Haven, CT: Yale University Press.

Dimock, M. E. (1936). The meaning and scope of public administration. In J. Gaus, L. D. White, & M. E. Dimock, *The frontiers of public administration* (pp. 1–12). Chicago: University of Chicago Press.

Dye, T. (1976). *Policy analysis: What governments do, why they do it, and what difference it makes*. Tuscaloosa: University of Alabama Press.

Flentje, H. E. (2000). State administration in cultural context. In J. J. Gargan (Ed.), *Handbook of state government administration* (pp. 67–105). New York: Marcel Dekker.

Friedrich, C. J. (1950). *Constitutional government and democracy*. New York: Ginn.

Gormley, W. T., Jr., & Balla, S. J. (2004). *Bureaucracy and democracy: Accountability and performance*. Washington, DC: CQ Press.

Hartmann, T. (2004). *A return to democracy: Reviving Jefferson's dream*. New York: Harmony Books.

Hayes, M. (1992). *Incrementalism and public policy*. New York: Longman.

Held, W. G. (1991). Decision-making in the federal government: The Wallace S. Sayre model. In J. S. Ott, A. C. Hyde, & J. M. Shafritz (Eds.), *Public management: The essential readings* (pp. 217–235). Chicago: Lyceum Books/Nelson-Hall.

Howard, C. (2002). Tax expenditures. In L. M. Salamon (Ed.), *The tools of government: A guide to the new governance* (pp. 410–444). New York: Oxford University Press.

Kingdon, J. W. (2003). *Agendas, alternatives, and public policies* (2nd ed.). New York: Longman.

Krane, D. (1985). Implementation of the Voting Rights Act: Enforcement by the Department of Justice. In L. S. Foster (Ed.), *The Voting Rights Act: Consequences and implications* (pp. 123-157). New York: Praeger.

Krane, D., & Koenig, H. (2005). The state of American federalism, 2004: Is federalism still a core value? *Publius: The Journal of Federalism, 35*, 1–40.

Krane, D., & Marshall, G. S. (2003). Democracy and public policy. In J. Rabin (Ed.), *Encyclopedia of public administration and public policy* (pp. 1–7). New York: Marcel Dekker.

Light, P. C. (1997). *The tides of reform: Making government work, 1945–1995.* New Haven, CT: Yale University Press.

Long, N. (1949). Power and administration. *Public Administration Review, 2,* 257–264.

Markoff, J. (1996). *Waves of democracy: Social movements and political change.* Thousand Oaks, CA: Pine Forge Press.

Mayo, H. (1960). *An introduction to democratic theory.* New York: Oxford University Press.

Mazmanian, D., & Nienaber, J. (1979). *Can organizations change? Environmental protection, citizen participation, and the Corps of Engineers.* Washington, DC: Brookings Institution.

Mazmanian, D., & Sabatier, P. (1983). *Implementation and public policy.* Palo Alto, CA: Scott Foresman.

McFarlane, D. R., & Meier, K. J. (2001). *The politics of fertility control: Family planning and abortion policies in the American states.* New York: Chatham House.

Meyerson, H. (2006, January 25). Bush the incompetent. *Washington Post,* p. A19.

Posner, P. L. (2002). Accountability challenges of third-party government. In L. M. Salamon (Ed.), *The tools of government: A guide to the new governance* (pp. 523–551). New York: Oxford University Press.

Sartori, G. (1965). *Democratic theory.* New York: Praeger.

Schattschneider, E. E. (1960). *The semi-sovereign people: A realist's view of democracy in America.* New York: Holt, Rinehart, & Winston.

Schneider, A. L., & Ingram, H. (1997). *Policy design for democracy.* Lawrence: University Press of Kansas.

Shafritz, J. M., & Russell, E. W. (2005). *Introducing public administration.* New York: Pearson Longman.

Smith, S. R., & Ingram, H. (2002). Policy tools and democracy. In L. M. Salamon (Ed.), *The tools of government: A guide to the new governance* (pp. 565–584). New York: Oxford University Press.

Stillman, R., II. (1996). *The American bureaucracy: The core of modern government* (2nd ed.). Chicago: Nelson Hall.

Van Meter, D. S., & Van Horn, C. E. (1975). The policy implementation process: A conceptual framework. *Administration & Society, 6,* 445–488.

Wayne, S. J. (2004). Issues of democratic governance. In S. J. Wayne (Ed.), *Is this any way to run a democratic government?* (pp. 3–19). Washington, DC: Georgetown University Press.

Weisberg, J. (2006, January 26). Drug addled: Why Bush's prescription drug plan is such a fiasco. *Slate.* Retrieved from www.slate.com/id/2134456/?nav=navoa.

Wilson, W. (1887). The study of administration. *Political Science Quarterly, 2,* 197–222.

Yates, D. (1982). *Bureaucracy and democracy: The search for democracy and efficiency in American government.* Cambridge, MA: Harvard University Press.

A Brief Tour of Public Organization Theory in the United States

Gary S. Marshall

Public administrative organizations in the United States rest on the twin pillars of management and democracy. Because the management processes of public organizations are not solely instrumental but involve the public interest, public agencies have to be more than mechanisms of rationality. Public administrative action has both an instrumental quality, i.e., its capacity for optimal technical rationality (technique), and a social quality—an underlying connection to the social bond between self and other.

With this backdrop, we begin the focus of this chapter which recounts the sociology of organizations with an emphasis on key democratic moments in the history of American public administration. Before doing so, we might ask how the central terms used in our discussion will be defined. What are organizations? For the purposes of this chapter, organizations are the basic unit through which virtually all social relations are formed in post-traditional society.[1] In that sense, all social life is understood as organizational life (Denhardt, 1981). Management, coterminous with any definition of organization, refers to the regularized relations within organizations. As will be developed in the chapter, the rationalization of work led to formal and informal relations within public organizations, and the "management" of those relations is the primary way in which the term management is used here.

Democracy, literally "rule of the people," is another term central to our discussion. As the book's editor, Richard Box, noted in the Introduction, "The practice of public administration in the United States is set within the context of a *liberal-capitalist, representative democracy*." On this point, our discussion of public organization theory reflects the dynamics of administrative institutions and their role within the general processes of societal governance. The prevailing view of democracy in relation to twentieth- and twenty-first-century public organizations is one of *overhead democracy*

(Redford, 1969). That is, both politicians and administrators are held accountable in a democratic society.[2]

A second important dimension in our discussion of democracy is the dramatic shift in the United States from an agrarian to an industrial society. Industrialism in western societies led to the rationalization of work and human relations with new forms of organization. Hence, the study of public administrative organizations is grounded in a tradition of industrial democracy.

A final point about democracy as it relates to this chapter is workplace democracy: the participatory dimension of internal organizational processes. Public organizations have been understood for the most part as administrative systems characterized by top-down legal-rational authority. This formal structure notwithstanding, the incorporation and practice of democratic principles and actions in the workplace have also been present within the public organizational setting, dating back to the anti-federalist ethos of the founding period of the U.S. Constitution.

Public Organizations and the Forging of the Administrative State

After the Civil War, American society transitioned to its modern form. The economy underwent a basic revision wherein regional monopolies disbanded and large corporate trusts developed. The political and social conditions of this period have been well documented (Bailyn et al., 1977; Hofstadter, 1955; Link & McCormick, 1983; McConnell, 1966; Wiebe 1967; Woll, 1977). The United States began to shift after 1830 from a predominantly agrarian society to an industrial society. By 1900, 40 percent of the American population was located in urban centers such as New York, Detroit, Chicago, and Philadelphia (Bailyn et al., 1977).

In addition, the structure of work changed. Bailyn et al. (1977) note that industrial technology, with its emphasis on specialization and the division of labor, melded man into an instrument of the manufacturing process. On the farm, the harvester replaced the scythe, and in the cities, machines and the technological assembly line processes revolutionized whole industries, as the Bessemer process did for the steel industry. Industrial and economic expansion occurred on all fronts, including mining, railroads, and industries in the cities. The result of this economic expansion was that by the end of the century, the largest business interests in each arena—steel, oil, agriculture, rail transport, and manufacturing—consolidated their market share to the point of monopoly. Technological changes and developments signaled the end of the period of rural democracy. This period of industrial expansion and subsequent consolidation created a set of diverse political expectations and social conditions. On the one hand there were the unregulated interests and concentrated economic power of the industrialists, and on the other hand there were the interests and distributed wealth of individuals who were farmers, local merchants, and industrial workers.

Until the late 1880s, there was little movement for a national authority to regulate economic activity. Rather, government had played a role in fostering economic development and as a result had a stake in continuing to promote the interests of business. More important, the reigning assumption of the period was that a natural economic equilibrium would occur independently of regulation. However, the social and political conditions eventually put government in an awkward position. As Woll (1977, p. 39) notes: "Having fostered industries with subsidies of various kinds, both national and state governments had to contend with political and social problems such as economic instability, deceptive business practices, and the growth of monopolies that were directly attributed to the activities of groups that they originally supported."

The Ethos of Technique

The field of public administration responded to the material requirements of a modern administrative state required in the wake of industrial expansion. Between 1870 and 1930, the number of federal employees rose from 73,000 to 700,000 (Mosher, 1975). During the period spanning from the turn of the century to 1935, many changes and developments took place in the field. The Taft Commission on Economy and Efficiency led the way for budget reform and an executive budget by 1921. The New York Bureau of Municipal Research became a clearinghouse for new research in public administration. Specialized knowledge about municipal governance was sought. The ideas generated from these reform efforts became known as the bureau movement and represented "the conviction that only through efficient government could progressive social welfare be achieved. . . . So long as government remained inefficient, volunteer, and detached, [any] effort to remove social handicaps would continue a hopeless task" (Mosher, 1981, p. 93).

The expanded role for public administrators was heralded by most because of their (1) subject matter expertise, (2) continuity as civil servants, and (3) commitment to the public interest. In addition, their application of scientific principles in the conduct of administration was seen as a positive step. It was assumed that the scientific method employed by the administrator would bring both impartiality and progress (better solutions through the ordered process of rationality) to an untenable situation. In their *Papers on the Science of Administration*, Gulick and Urwick (1937, p. 49) wrote: "There are principles which can be arrived at inductively from the study of human organizations. . . . These principles can be studied as a technical question, irrespective of the enterprise." In an essay entitled "Notes on the Theory of Organization," Gulick articulated the principles of administration known by the acronym POSDCORB—Planning, Organizing, Staffing, Directing, COordinating, Reporting, and Budgeting.

The ethos of technique as evidenced by the above discussion dominated this period of research and theorizing about public organizations. This emphasis on the technical character of administration did not mean, however, that the democratic nature of public institutions had been foreclosed. Rather, it reflected the predominantly Wilsonian view at the time that there ought to be a clear separation between politics and administration. As Gulick wrote, the place of the administrator with his/her expertise is "on tap, not on top" (Gulick, in Harmon & Mayer, 1986, p. 127). The view was that the United States would thrive as a democracy if its strong political leadership was supported by administrative agencies with strong institutional capacity.

Scientific Management and Early Organization Theory

The specter of scientific management and its emphasis on the instrumental, in retrospect, haunts the twentieth century. But, in the first two decades of that century, efficiency was a word that portended apolitical social change, scientific progress, and increased material wealth. During this period of industrialization and modernization, bureaucracy and its corollary, scientific management, were understood as humane alternatives to the autocratic patterns of earlier decades wherein there was little regard to safety and systematization of work. The so-called rationalization of work allowed a heavy workload to be accomplished by the fewest people in the most efficient way possible. As Weber (1991, p. 214) noted: "The decisive reason for the advance of bureaucratic organization has always been its purely technical superiority over any other form of organization. The fully developed bureaucratic organization compares with other organizations exactly as the machine with the non-mechanical modes of production."

Frederick Taylor, with his work at the Midvale and Bethlehem Steel companies, was the strongest proponent of these ideas. Taylor's efforts all focused on strategies to limit worker autonomy and individual discretion in the production process in favor of a model that valued one best way to carry out a task as determined by scientific expertise. His view of human nature portended the behavioral revolution in social science. While one might not be able to fully explain people's motives, one could direct their behavior through economic motives and scientific expertise. Taylor held that "man is an economic animal who responds directly to financial incentives within the limits of his physiological capabilities and the technical and work organization which is provided to him" (Silverman, 1971, p. 176). A famous conversation between Taylor and one of the Bethlehem workers found in the essay *Principles of Scientific Management*, gives one a flavor:

> What I want to find out is whether you are a high-priced man or one of those cheap fellows here . . . whether you want to earn $1.85 a day or . . . are you satisfied with $1.15 just the same as all those cheap fellows. . . . Oh you're aggravating me. Of course you want $1.85—everyone wants it. . . . Well if you are a high-priced man, you will do exactly as this man tells you to-morrow, from morning till night. . . . And what's more, no back talk. . . . Do you understand that? (1947a, p. 45)

In Taylor's view, man is not capable of accomplishing work without an expert to direct his/her behavior. Hence, he calls for the "one-best way of the scientific method." This reflects, in spite of Taylor's lionizing of the worker, a profound distrust in human beings. In his classic paper "Shop Management," he wrote about the "social loafing" of workers. This loafing or soldiering proceeds from two causes. First, from the natural instinct and tendency of men to take it easy, which may be called natural soldiering. Second, from more intricate second thought and reasoning caused by their relations with other men, which may be called systematic soldiering (1947b, p. 30).

Not only did Taylor have disdain for subordinates, but for their superiors as well. He wrote extensively about the "indifference" of employers to the plight of good management. Taylor sought to shift authority from management to the expert, whose sphere of authority was legitimated through the planning departments of organizations. As satirized in Chaplin's *Modern Times*, work processes are analogous to the pieces of a mechanical clock. All the parts are discrete entities, some parts are more important than others, but in the final analysis all fit together to make it work. In this analogy, the scientific expert plays the role of the watchmaker.

Taylor's legacy remains firmly in place today not only in his view of worker-management relations but also in the form of systems from managerial accounting, organizational form and function, artificial intelligence applications, and many other organizational systems. His approach required nothing less than a mental revolution. As his testimony before a House Special Committee investigating the union strikes at the Watertown Arsenal reflects:

> Now, in essence, scientific management involves a complete mental revolution on the part of the working man engaged in any particular establish-

ment or industry—a complete mental revolution on the part of these men as to their duties toward their work, toward their fellow men, and toward their employers. And it involves the equally complete mental revolution on the part of those on the management's side—the foreman, the superintendent, the owner of the business, the board of directors—a complete mental revolution on their parts as to their duties toward their fellow workers in the management, toward their workmen, and toward all of their daily problems. And without this complete mental revolution on both sides scientific management does not exist. (1947c, p. 27)

To summarize, scientific management reflects these four elements: organizations exist to accomplish production-related and economic goals; there is one best way to organize for production, and that way can be found through systematic, scientific inquiry; production is maximized through specialization and division of labor; and people and organizations act in accordance with rational economic principles (Shafritz & Ott, 1996).

The Early Human Relations Movement

"But scientific management has never studied the facts of human social organization, it has accepted the 19th century economic dictum that economic interest and logical capacity are the basis of the social order" (Henderson & Mayo, 2002, p. 311). This quotation, in an essay by L. J. Henderson and Elton Mayo, reflects the assessment of a group of researchers at Harvard University who, in part due to Henderson's championing of Vifredo Pareto's concept of social equilibrium (Heyl, 1968), wrote about organizations as social systems.

The work of Henderson, Mayo, Roethlisberger, and Dickson at General Electric's Hawthorne Plant represents an important development in the history of organization theory. These so-called early human relationists sought to emphasize the interpersonal dimension of work life, i.e., the relationships that people form with one another in the workplace and the meaning made through those relationships and work experiences. The major point was that the underlying social bond between and among individuals is extremely powerful and not necessarily malleable to the rapid changes that the technical dimension of the organization projects upon it. A further quote from Henderson and Mayo makes this point quite well:

Now the social codes which define a worker's relation to his work and to his fellows are not capable of rapid change. They are developed slowly and over long periods of time. They are not the product of logic, but of actual human association, they are based on deep rooted human sentiments. Constant interference with such codes is bound to lead to feelings of frustration, to irrational exasperation with technical change of any form. (2002, p. 311)

These researchers brought into stark relief the disjuncture between the technical demands of the organization and the rapidity of functional changes with regard to management processes within an organization on the one hand, and the informal long-term social and psychic relationships of one human being to another. This "social dimension" of human association had (has) a logic all its own that bears little relationship to the functional or formal organizational design that is configured according to the goals, objectives, and production processes of the organization. No doubt, the work itself is central to the group dynamics of those working in the organization, but the functional relationships are in some sense artificial as compared with the underlying social bond of those in the workplace. This social bond follows a psychological path rather than a functional path.

The "solution" offered by the Harvard group might be labeled a benignly corporatist one. As Harmon and Mayer note:

> The thrust of these interpretations [by the Harvard group] is clear: The dissatisfied individual (the source of the complaint) is to be manipulated by alterations in his or her position or status; this is achieved by manipulation, to the extent possible, of the social organization, etc. . . . Essentially, people are seen as socially motivated and controlled. Any increase in morale (and therefore in productivity) is, thus, necessarily related to change in the human and social conditions, not the physical or material condition. (1986, p. 101)

This perspective is more fully developed by Chester Barnard. Barnard's book, *The Functions of the Executive*, is considered a classic in the organization theory literature. It builds on insights about the social dimension of organizational life and presents organizations as systems of cooperation that must be well managed by the organization's leaders. Barnard writes:

> A part of the effort to determine individual behavior takes the form of altering the conditions of behavior, including a conditioning of the individual by training, by the inculcation of attitudes, by the construction of incentives. This constitutes a large part of the executive process. . . . Failure to recognize this position is among the most important sources of error in executive work. (1968, p. 15)

Thus for Barnard the executive must act as sea captain, ready at the helm to guide the human systems—formal and informal—to propel the organizational vessel in the appropriate direction. This view reinforced a top-down view of government institutions, wherein a responsive public executive ensured democratically accountable administrative practices.

Mary Parker Follett

The pioneering work of Mary Parker Follett represents an alternative perspective on knowledge that human relationships are the central factor in organizational action. Although the compelling quality of Follett's work went largely unheralded in her day, Follett is an important contributor to an understanding of the social dimension of organizational life (Drucker, 1995). She lectured and wrote extensively and was a compatriot of the members of the Harvard group. Like her colleagues, she saw social cooperation as an important and underdeveloped criterion in the study of group processes. Follett however, did not see social cooperation as merely a functional element of industrial organization. Rather, she saw it as evidence of the vital human bond between people. In a word, social process—the process of relating to others, an engagement of social experience—was a prerequisite to all human action. For Follett, relationship is the primary unit of analysis and the wellspring from which all else unfolds.

The social process is the interaction that occurs between human beings. It is in Follett's language the having and digesting of social experience. This social process is the basis through which common agreement and common action can be undertaken. As she notes: "We have seen that the common idea and the common will are born together in the social process. . . . They complete themselves only through activity in the world of affairs, of work and of government" (Follett, 1995a, p. 247).

Writers who have championed Follett's work emphasize the integrative dimension of her approach. The use of the term "integrative" refers to a key insight by Follett that human activity resists reduction to causal analysis. In the Pavlovian stimulus-response equation, the response "is not merely the activity resulting from a certain stimulus and that response in turn influencing that activity; it is because it is response that it influences that activity, that is part of what response means" (Follett, 1995b, p. 41). Social relations are never static. Rather, they are an evolving situation—a situation of constant interdependent reciprocal influence. As she notes:

> In human relations . . . I never react to you but to you-plus-me; or to be more accurate, it is I-plus-you reacting to you-plus-me. "I" can never in-

fluence "you" because you have already influenced me; that is, in the very process of meeting, by the very process of meeting, we both become something different. (Follett, 1995b, p. 42)

Integration refers to the constant integrating of experience. Social process then is a platform under which all human process takes place, or more properly stated, evolves. Organizations are institutions of social process wherein goal-directed behavior on the part of leaders, managers, supervisors, and workers does not accurately account for the way in which events unfold. This basic approach serves as the grounding for all of Follett's work, including her well-known analysis on the concept of power, the giving of orders, the law of the situation, and the quality of twentieth-century democracy.

Central to this chapter is the view of the self as understood by the management theories under review. Follett's perspective represents a radical departure because she posits the self as constantly in process, constantly evolving. Such a view is diametrically opposed to the self as economic man: a rational calculating being who knows what he wants or whose wants can be predicted. For Taylor, the worker was motivated by a higher wage. For the early human relationists, workers were also social beings whose "sentiments" were to be afforded a certain degree of attention in service of organizational productivity.

This emphasis on the interpersonal dimensions of organizational life paved the way for an increased study of groups and group dynamics. Beginning with the work of Jacob Moreno, whose pioneering sociometric methods gave researchers a way to analyze the patterns of verbal and non-verbal behavior in small groups, group dynamics validated Follett's insight of a live social process beneath the formal structure of the organization. More specifically, the insight of group dynamics is that groups are discrete entities that foster behavior that would not occur otherwise.

Kurt Lewin

Kurt Lewin is the best-known writer on the study of groups and the contribution of group dynamics to organizational theory and organizational change. Why was his work so pivotal? First, like the early human relationists, he championed the human dimension in the workplace. In Lewin's earliest work as a researcher at Berlin University, he demonstrated in his study of the work processes of Silesian textile workers that technique based on manual dexterity—the central claim of scientific management—was not the overriding factor in creating a productive workplace. Rather, when one considers total job demands, including the intrinsic value of the work itself, the worker's self-perception, and motivation and commitment, scientific management's rigid criterion of technical competence was too narrow (Weisbord, 2004, pp. 85–86).

In 1933, Lewin immigrated to the United States and began a fruitful period of research at the University of Iowa, where he worked with the sociologist Margaret Mead among others. One of their key findings was that organizational processes are more likely to succeed when the decision-making process is an inclusive one. Mead and Lewin determined that to get families to eat other kinds of meats than the types subject to severe rationing during World War II, so-called gatekeepers (typically moms in this case) needed to be a part of the decision-making process. As Mead so famously noted: "you cannot do things to people but only with them" (Mead, in Weisbord, 2004, p. 94). Their research demonstrated that meaningful inclusion in the decision-making process leads to sustained organizational commitment.

While the notion of the "group mind" can be attributed to the work of Gustave LeBon and his famous work *The Crowd: A Study of the Popular Mind* (1982), Lewin pioneered the study of groups and the principle that feedback and therefore participatory processes were requisites to organizational productivity and success. With the establishment of the National Training Laboratories (NTL) in Bethel, Maine, T-Groups or "training groups" became a vehicle by which the ideas of participative management were disseminated into the workplace. The current emphasis on teams in the workplace is a direct result of this work. Further, better insights into group dynamics were developed as a result of the T-Group phenomenon, e.g., the stages of group development.

Lewin's legacy also lives on in the action research model of organizational analysis. Consistent with his famous dictum "there is nothing so practical as good theory," the action research model incorporates worker feedback into its framework, particularly in the problem definition and clarification stages. Worker participation is also central to the joint problem-solving and implementation stages of action research. Lewin's work is central to the sociology of organizations because he saw human beings as goal directed but profoundly affected by the context.

The concept of workplace democracy can most directly be attributed to Lewin. His research showed that democratic workplace processes, characterized by group goal setting and mutual feedback, led to stronger task completion, synchronicity, and innovation. While he advocated participation (workplace democracy), he was not an advocate of unstructured participation. Lewin's field research showed that so-called laissez-faire management (wrongly assumed to be "democratic") led to drops in productivity far lower than the drops demonstrated in long-terms studies of authoritarian management environments.

Herbert Simon and the Rational Model of Organization

After World War II a refined discourse of rationalism and efficiency took hold in conjunction with the technological innovation occurring after the war. Early in the twentieth century, in the social sciences, science was essentially understood as a rationalizing technology, that is, making systems work more efficiently by ordering the processes to accomplish maximum output using the least resources. Technical solutions were very appealing given the scale of the changes that occurred in the wake of industrial expansion, the Great Depression, and two World Wars.

As gains in natural science took hold, there was a push by social scientists to effect the same rigor in the social sciences. As Denhardt notes:

> In keeping with the general scientism of the period, many political scientists felt their earlier studies of government institutions lacked the rigor (and therefore, presumably the dignity) of work in such "real" sciences as physics and chemistry. To correct the situation, they argued on behalf of an approach to science based on the philosophical perspective of logical positivism. This approach held that regularities in human behavior, as in the behavior of physical objects, could be determined by the careful and objective observation of exhibited (or manifest) behavior and that scientific theories could be logically derived from such observations. Just as one could observe the behavior of molecular structures, and then develop theories concerning physical life, so it was argued, one could observe the behavior of human beings "from the outside," then develop theories concerning social life. (2004, p. 68)

This led to a push toward a so-called science of administration. A major contributor to such an approach was Herbert A. Simon. Simon's book *Administrative Behavior* shaped the post–World War II view of organizations. In his famous article "The Proverbs of Administration," he trivialized as naïve the management theory of the early twentieth century. Probably the most significant effect of Simon's work was that prior to *Administrative Behavior* (1976), theorists sought to control work processes. After Simon, theorists sought to control decision processes. Using behaviorist methods, if one could predict and control human behavior in organizations, then one could predict and create successful organizational outcomes.

The crucial argument made by Simon is that one should design theories of organization to focus only upon the so-called rational component of the mind. That is, what is most predictable about human behavior is our capacity to be rational: to act with conscious intention. Simon later went on to show how decision support systems and artificial intelligence models could enhance the vital but limited capacity of humans to act rationally. As Denhardt notes in a quotation from Simon: "The rational individual is, and must be, an organized and institutionalized individual" (2004, p. 74).

The prototype for Simon was *administrative man*. Denhardt recounts a definition for us:

> The classical utility-seeking "economic man" is replaced by a more modern and more institutionalized "administrative man": administrative man accepts the organizational goals as the value premises of his decisions, is particularly sensitive and reactive to the influence upon him of other members of his organization, forms stable expectations regarding his own role in relation to others and the role of others in relation to him, and has high morale in regard to organizational goals. (2004, p. 76)

The acceptance of organizational goals as value premises is and has been a controversial point. Which trumps which when the values of efficiency and democracy collide? Simon attempted to finesse this vital debate by suggesting a separation between policy and administration. He argued that the administrator's task is to optimally implement the stated policy directions that have been democratically decided upon by the elected representatives of government. Such an argument avoids the artificial nature of such a split, as administration is clearly governance. In addition, it is hard to argue with Dahl's (1947) point that the application of the value of efficiency as an overriding criterion in the conduct of administration is a policy decision in its own right. Both Dahl and Dwight Waldo (1948; 1952) sought to refute Simon's push for an administrative science that discounted the normatively democratic character of public administration.

This period in the history of the study of organizations is often called the golden age of organization theory. In this period, organizational roles were understood as a unit within the broader social system of organization. Such a view held the organizational role as relatively unproblematic. As McSwite suggests, the role is "defined as the set of stabilized expectations that organizations comprise. Human beings are seen simply as role players who respond to 'role senders' who transfer expectations to them" (1997, p. 185).

The logic of this view was structural-functional (Burrell & Morgan, 1979; Parsons, 1951). That is, the organization was understood as a tangible, typically biological, structure composed of subunits that ensured its survival. Parsons, in an effort to describe human action, argued that while social scientists were often at odds to explain the particular behavior of individuals, a coherent explanation of human action could be ascertained if one examined the roles (the functions) that individuals carried out within the context of the larger society. From this perspective, one's identity or "self" was based on one's societal roles. As such, "One is a mother, a son, a Texan, a Scot, a professor, a sociologist, a Catholic, a lesbian—or a combination of these social roles and possibilities" (Kellner, in Anderson, 1997, p. 107). This view, dominant at the time, emphasized the *functions* of a society and the way in which an individual's "values" either facilitated or complicated an individual's socialization and integration into the social order. It emphasized the values that established and maintained the social order. Entities such as the home, the nuclear family, and the school were understood as sites for the reinforcement of this perspective.

Such a view also framed the worker, as we see with Simon above, as an information processor, a rationally choosing entity able to consciously identify its interests and choose how to act in accordance with those interests. This view serves as the foundation for the self as developed by those in the field of artificial intelligence. It was also the base for early work in cognitive science.

During the 1950s and 1960s, the organization as a system was the dominant metaphor. As work in this area developed, theorists moved from closed systems to open systems. This in part reflected the importance of the environment outside of the organization's functional or technical operations. As Katz and Kahn wrote in their classic *The Social Psychology of Organizations:* "Social systems are flagrantly open systems in that the input of energies and the conversion of output into further energic input consists of transactions between the organization and its environment" (1966, p. 18). The result of this perspective was a focus on a variety of "environmental effects" and the "feedback" from those external environments.

A concomitant influence during this period was general systems theory (GST) (Kast & Rosenzweig, 1972). GST is a meta-theory that incorporates all types of biological, physical, and social systems. The creation of such a meta-theory in the natural sciences led to so-called second order theorizing about organizational systems, thereby yielding contingency theory. This approach, attributed to Harvard researchers Paul Lawrence and Jay Lorsch, looked for patterns of relationships in organizational subsystems. The lessons learned from these patterns would allow a manager to respond to specific contingencies or situations with the right mix of task, technology, and people. As another well-known organization theorist, J. D. Thompson, wrote:

> The contingency view seeks to understand the interrelationships within and among subsystems as well as between the organization and its environment and to define patterns of relationship or configuration of variables. It emphasizes the multivariate nature of organizations and attempts to understand how organizations operate under varying conditions and in specific circumstances. (1967, p. 157)

The systems and neo-classical approaches to the study of organizations had the organization's efficient function as their raison d'être. This perspective was matched with a value-neutral approach to public service. That is, the expertise of the administrator, coupled with his or her ability to manage for efficiency, was the ideal type of the period. Social and political events in the United States in the 1960s revealed the dilemma of viewing public organizations as purely rational instruments. A classic example is the Defense Department's use of "body count" during the Vietnam War. American success in the war was measured by the number of enemy killed. Such an operational variable "made sense" in the parlance of organizational goals and objectives, but giving primacy to this instrumental view led to a distorted picture of events on the ground to say nothing of the public's response to the detached analytic posture of its politicians and administrators.

Public administration writers of this period sought to establish a New Public Administration to respond to a seemingly changed social order. The core view that animated the New Public Administration was that "the purpose of public organization is the reduction of economic, social and psychic suffering and the enhancement of life opportunities for those inside and outside the organization" (LaPorte, 1971, p. 32). The core dialectical themes that animate the public administration field—politics and administration; facts and values; efficiency and equity; hierarchy and participation—all seemed out of balance. As the organizational theorist Chris Argyris wrote in *Public Administration Review*:

> Organizational theory in public administration may be undergoing an important transformation. The new critics find much administrative descriptive theory to be nonrelevant to many critical problems of organizations. They suggest that the present theories are based on a concept of man, indeed a morality, that leads the scholar to conduct research that is, intentionally or unintentionally, supportive of the status quo. . . . The newer critical writings are also concerned with individual morality, authenticity, human self-actualization. The scholars are not only asking what makes an organization more effective; they are concerned with the issues: For whom are the organizations designed? How humane can organizations become and still be effective? (1973, p. 253)[3]

Organizational Humanism

Argyris's work gained prominence in light of the critique of the rational model of organization. The so-called later human relationists reasserted the primacy of the individual in organizational theorizing. The early human relationists like Henderson, Mayo, Roethelisberger, and Barnard introduced the importance of the individual in organizational life. However, their view was that human "sentiment" was a dimension of organizational life to be managed in the accomplishment of organizational goals and objectives. The rational model of organization in its neo-classicist and systems forms sought to predict and control the work of its members by using the organizational structure as a means to produce rational behavior. Argyris, whose work built on that of Maslow's Hierarchy of Needs and McGregor's Theory X and Theory Y, heralded an expanded role for member participation in organizations.[4] In his famous book *Personality and Organization* (1957), he argued that because the trajectory of individual human development would always differ from the trajectory of the organization's goals and objectives, the task of management should be to mediate the gap of this inherent disparity.

This perspective, also known as organizational humanism, led to significant changes in organizational design. Ideas about worker autonomy and participation that we now take for granted were ushered in in this period. Among works in public administration, Robert Golembiewski's *Men, Management and Morality* (1967) is continually cited as best expressing the elements of organizational humanism within public organizations.[5] The following five tenets reflect the normative stance taken by Golembiewski:

1. Work must be psychologically acceptable to the individual . . .
2. Work must allow man to develop his own faculties . . .
3. The work task must allow the individual considerable room for self-determination . . .
4. The worker must have the possibility of controlling, in a meaningful way, the environment within which the task is to be performed . . .
5. The organization should not be the sole and final arbiter of behaviour; both the organization and the individual must be subject to an external moral order (1967, p. 65).

The Economists' Response to Bureaucracy

The very large bureaucracy will (1) become increasingly indiscriminating in its response to diverse demands, (2) impose increasingly high social costs upon those who are presumed to be its beneficiaries, (3) fail to proportion supply and demand, (4) allow public goods to erode by failing to take actions to prevent one use from impairing other uses, (5) become increasingly error prone and uncontrollable to the point where public actions deviate radically from rhetoric about public purposes and objectives, and (6) eventually lead to a circumstance where remedial actions exacerbate rather than ameliorate problems. (Ostrom, 1989, p. 56)

In a sweeping analysis of the way in which public organizations have been viewed, Vincent Ostrom's book *The Intellectual Crisis in Public Administration* (1989) argued that large-scale bureaucracies are not the sole instruments capable of delivering public goods and services. Ostrom championed a public choice approach to organization theory. Public choice theory developed by James Buchanan and Gordon Tullock applies economic decision-making to the realm of politics and public policy. Ideas that have now gained acceptance such as education vouchers, pollution credits, and open competition for the provision of public services had their genesis in Buchanan and Tullock's book the *Calculus of Consent* (1962).

The themes of public choice theory that undergird a public choice theory of organizations are methodological individualism and decentralized organizational arrangements. Methodological individualism refers to the individual as the unit of analysis in the examination of all social phenomena (Donaldson, 1996, p. 342). Moreover, the definition of the individual is tightly circumscribed. He/she is (1) motivated by self-interest, (2) rational in his/her ability to rank alternatives, and (3) seeks to maximize his/her net benefit in any given situation (Ostrom, 1989, pp. 44–46).

Public choice organization theory centers on decentralized organizational arrangements. The rationale for such arrangements is based on an economic argument about the delivery of goods and services. Between purely private transactions, purchasing a toaster for example, and purely public transactions, defending the nation's citizens, for example, there is a vast middle range, which Ostrom suggests should be subject to economic models of collective action rather than other forms of decision-making (Ostrom, 1989, pp. 46–47). In this sense, "public agencies are viewed as a means for allocating decision-making capabilities in order to provide public goods and services responsive to the preferences of individuals in different social contexts" (Ostrom & Ostrom, in Denhardt, 2004, p. 207). Hence, for a broad range of public-sector-related activities, bureaucratic systems ought to be replaced by decentralized market-like mechanisms. This approach, in Ostrom's view, is not only more responsive to individual choice, but more closely aligned with Madison's and Hamilton's design for American government than with Woodrow Wilson's interpretation of the relation between politics and administration.[6]

The public choice model represents an exchange-based view of human behavior that has maintained its prominence. New Public Management practices across all western governments have approached the reform of public sector organizations in the tradition of public choice's principal-agent model. Put simply, these theories argue that each actor possesses an asset another actor needs, and this interdependence spurs an exchange; that leaders establish the terms of exchange with other actors whose cooperation is important for achieving goals; and that both parties of the exchange (principals and agents) are opportunistic, seeking to maximize their gains. The principal's primary task is to monitor the agent closely to ensure compliance and cooperation (Reitan, 1998).

From the standpoint of organization theory however, it is not clear whether the public choice cum new public management model provides any real innovation in terms of its view of human behavior. In all its varieties, the principal-agent model is based on the unwavering view that in an effort to maximize his/her self-interest, the agent will try to shirk his/her responsibilities to the principal. Echoing Oliver Williamson (1985), the agent is "an individual who has the inherent propensity to *shirk*, to be *opportunistic*, to maximize his or her self-interest, to act with guile, and to behave in ways that constitute a *moral hazard*" (Donaldson, 1996, p. 340). Such a view, so reminiscent of Taylor's systematic soldiering claims, leads one to wonder whether much has changed in the study of organizations.

The Network Model of Organization Theory

Since the mid-1990s, there has been a proliferation of writing about the network model of organization. From the organizational structure standpoint, the network model creates the possibility for reduced layers of communication, ease of information flow, and, ideally, better access to services. The value of such a model is the optimization of resources, including human resources. Catherine Alter and Jerald Hage's notable text, *Organizations Working Together* (1993, p. 46), defines organizational networks as "the basic social form that permits interorganizational interactions of exchange, concerted action, and joint production. Networks are unbounded or bounded clusters of organizations that, by definition, are nonhierarchical collectives of legally separate units." In Alter and Hage's definition, two overriding characteristics of the network model are an emphasis on horizontal rather than hierarchical relationships and an emphasis on exchange-based assumptions about human behavior.

To a large degree, the network model is an extension of the decentralized approach to organizing. As Goldsmith and Eggers note in their widely read *Governing by Network:*

> The hierarchical model of government persists, but its influence is steadily waning, pushed by governments' appetite to solve ever more complicated problems and pulled by new tools that allow innovators to fashion creative responses. This push and pull is gradually a new model of government in

which executives' core responsibilities, no longer center on managing people and programs but on organizing resources, often belonging to others, to produce public value. Government agencies, bureaus, divisions, and offices are becoming less important as direct service providers, but more important as generators of public value within a web of multiorganizational, multigovernmental, and multisectoral relationships that characterize modern government. (Goldsmith and Eggers, 2004, p. 8)

As networks seek the optimal mode of operation, each component of the network tries to function in its best possible fashion. There is an emphasis on lean operations and optimal linkages. Hierarchical organizations are flattened; redundant systems are exorcized. How does today's public administrator cope with the demands of administering in a decentralized system wherein both normatively and operationally lines of authority are more fluid and where democratic representativeness and accountability—the staples of administrative legitimacy—are rendered both more complex and more ambiguous? Two answers surface in the literature. In the United States the emphasis has been primarily instrumental. That is, the focus has been on techniques for network managers (Agranoff & McGuire, 1999; Berry et al., 2004; McGuire, 2002).

McGuire (2002) maintains that there is a core set of behaviors that the current public administrator must possess in order to manage successfully in the network setting. First, an administrator must hold activation skills. Activation is a set of behaviors employed for identifying and incorporating the persons and resources (such as funding, expertise, and legal authority) needed to achieve program goals. The single organization parallel to activation would be personnel issues of staffing. Activating involves identifying participants for the network and including key stakeholders in the process. The removal of network participants is known as "deactivating." Second, McGuire claims an administrator must also have framing behaviors. Framing behaviors are used to arrange and integrate a network structure by facilitating agreement on participants' roles, operating rules, and network values. Third is mobilization. Mobilizing develops commitment and support for network processes from network participants and external stakeholders. The last core behavior is synthesizing. Synthesizing behaviors build relationships and interactions that result in achieving the network purpose. The crowded schedule of the public manager must include room for these support-building activities.

In the European literature, there is an emphasis on democratic network governance. Sørensen and Torfing define a governance network as: (1) a relatively stable horizontal articulation of interdependent, but operationally autonomous actors, (2) who interact through negotiations, (3) that take place within a regulative, normative, cognitive, and imaginary framework, (4) that to a certain extent is self-regulating, and (5) that contributes to the production of public purpose within or across particular policy areas (2005). This broader definition reflects their view that network models of organization do not operate solely based on the heretofore-discussed principal-agent model but have the potential to operate from various epistemological frames.

Sørensen-Torfing Model:
Four Basic Theories of Network Governance

	Calculation	Culture
Conflict	Interdependence theory	Governmentality theory
Coordination	Governability theory	Integration theory

At the level of social theory, they distinguish between theories of rational calculation and theories that presume culture influences social action. The authors then juxtapose these dimensions of social theory with assumptions operative within networked systems: network approaches that emphasize coordination and network models that assume that conflict is the logic behind interaction within the network. Such a juxtaposition offers a more nuanced view of relations within a network.

A second major component of Sørensen and Torfing's analysis is their engagement of post-liberal theories of democracy. Whereas the U.S. public management network literature takes the question of democratic network governance as a given, Sørensen and Torfing convincingly argue that the network model of governance affects the traditionally understood democratic practices within both the administrative sector and the larger political structure of society (Sørensen, 2002; Sørensen & Torfing, 2005). Although the public management movement within the United States has not been silent on, for example, the question of substantive versus procedural democracy, it has typically understood its research agenda as standing outside the work done by democratic theorists (Box, Marshall, Reed & Reed, 2001).

Conclusion

So ends our brief tour of public organization theory in the United States. Public organizations today are increasingly decentralized and multisectoral. This creates new challenges for organizing and managing and also for sustaining the democratic character of public administration. With regard to the former—organization and management—the network structure is not without its limitations and as such, horizontal coordination is vital. With regard to the latter—democracy—there are implications for the normative dimensions of democratic governance and for the possibility of workplace democracy.

The decentralized model of organization changes the normative equation. Rather than large administrative institutions as symbols—both physically and socially—of the public interest, we have multiorganizational arrangements. These multisectoral arrangements are understood to be more democratic because of their capacity to be responsive to citizen preferences. These new arrangements may perhaps also provide new opportunities for workplace democracy, if the lessons of Kurt Lewin's work on groups are applied and if the type of collaborative social process described by Mary Parker Follett is realized. Equally possible in the largely networked organization environment on the horizon is the expanded application of the principal-agent model to all types of organizational forms and relationships. In such a scenario, the social bond that is characteristic of public life will take on an increasingly exchange-based rather than substantively democratic quality.

Notes

1. I am using the term post-traditional society to refer to both modernity and its echo: postmodernity. Central to this definition is an understanding of modernity. According to Giddens (1991, p. 15), there are four key aspects to modernity. That is, four main discourses: (1) industrialism—the social relations implied in the widespread use of material power and machinery in production processes; (2) capitalism—a system of commodity production involving both competitive product markets and the commodification of labor power; (3) surveillance—the supervisory control of subject populations, whether this control takes the form of "visible" supervision in Foucault's sense or the use of information to coordinate social activities; and (4) organization—the regularized control of social relations across indefinite time-space distances.

2. Redford's argument is that administrative agencies play a crucial role in sustaining a democratic society. As Orion White noted of his mentor: "Emmette Redford represented the idea that effective governance, performed by responsible officials and of which administration was an indispensable and legitimate part, was a vital part of social life and societal well-being" (McSwite, 1997, p. 7). A different interpretation is offered by Meier and Krause (2003), who argue that Redford's overhead democracy is a precursor to the principal-agent literature in organization theory.

3. In using this particular quote from Argyris, I want to highlight the broader discussion of Argyris's work developed by Mike Harmon and Rick Mayer in their excellent book *Organization Theory for Public Administration*. Mike Harmon was the scholar who introduced me to the field of public organization theory. His superb scholarship and excitement for this field of study has had a lasting effect on me. The logic of this chapter is grounded in Mike's teaching.

4. As is well known, the hierarchy of needs moves from very basic survival and economic concerns to the higher plane of psychological satisfaction: physiological needs, safety needs, love (affiliation) needs, esteem needs, and self-actualization.

Maslow's premise is that "man is a perpetually wanting animal." His theory assumes that people are not unlike organisms who have biological "needs" that they seek to reduce or "satisfy"(McSwite, 1997).

Douglas McGregor's book *The Human Side of Enterprise* (1960) was extremely well received, albeit dismissed as facile by some management science types. While the theory in the book was developed early on, the examples and the tone of the book were forged by McGregor's practical experience both as a consultant and as president of Antioch College in Ohio. In addition, he actively wrote and consulted during a period of unprecedented industrial growth in the United States. It was for America, the zenith of modernism. As a result, McGregor more than others successfully influenced the corporate and governmental sectors because his practices became institutionalized in a variety of workplace settings. Weisbord argues that McGregor introduced the idea that social (and organizational) change starts deep inside each of us (2004, p. 113). This leads directly into his famous Theory X and Theory Y. Most of us have learned about the theory and understand it as a contrast between two management styles, with Theory X being the big stick authoritarian approach and Theory Y the "carrot giving" sensitive approach. These broad characterizations lead us back to questions of authority and participation. More than anything else, McGregor's book fit the robust post–World War I economy in the United States. After decades of Taylorism (Weisbord, 2004, p. 137), workers were sufficiently inculcated with segmented, expert-based work systems. However, they were also ready for more inclusive approaches. The six core assumptions of Theory Y are as follows:

- Work is as natural as play. People like or dislike it based on conditions that management can control.
- External control is not the only way to achieve organizational goals. People will exercise self-control toward objectives they feel committed to.
- Commitment comes from rewards based on satisfying people's needs for status, recognition, and growth.
- Under the right conditions the average person will seek and accept responsibility rather than avoid it.
- Many people have the ingenuity and creativity needed to solve organizational problems. These qualities are not the rare province of a gifted few.
- Modern industry uses only a part of the ability, talent, and potential brainpower of the average person (Weisbord, 2004, p. 140).

The final observation about McGregor's work that I want to highlight is the present-day discussion of Theory X and Theory Y. Rather than narrowly categorizing one person as completely devoted to one management style or another, one might also read McGregor's work as suggesting that each of us has some of the elements of the other. For example, a person who sees him/herself as a no-nonsense realist (Theory X) may in fact have a nonconformist creative side even thought he/she projects all Theory Y types to be self-absorbed and anarchic. Similarly, a person who sees him/herself as sensitive, empathic, and open may in fact be strong willed and objectivist, even though he/she would claim that all Theory X types are boring and unaware (Weisbord, 2004, p. 141).

This point is important because not only does it problematize the oppositional talk (Theory X managers are bad, Theory Y managers are good or vice-versa), it also makes the point that managers and/or supervisors are not neutrals who apply a particular management technique. Rather their singularity, their strengths and weaknesses make them who they are and the person to whom their employees will react (respond).

5. This view follows the two long-standing textbooks of public administration theory, Harmon and Mayer's *Organization Theory for Public Administration* (1986) and Denhardt's *Theories of Public Organization* (2004).

6. Wilson's admiration for the British civil service is well known.

References

Agranoff, R., & McGuire, M. (1999). Managing in network settings. *Policy Studies Review, 16,* 19–41.

Alter, C., & Hage, J. (1993). *Organizations working together.* Newbury Park, CA: Sage.

Anderson, W. (1997). *The future of the self: Inventing the postmodern person.* New York: J. P. Tarcher.

Argyris, C. (1957). *Personality and organization.* New York: Harper & Row.

Argyris, C. (1973). Some limits of rational man organization theory. *Public Administration Review, 33,* 253–267.

Bailyn, B., Dallek, R., Davis, D. B., Donald, D. H., Thomas, J. L., & Wood, G. S. (1977). *The great republic* (4th ed.). Lexington, MA: D. C. Heath.

Barnard, C. (1968). *The functions of the executive.* Cambridge, MA: Harvard University Press. (Original work published 1938)

Berry, F. S., Brower, R., Choi, S. O., Gao, W. X., Jang, H. S., Kwon, M., & Word, J. (2004). Three traditions of network research: What the public management research agenda can learn from other research communities. *Public Administration Review, 64,* 539–552.

Box, R. C., Marshall, G. S., Reed, B. J., & Reed, C. M. (2001). New public management and substantive democracy. *Public Administration Review, 61,* 608–619.

Buchanan, J. M., & Tullock, G. (1962). *The calculus of consent.* Ann Arbor: University of Michigan Press.

Burrell, G., & Morgan, G. (1979). *Sociological paradigms and organisational analysis: Elements of the sociology of corporate life.* London: Heinemann.

Dahl, R. A. (1947). The science of public administration. *Public Administration Review, 7,* 1–11.

Denhardt, R. B. (1981). *In the shadow of organization.* Lawrence: Regents Press of Kansas.

Denhardt, R. B. (2004). *Theories of public organization* (4th ed.). Belmont, CA: Wadsworth/Thomson Learning.

Donaldson, L. (1996). The ethereal hand: Organizational economics and management theory. In J. M. Shafritz & S. O. Ott (Eds.), *Classics of organization theory* (4th ed., pp. 340–351). Ft. Worth: Harcourt Brace.

Drucker, P. (1995). Introduction: Mary Parker Follett: Prophet of management. In P. Graham (Ed.), *Mary Parker Follett: Prophet of management* (pp. 1–10). Boston: Harvard Business School Press.

Follett, M. P. (1995a). The individual in society. In P. Graham (Ed.). *Mary Parker Follett: Prophet of management* (pp. 247–263). Boston: Harvard University Press.

Follett, M. P. (1995b). Relating: The circular response. In P. Graham (Ed.). *Mary Parker Follett: Prophet of management* (pp. 35–65). Boston: Harvard University Press.

Giddens, A. (1991). *Modernity and self-identity: Self and society in the late modern age.* Cambridge, UK: Polity Press.

Goldsmith, S., & Eggers, W. D. (2004). *Governing by network: The new shape of the public sector.* Washington, DC: Brookings Institution.

Golembiewski, R. (1967). *Men, management, and morality.* New York: McGraw Hill.

Graham, P. (Ed.). (1995). *Mary Parker Follett: Prophet of management.* Boston: Harvard University Press.

Gulick, L., & Urwick, L. (1937). *Papers on the science of administration.* New York: Institute of Public Administration.

Harmon, M. M., & Mayer, R. T. (1986). *Organization theory for public administration.* Boston: Little Brown.

Henderson, L. J., & Mayo, E. (2002). The effects of the social environment. In S. Clegg (Ed.), *Central currents in organization studies I: Frameworks and applications* (pp. 299–313). Thousand Oaks, CA: Sage.

Heyl, B. (1968). The Harvard Pareto circle. *Journal of the History of the Behavioral Sciences, 4,* 316–334.

Hofstadter, R. (1955). *The age of reform.* New York: Vintage.

Kast, F. E., & Rosenzweig, J. E. (1972). General systems theory: Applications for organization and management. *Academy of Management Journal, 15,* 447–465.

Katz, D., & Kahn, R. L. (1966). *The social psychology of organizations.* New York: John Wiley.

LaPorte, T. R. (1971). The recovery of relevance in the study of public administration. In F. Marini (Ed.), *Toward a new public administration: The Minnowbrook Perspective* (pp. 17–48). Scranton, PA: Chandler.

LeBon, G. (1982). *The crowd: A study of the popular mind.* Flint Hills, VA: Fraser. (Original work published 1895)

Link, A., & McCormick, R. (1983). *Progressivism.* Arlington Heights, IL: Harlan Davison.

Maslow, A. (1962). *Toward a psychology of being.* Princeton, NJ: D. Van Nostrand.

McConnell, G. (1966). *Private power and American democracy.* New York: Knopf.

McGregor, D. (1960). *The human side of enterprise.* New York: McGraw-Hill.

McGuire, M. (2002). Managing networks: Propositions on what managers do and why they do it. *Public Administration Review, 62,* 599–609.

McSwite, O. C. (1997). *Legitimacy in public administration: A discourse analysis.* Thousand Oaks, CA: Sage Publications.

Meier, K. J., & Krause, G. A. (2003). The scientific study of bureaucracy: An overview. In G. A. Krause & K. J. Meier (Eds.), *Politics, policy, and organizations: Frontiers in the scientific study of bureaucracy* (pp. 1–19). Ann Arbor: University of Michigan Press.

Mosher, F. C. (Ed.). (1975). *American public administration: Past, present and future.* University, AL: University of Alabama Press.

Mosher, F. C. (1981). *Democracy and the public service* (2nd ed.). New York: Oxford University Press.

Ostrom, V. (1989). *The intellectual crisis in public administration* (2nd ed.). Tuscaloosa: University of Alabama Press.

Ostrom, V., & Ostrom, E. (1971). Public choice: A different approach to the study of public administration. *Public Administration Review*, *31*, 203–216.

Parsons, T. (1951). *The social system.* New York: Free Press.

Redford, E. S. (1969). *Democracy and the administrative state.* New York: Oxford University Press.

Reitan, T. C. (1998). Theories of interorganizational relations in the human services. *Social Service Review*, *37*, 285–309.

Shafritz, J. M., & Ott, S. O. (1996). *Classics of organization theory* (4th ed.). Ft. Worth: Harcourt Brace.

Silverman, D. (1971). *The theory of organisations.* New York: Basic Books.

Simon, H. A. (1976). *Administrative behavior: A study of decisionmaking processes in administrative organizations* (3rd ed.). New York: The Free Press.

Sørensen, E. (2002). Democratic theory and network governance. *Administrative Theory & Praxis*, *24*, 693–721.

Sørensen, E., & Torfing, J. (2005). Network governance and post-liberal democracy. *Administrative Theory & Praxis, 27,* 197–237.

Taylor, F. W. (1947a). The principles of scientific management. In F. W. Taylor, *Scientific management* (pp. 1–144). New York: Harper & Brothers.

Taylor, F. W. (1947b). Shop management. In F. W. Taylor, *Scientific management* (pp. 17–207). New York: Harper & Brothers.

Taylor, F. W. (1947c). Taylor's testimony before the special House committee. In F. W. Taylor, *Scientific management* (pp. 5–287). New York: Harper & Brothers.

Thompson, J. D. (1967). *Organizations in action.* New York: McGraw Hill.

Waldo, D. E. (1948). *The administrative state: A study of the political theory of American public administration.* New York: Ronald Press.

Waldo, D. E. (1952). Development of theory of democratic administration. *American Political Science Review*, *46*, 81–103.

Weber, M. (1991). Bureaucracy. In H. H. Gerth & C. W. Mills (Eds. & Trans.), *From Max Weber: Essays in sociology* (pp. 196–244). London: Routledge.

Weisbord, M. (2004). *Productive workplaces revisited: Dignity, meaning and community in the 21st century.* San Francisco: Jossey-Bass.

Wiebe, R. H. (1967). *The search for order: 1877–1920.* New York: Hill & Wang.

Williamson, O. E. (1985). *The economic institutions of capitalism.* New York: Free Press.

Woll, P. (1977). *American bureaucracy.* New York: Norton.

Citizens, Citizenship, and Democratic Governance

Cheryl Simrell King

We have met the enemy and it is us.

—Pogo

Is it more a matter of political courage, to appeal to the best instincts of people, not the worst? And, perhaps rather than new laws, [the absence of] staffing levels and training in local support services are part of such problems, just as the roots of the problems of poor education and lawlessness . . . are largely economic. . . . There must be some better democratic, not simply populist, way of deciding matters. The populist mode of democracy is a politics of arousal more than of reason, but also a politics of diversion from serious concerns that need settling in either a liberal democratic or a civic republican manner.

—Bernard Crick (2002). Democracy:
A Very Short Introduction

There is a purported ancient Chinese blessing/curse that says: "May you live in interesting times." We are, indeed, blessed and cursed to be living in interesting times when it comes to the questions of, and confluences amongst and between, citizens, citizenship, democracies, and governments in the United States.

Those of us researching and practicing in this area in the 1990s and into the early years of the new century have seen the calls for increased citizen participation and engagement shift and change a bit: the context of ten years ago was very different from today and the reasons for why these are such essential topics have changed. Nonetheless, the questions of citizens and citizenship and the roles, relationships, and responsibilities amongst and between citizens and their governments—in the United States—remain as relevant and fresh today as they were ten years ago. Indeed, they remain as essential as they were more than two hundred years ago.

The need for genuine and authentic roles for citizens in their governance is not new. Nor is it a new subject for students and practitioners of public administration. Louis Gawthrop (1984) pointed out that each generation in U.S. history produces its own call for a renewed sense of the public interest among citizens. But, as Gawthrop notes, in the past, not enough attention has been given to the potential for public administration as a means to achieve this revivified public:

> To run the risk of advancing a tautology, public management is public service, or service to the public. Hence, if the concept of democracy is to have any meaning at all, public managers are the servants of the public where the primacy of the body politic is explicitly recognized as the linchpin of our democratic ethos. Therefore, to argue that the primary mission of public management is to serve the public, while not particularly novel or unique, is, nonetheless, somewhat of a radical departure from the notions of the aggregate groupings that have constituted a phantom public in the minds of many professional public administrators. (p. 103)

According to McGregor, within certain limits "in a democracy practitioners must constantly seek ways to make themselves unnecessary" (1984, p. 128). The contemporary calls for increased democracy and citizenship in the public realm require public administrators to use their authority to make themselves somewhat less—and citizens much more—necessary. In this way they, potentially, transform citizens from Gawthrop's "phantom public" to real actors in public affairs.

At the risk of reifying the classic "politics/administration" dichotomy, discredited by Waldo (1948) and others, it is important to clarify to whom this chapter is intended to communicate and to define public administration and public service. The classic definition of the politics/administration dichotomy situates the two at opposite ends of an engagement spectrum: politics is the field of citizen engagement and the place where multiple, and often conflicting, desires and needs are mediated using political processes. It is here—in the political realm—that citizenship is classically practiced, with the ideal citizen being an active shaper and player in politics. Citizens' political roles are not limited to voting, but voting is the ultimate engagement act. On the other hand, administration, according to the classic definition of the dichotomy, is the place where political aims and ends are implemented. Administration was once seen as a sterile, objective, and nonpolitical process wherein citizens had no substantive roles.

The politics/administration dichotomy no longer carries much weight, and administrators know that citizens are asking, even demanding, that they be involved in administrative decisions and processes. This is where the rubber meets the road for contemporary administrators of the public good, be they operating in public, private, or nonprofit organizations.

It is also necessary here to elucidate the use of the terms *citizens* and *citizenship*. It is common, in contemporary conversation, to refer to subjects of government as "clients," "customers," "taxpayers," or even "the public." These terms are purposively avoided here because of the way they shift and change the relationships amongst and between citizens and their governments. In using the term *citizen*, the intention is not to proffer a term that, by definition, excludes those who are not legal citizens. Instead, it suggests that citizenship is both a legal status and a practice.

The idea of citizenship has a long history in western political philosophy, beginning with the city-states of ancient Greece. Within this historical framework, citizenship has long been thought of as both a status and a practice (Stivers, 1990). As *status*, it connotes formal relationships between the individual and the state, including rights (voting, free speech, and freedom of association), but few, if any, responsibilities. As *practice*, citizenship entails obligation, responsibilities, and activities that make up the essence of political life, such as participation in governance and the duty to consider the general good.

The last essential term that needs defining is *democracy* or *democratic governance*—this will be done in the next section. It is important to mention, before moving to the next section, that this chapter is purposively United States–centric. This is not to indicate that democracy and citizenship, as practiced in the United States, are somehow superior to the ways they are practiced elsewhere, no matter what the popular rhetoric of our federal government. The point is we practice democracy and citizenship in unique ways in the United States; we have a particular brand of democracy here, well influenced by continental and classic traditions, but filtered by uniquely American values that put a particular spin on democracy and citizenship often not seen in other countries. To conflate one version of democracy and citizenship with another, without recognizing how different national and cultural values make for very different practices, is to engage in a naïve and colonial analysis. Therefore, then, this discussion will focus only on citizenship and democracy in the United States.

History of Democracy and Citizenship in the United States

Historical accounts of citizenship and democracy in the United States abound with examples of active citizenship, starting with the founding of the country and continuing through the social movements of the twentieth and twenty-first centuries. It is part of our common lore that Alexis de Tocqueville, a French aristocrat visiting the United States in the early 1800s and author of *Democracy in America* (1945/1830), found a place inhabited with a deep democratic and egalitarian spirit. Tocqueville, somehow, occupied an in-between of "right" and "left" views: his experiences in the United States made him both a critic of addiction to material well-being and an apostle of civic engagement as well as a critic of big government and doctrinaire egalitarianism (Kimball, 2000). Nonetheless, his experiences in the United States led him to believe that a deeply engaged populace is essential for democratic freedom and liberty.

As Tocqueville observed in the 1830s and others have observed since, we have, historically, been a country of active citizenship and active dissent. Yet, how active citizenship and dissent are practiced differs depending on the historical period. The history of democracy and citizenship in the United States could be seen as occurring in four eras:

1. Founding (Birth–1830s)
2. Populist (1830s–1890s)
3. Progressive Movement (1890s–1950s)
4. Awakening from the American Dream (1960s–today)

Founding (Birth–1830s)

In general, citizenship in U.S. history has leaned toward classical liberalism, giving citizenship a constricted and instrumental role, one apparent in the limited and distanced part for citizens in government today. The founders believed that the extended geographic scope and social complexity of the new American state made direct participation by citizens unworkable. The founders were deeply influenced by the Greeks (Aristotle and Plato) and continental political philosophers such as John Locke, Thomas Paine, Montesquieu, Voltaire, and others.

James Madison, one of the authors of *The Federalist Papers*, argued that popular governance could only work in "a small spot" (Cooke, 1961, p. 84). More important, however, in Madison's view, echoing Aristotle and Plato, was the propensity of popular governments for the "violence of faction" and their tendency to produce decisions based on "the superior force of an interested and overbearing majority" (p. 57).

The founders were advocates of representative government because representation makes it possible to extend government over a large area and serves to "refine and enlarge the public views, by passing them through the medium of a chosen body of citizens, whose wisdom may best discern the true interest of their country" (Cooke, 1961, pp. 62–63). The Federalists believed that ordinary people were neither qualified for, nor interested in, participating directly in governance other than through voting. Instead of a government "of the people, by the people, and for the people," the founders' government would be an "elite *republic* of elected representatives who would deliberate together and speak *for* the people" (Fishkin, 1995, p. 21).

During the early years of the American republic, ordinary people's public role was sharply restricted. Only a select group of white male property owners was allowed to vote. Governing was left safely in the hands of wise leaders; what Mosher (1982) has called "government by gentlemen" prevailed. Governments, in general, during this period were small and weak. The federal government mostly delivered mail, fought wars, secured new territories, and collected customs and excise taxes. Administrative agencies were organized in a semi-aristocratic rather than bureaucratic fashion. Kinship and class shaped membership in the early administrative agencies. New England town hall style of local governance was being practiced along the Atlantic seaboard (Box, 1998); beyond this, local governance was weak and dispersed.

Populist (1830s–1890s)

It was not until the presidency of Andrew Jackson that thinking about the capacities and proper role of citizens and administrators changed. Jacksonian thinking expanded the pool of fit candidates for administrative office, from the wellborn to any citizen who had demonstrated his loyalty to the political party in power. The door to direct involvement in governmental processes was opened to ordinary citizens.

This expanded view of citizenship led to an increase of public activity. At about the time Tocqueville visited the United States, citizen participation in public activity was at a high point. For those who qualified, the citizen role was not just a legal status, but a performance. In small towns across the country, the New England town hall style of local governance and activities migrated and was put into place. Citizens and officials worked closely together to govern their communities, although we know, in retrospect, that only a select group of citizens was actually involved (Skowronek, 1982; Wiebe, 1967). For every person who felt a part of the government, there were handfuls more on the outside: slaves or those one step from slavery—indigenous peoples, women, immigrants, and other marginalized people.

For the most part, ties to political parties defined the administrative role during this time, still limited by the restricted scope of government responsibilities. Jackson sought to systematize agency processes somewhat in order to make good on his statement that anyone could do government work (Morone, 1990), thus beginning the movement toward bureaucratization.

Progressive Movement (1890s–1950s)

In the late nineteenth and early twentieth centuries another significant change occurred in citizenship and administration, one that reversed the emphasis on direct involvement of ordinary citizens and the simplicity of government work, arguing, instead, the need for administrative expertise. This is the birth of Progressive-era administration.

Woodrow Wilson's (1887) famous essay, "The Study of Administration," is emblematic of Progressive ideals. Wilson argued that administrators should be given considerable latitude in the execution of their duties, a freedom that was defensible because administration was not political (the genesis of the politics/administration dichotomy). Administrators carried out the laws, holding themselves accountable to the citizenry at large. Citizens were to serve as the ultimate source of legitimacy and not to become meddlesome. Citizens became the source of something called public opinion.

Progressive reformers called for administrative practices based on scientific knowledge. In their view, the proper role of citizens in the reform process was to inform themselves about issues and rally round the quest for efficient, expert government methods. Progressives sought to improve public opinion by making it judicious. Citizens were assured that the experts and professional administrators were more capable of handling public problems and situations and better able to make decisions than common folk. The public service, growing rapidly due to the need for infrastructure and services, was developing into a government "of the technocrats, by the technocrats, and for the technocrats" (Kearny & Sinha, 1988, p. 571).

Most of the growth of government, federal and local, occurred during this historical period. It was related to increased needs for public infrastructure in urban areas, which were experiencing significant growth and expansion, the rapid expansion of the nation and dense population settling in the West, and the federal government's response to the Depression (Keynesian economics), which expanded government to stimulate the private economy. This was the historical period of Roosevelt's New Deal, and, to some extent, Johnson's Great Society. Government, and the experts making it happen, were seen as positive solutions to social and economic ills. This period could be considered the golden age of U.S. government and was short-lived. It was also the period in which most of the contemporary practices of administration —our systems, processes, and structures—were developed and put into practice, developed out of scientific studies and professional rationality/expertise

(Stivers, 2000). Most of these practices are still in use today, and administrators are likely to bump up against them when trying to shift and change administrative practices to better account for the contemporary role of citizens and citizenship in the practices of public service (Denhardt & Denhardt, 2003).

Awakening from the American Dream (1960s–Today)

In the 1960s and into the 1970s, the dialogue about citizenship and administration shifted once again. Growing public distrust of governmental institutions drove many citizens to challenge the legitimacy of administrative and political processes. This distrust, coupled with federal mandates requiring more public participation, opened the door for citizens to become more involved in administrative processes. However, this participatory moment was short-lived; it more or less expired when federally supported citizen action threatened the power base of local officials. Meaningful citizen involvement lived on here and there and in a plethora of administrative regulations aimed at getting citizen "input," usually through largely ineffective public hearings.

It was during this time that citizens became seen as clients or consumers —as passive recipients of governmental services. Requirements for citizen participation were generally treated in administrative agencies as a cost of doing business instead of as an asset to effectiveness or a responsibility worth carrying out for its own sake (Jones, 1981; Mladenka, 1981). At best, citizens were viewed as a constituency, the source of important political support (McNair et al., 1983) or of important values to guide policy decisions (Stewart et al., 1984). As a result of seeing citizen participation as a cost of doing business, by the early 1980s public participation was beginning to be perceived negatively, as not necessarily enhancing administrative processes, especially since participation detracted from administrative expertise.

Treating citizens as a business cost led to a kind of citizenship that Rimmerman (1997) calls "outlaw" citizenship. As Rimmerman indicates, the failure to integrate citizens into the governance process led to "new movements of Left and Right with a strategy for promoting political, social, and economic change" (p. 72). Both the Left and Right in these outlaw citizenship movements practice carefully choreographed "disruptive politics and potential threats to system stability" (p. 62).

In the 1990s, these movements along with environmental activism, new class social movements, neighborhood action in response to crime and other urban problems, and political organization around ideological issues led to a resurgence in public participation (Thomas, 1995; Timney, 1996) and to changes in the citizen-administrator relationship. Ironically, although participation in voting is at an all-time low, and observers are decrying a general lack of civic involvement (e.g., Putnam, 1995), some citizens are demanding a place at the table in administrative decision-making.

Citizens in the United States are awakening from the American Dream and finding that they need and desire to be involved with the public decisions and services that affect their quality of life. Partly this comes from the significant distrust in government that has developed over the last thirty years or so; partly this is due to a host of other factors including the decentering of expertise and the information explosion. Seeking to regain the particular kind of trust that citizens practiced back when the majority believed the government was always "right" is probably a wrong-headed intention, albeit sympathetic. As citizens, we are, paradoxically, both more unengaged and more engaged than we have been in a very long time, perhaps since the founding. It is no longer possible to practice a Progressive-era type of administration where the citizen is merely a vague player in the mix or a cog in the wheel of a massive bureaucratic machine. Something else is called for.

This Moment

In such a climate, it is not surprising that both administrators and citizens are frustrated and often at loggerheads with each other. Citizens believe the information they receive is managed, controlled, and manipulated in order to limit their capacity to participate. Citizens see the techniques of participation (public hearings, surveys, focus groups) as designed, at best, to generate input and, at worst, to keep them on the outside of the governance process (Innes & Booher, 2004). Citizens are particularly sensitive to vacuous or false participation efforts that ask for, and then discount, public input. Such inauthentic processes simply lead to greater tension between administrators and citizens. It is better not to work with citizens at all than to work with them under false, purely instrumental, pretenses (King, Feltey, & Susel, 1998).

Administrators, for their part, know that citizen involvement is desirable but are, at best, "ambivalent about public involvement or, at worst, they find it problematic" (King, Feltey, & Susel, 1998, p. 319). Citizen participation is time consuming, costly, and a burden—it gets in the way of doing one's work! Administrators are not, necessarily, trained or socialized to be good facilitators of participation and engagement. Indeed, there is an inherent conflict between the values of citizen participation and engagement and the structure and processes of bureaucratic government, creating significant obstacles for meaningful citizen engagement with government (Callahan, 2002) and no end of trouble for administrators who have good intentions about direct participation. We are, after all, a representative democracy, not a direct democracy. And, participatory or engagement efforts do not, necessarily, guarantee positive results or any results at all (Berkshire, 2003); sometimes they simply make a messy situation even messier.

Recent empirical research gives us a good picture of citizen participation efforts, at various levels. While participation and engagement efforts are happening all over the country, at all levels and scale of government, most often what administrators view as participation efforts may be more adequately described as public relations or communications (Ebdon, 2002; Wang, 2001). In addition, the arenas within which participation is sought or facilitated tend to be limited. In his study of chief administrative officers of cities with populations over 50,000, Wang found that most respondents do seek citizen input, or communicate with citizens, on processes and projects (certain functions), but only one third agreed that citizens were involved in agency goals and objectives setting. Wang's results were validated in a later, somewhat different study (Yang & Callahan, 2005) of smaller cities: citizen involvement is more likely to be sought in the areas of planning, parks and recreation, and public works; involvement is less likely to be sought (or to happen) in goal setting, strategic planning, and goal measurement. In addition, citizen involvement is more likely to be sought when there is significant pressure from citizens to include them (push rather than pull).

While it may be the case that our current problems are not any less complex than those of the past, administrators are no longer trying to simplify problems with relatively simple answers. Administrators are grappling with "wicked problems—with no solutions, only temporary and imperfect resolutions" based upon how we interpret the presenting situation in this particularized moment (Fischer, 1993, p. 172). Administrators are no longer addressing a public that can situate its identity collectively (even if our collective identity of the past was a façade, covering over marginalized groups). As Lance Bennett sees it, the "breakdown of broadly shared social and political experience, and the rise of personalized realities" (Bennett, 1998, p. 741) changed the nature of politics and administration. When we moved away from "collective" politics (political parties, broad-based identity groups organized around values) to what Bennett calls "lifestyle" politics (fragmented identities, narrow identity groups organized around lifestyle issues), the connection between people and their governments fragmented even more.

In a time of wicked problems and fragmented identities it is no longer feasible to seek out simple solutions to our citizenship and governance challenges. While we may long for simple solutions to complex problems, they no longer exist (if they ever did!)—"if only we could get the *right* administration in the White House, all would be solved." Or, "if only we could get the couch potato citizens off the couch, all would be solved." Or, "if only we could fix our broken legislative systems, all would be solved." Etc.

Talking about solutions begs the question of a need for solutions. What are the conditions of these particularly interesting times in which we are both blessed and cursed to live? Why do we need solutions to governance and citizen/citizenship wicked problems? While one's perception of what is wrong is framed by one's values and philosophical/metaphysical orientation, there does seem to be agreement between the various warring camps on the significant problems in the United States.

We seem to be a large, lumbering, slow, and disconnected nation. Big money talks while the many voices of the citizenry seem to only whisper. We lock ourselves away from the things that scare us and make us feel vulnerable, often in gated communities that serve to further our isolation and separate us from those that are different from us, fueling our fears instead of calming them. Forces bigger than us (nature, globalization) tell us we can run but we cannot hide, but we do not seem to listen. Poor people stay poor; rich people get richer, and the middle class shrinks as more folks slide into the ranks of the poor. Citizenship is contextualized as consumption—citizens are now tax-paying "consumers" of government services; to be a better citizen, one is exhorted to go out and stimulate the economy, making a contribution to the gross domestic product (GDP). We live in a culture that fears the "other" (and our government) and manipulating and spinning that fear keeps citizens in their place (Glassner, 2000). Terrorism has exacerbated the fear of the other; our leaders trade on this fear to garner political power. Public policy is mostly made behind closed doors, without engagement of the citizens, with special interests and corporations trumping all other input.

We have lost an ideological center and are adrift, searching for a new value or group of values upon which to hang our collective identity (God, patriotism, colonialism?). Most of us are not active politically or active within our communities unless we are *reacting* to something that threatens our liberty, freedom, and security, often misusing citizen initiative processes in our reactionary modes. We fight amongst ourselves—each of our "identity" causes working to trump other "identity" causes. With good intentions and for good reasons, progressive advocacy work tends to pit activist against activist vying for the same scarce resources and attention, ironically creating a void into which other versions of activism have flowed, particularly neo-conservative activism.

Things are marginally better at the local and regional level; scale does matter and we seem to be somewhat better at practicing democracy at a more local level. Still, one may argue that while we have created localities and regions that reflect citizen desires and engagement, these pockets of community tend to be deeply value-driven. Often, nationally speaking, they are separatist enclaves where there is tacit (or active) agreement amongst the locals that only certain behaviors and ways of orienting oneself toward the world are accepted or tolerated. We are a fragmented nation populated by fragmented peoples.

Progress has served, but it has also cost us. The costs to the environment and sustainability are well known and well documented in the alternative and, increasingly, mainstream literature (Portney, 2003). There are other significant costs to unquestioned progress. Many of these costs are relational. As we get further away from a political economy that requires people to work and interact together to meet their daily needs, we dilute and dull our relational capacities. In a consumption-based economy, our well-being is measured by what we have (what Eric Fromm, 1979, calls "having") versus what we are (or, in Fromm's language, "being"). Late-twentieth-century consumption-based capitalism exacerbated the conditions that subtract from citizenship: inequalities of income, status, and prestige in the market and workplace; an excessive focus on the economic self; and a lack of "we thinking" (Barber, 1984). When active citizenship interferes with the workings of profit and accumulation, then those who desire profit and accumulation will work to limit citizen engagement. Indeed, as active citizenship has declined in the United States, the powers of corporations and other special interests have increased (and vice versa).

And, yet, in the midst of all of this are active citizen movements, many of them manifesting in the initiative or referendum processes. Ironically, while one may call initiatives and referenda citizen engagement or *action*, they often are more aptly described as citizen *reaction*, a more staid version of Rimmerman's "outlaw citizenship" (1997). For example, in the state of Washington, as well as in many other western states, citizens govern through initiative processes. Antigovernment movements and ideological special interests are currently working to limit the power that public officials (legislators and administrators alike) have over taxation and other resource-allocation decisions. In an ironic appeal, using "taxpayers" as their audience rather than "citizens," these reformers argue that the government takes too much from them to fund a beast that is growing too powerful and too big. This movement speaks to a certain kind of "knee-jerk" citizen who falls anywhere on the ideological spectrum, from the left to the right. The desire to limit the funding of government seemingly does not belong to only one party or one side of the ideological spectrum.

As a columnist writing in the Olympia, Washington, local paper put it: "The problem is more fundamental—'We the People' have lost control of the reins of government" (Preble, 2000, p. 9). People do not trust their governments to make decisions that are in the best interest of the people. While one response calls for more democratic, deliberative, and inclusive governments, driving decisions down to the people, the most prevalent response to this loss of trust and control is to talk the language of accountability, performance evaluation, and measurement and transparency.

For example, in 2003, the Washington State House of Representatives unanimously passed a bill to require performance audits of all state agencies and functions in a response to citizens' calls for greater accountability in government. The unanimity of this move was surprising; not one legislator looked beneath the surface of the accountability issue. Yes, citizens are asking for greater accountability, but are they asking for performance audits (superficial accountability) or for a deeper connection to and with government and the governance of civil society (deep accountability)? Will published reports of performance audits satisfy citizen desires for accountability, or is something deeper needed?

It may well be that citizens are calling for a deeper response from government. Nonetheless, performance audits are what they are getting. Performance audits as a response to a call for accountability reflect the contemporary management orientation toward public service that is founded in the idea of the free market where good government is government that runs like a business and creates public value (Moore, 2000). In this context, do citizens, as a rule, make decisions about these initiatives based upon thirty-second sound bites and inflammatory advertising? Are voters making decisions based upon appeals to their pocketbooks and to their personal frustrations? Informed decision-making requires considering options (e.g., what are the consequences of making decision A over decision B?). Active citizenship requires being *engaged* in a process that leads to making informed decisions that have the public good in mind rather than private gain. Citizens are *participating* in governance through voting, but are usually not *engaged* in a deliberative process that informs their decisions. Because citizens are not engaged with their governance, participation tends to be an action *against* government, instead of an action *with* government. Participation that comes out of anger and discontent may focus on individual aims and purposes. The preferred alternative comes out of an engaged process that has, as its intended ends, outcomes that serve the public good.

This, then, is our administrative context. If we do not work to engage citizens, they will practice forms of participation that stymie or limit the ability of government to do the work of the public good. If we do not engage citizens, the possibilities of despot-democratic governments increase. If we do not engage citizens, we are not going to be very successful at working to ameliorate the wicked problems of our times.

Where Do We Go From Here?

Engaged citizenship requires that one view, as discussed earlier, citizenship as both a status and a practice. Citizenship as practice empnasizes "freedom to." Engaged citizens have the potential to make public decisions based on their sense of the public interest, using *phronesis*, or practical wisdom, and experiential knowledge relevant to the circumstances. Through engagement in governance, citizens can develop capacities and skills important to the effective conduct of public affairs. Because they have to wrestle with problems larger than their own private concerns, they may develop the kind of broad understanding and judgment that will ensure that their decisions are well made. As John Stuart Mill put it, the citizen "is called upon . . . to weigh interests not his own; to apply, at every turn, principles and maxims which have for their reason of existence the common good" (1972, p. 233). Tocqueville argued in a similar way that through this educative process of having to make public decisions, initial self-interested participation would be transmuted to something approaching classical virtue (1945, vol. II, p. 112). While these shifts in citizens as a result of engagement are potential, not absolute, they certainly seem a step up from where we are today.

Furthermore, by joining together in civil and political organized activity, citizens may come to value not agreement but collaboration. As Benjamin Barber suggests, through "strong democratic talk," which may often involve disagreement, citizens can become "capable of genuinely public thinking and political judgment and thus able to envision a common future in terms of genuinely common goals" (1984, p. 197). Barber explicates this kind of citizenship further:

> [It is] a dynamic relationship among strangers who are transformed into neighbors, whose commonality derives from expanding consciousness rather than geographical proximity. Because the sharp distinction that separates government and citizenry in representative systems is missing, the civic bond under strong democracy is neither vertical nor lateral but circular and dialectical. Individuals become involved in government by participating in the common institutions of self-government and become involved with one another by virtue of their common engagement in politics. They are united by the ties of common activity and common consciousness— ties that are willed rather than given by blood or heritage or prior consensus on beliefs and that thus depend for their preservation and growth on constant commitment and ongoing political activity. (1984, p. 223)

A recent example of this is the Listen to the City project, designed and facilitated by the nonprofit AmericaSpeaks (www.americaspeaks.org), where

4,300 people came together in an electronic town meeting format to review and respond to proposals for the reconstruction of the World Trade Center site (Lukensmeyer & Brigham, 2002). *New York Daily News* columnist Peter Hamil (cited in Lukensmeyer & Brigham, 2002) speaks to the power of deliberative processes: "Because the process was an exercise in democracy, not demagoguery, no bellowing idiots grabbed the microphones to perform for the cameras. . . . In this room, 'I' had given way to 'we'" (p. 366).

Moving toward engaged citizenship requires that we, as administrators, think about citizen participation and involvement in new ways. This is not an easy task. We are poised on a precipice of significant transformation and, to quote the great philosopher Pogo, "we have met the enemy and it is us." Much of what is required to move to administrative models that create and encourage citizen engagement (neither participation nor input, as indicated below) is related to the *who* we bring to our administrative work and the *how* we practice administration. If we want a different relationship between citizens and governments—if we want or have to practice some form of democratic governance—we must do things differently and we must be different kinds of administrators.

Transformative movements seem to happen in stages. The first stage involves *coming to consciousness*—where we recognize that transformation and change is needed—and includes calls for change that are often ideological, theoretical, and dogmatic. The questions of *why* or *whether* get answered in this first stage. The first stage of the current citizen participation movement in the United States has been in process for over thirty years, although, as we know, the question of the appropriate involvement of citizens in their government has been a topic of debate since the founding of this country.

In review, the contemporary movement began, more or less, with the community-based reforms of the Great Society programs, including the reforms suggested by the New Public Administration movement (Frederickson, 1980; Marini, 1971), and continuing in contemporary "citizen-centered governance" movements (see: Barber, 1984; Box, 1998; Frederickson, 1997; Gawthrop, 1998; McSwite, 1997; Thomas, 1995). In the last thirty years or so, public administrators and public administration scholars have become conscious of the importance of citizen involvement in administration. The question of why, or whether, citizens *should* be involved in administrative governance seems to be argued with less regularity of late. We know that governance processes are generally improved with citizen involvement and that citizens *should* be involved in some way. If administrators, and the administrative processes, do not invite citizens in, then citizens will seek involvement in other ways.

In the second stage of transformation, consciousness is put to practice and the thorny questions of *how, who, in what, where,* and *when* come into play. At this stage, the dogmatic claims that transformation always results in positive outcomes (usually posited in the coming-to-consciousness stage) are interrogated and deconstructed. We start experimenting with transformative practices and are quickly embroiled in the wicked conundrums that arise, as a result.

With regard to citizen involvement in administrative practices, this second stage has been occurring in tandem with the first stage and overlapping for a number of years. We might agree that citizens *should* be involved but we cannot agree about *how* to do this, *in what* processes, and *where* or *when* citizens should be involved. For example, perhaps citizens should be involved in making decisions about the siting of waste facilities, but not in the more traditional administrative functions like staffing and budgeting, among others. And even deeply engaging citizens in siting decisions is thorny and does not guarantee a successful result, or any result at all (Berkshire, 2003).

These thorny questions are at the core of many of the ideological differences between advocates of citizen involvement in administrative governance. Most contemporary movements in public administration advocate increased citizen participation or involvement in administrative governance, yet have significantly different definitions of citizen participation. New Public Management advocates view participation from a managerial perspective, building citizen participation into managerial techniques often drawn from "total quality Management" and similar management movements in the private sector (Osborne & Hutchinson, 2004; Popovich, 1998). In these models, citizens are the consumers or customers of government service and their input is important in order to deliver high-performance products and services. Citizen participation is encouraged in the form of citizen satisfaction panels or surveys, and in performance measurement. Like in contemporary politics, and borrowing from classical marketing techniques, new ideas are "focus grouped" with citizens to test their viability. Citizens, in a classic managerial model, are one of the inputs of the managerial process. What is important here is to see that participation is defined as input and as one of the pieces of raw material used in the production process, separate from the machinery that produces the public or civic good.

Another way of looking at citizen participation is as an instrument of production—as a piece of the machinery that produces the public good or civic good. For citizen-based-governance scholars, citizen engagement is an essential part of the machinery that produces governance, not a raw material input or an add-on to the already existing machinery. Achieving this kind of citizen participation or engagement requires that we not only shift the way we think about citizens and their roles in governance processes, but shift the way we govern itself—shifting the administration processes and structures such that citizen engagement is possible.

There is no doubt that government needs reform with respect to efficiency, effectiveness, and citizen engagement. And, there are many excellent recent movements to increase citizen involvement and engagement in government, particularly in local-level activities and alongside performance measurements efforts (Epstein, Coates, Wray, & Swain, 2005). Still, the emphasis of the reform work being done in the fields of public administration and public policy—in scholarship and in practice—is on *how* we administer to improve accountability, efficiency, and effectiveness in our work. This makes sense as we are, after all, about administering. Yet, many of these reform movements are off target. The contemporary shortcomings of American public administration happen around failures in policy and administrative practices that were designed in the tradition of classical liberalism. Models (solutions) of new governance are responses to the limitations of democracies built in the classical liberal tradition. These solutions tend to lean toward the benefits of classical liberalism—protecting individuals, magnifying personal property, and minimizing the ability of authorities to limit individual rights (Heying, 1999). Government is, by design, at the periphery, and nongovernment institutions, particularly the market, are at the center.

We see this reflected in the mainstream of contemporary American public administration. Here, one finds mostly private (individualized) solutions to our contemporary dilemmas, following on our classical liberal roots. As movements to perfect the science of administration, these responses do not threaten our root values and assumptions. Yet, they miss the point that we need less emphasis on the private individual and more emphasis on the public collective or public good. We do not need to make government more individualistic, more corporatized, and more disconnected from the people. We do not need to make governments more administrative. We need to make our governments more democratic. And, we need a citizenry that practices citizenship in other than reactionary ways.

While we know that a more engaged citizenry serves government and governance, we are firmly ensconced in the second stage of transformation, the stage at which the dogmatic assumptions of the ideological first state are interrogated and deconstructed and the thorny problems emerge. We agree that citizen engagement is a good thing, yielding good results (Kweit & Kweit, 2004; Lukensmeyer & Brigham, 2002; Roberts, 2004). We cannot agree upon what participation/engagement means and what it looks like in various levels of government. For some, as indicated above, it is merely another managerial input; for others, it means completely remaking the administrative/managerial processes such that engagement is an essential part of the processes. Furthermore, as we experiment with practices that are participatory, engagement-oriented, and deliberative, more of the dilemmas and thorny problems are exposed.

Practicing more democratic administration, shaped by an engaged citizenry, is no small challenge. While it is relatively easy to acquire citizen input on policies and projects, particularly at the local level, it is quite another thing to engender an engaged citizenry and to incorporate citizen engagement into mission and goal-setting work. To do so is to further challenge the politics/administration dichotomy. The Founding Fathers purposively set in place a system of checks and balances and left the policy decisions in the hands of those who are most likely to be able to make informed and reasoned decisions—those who represent us in our legislative bodies. "Extra-formal democracy" (Bogason, Kensen, & Miller, 2004), that which takes place outside of the formal representative democratic system, was not a part of the founding models of governance and government. Administrators, many of whom are protected under civil service laws and regulations, are not elected to their positions and are not considered to be representatives of the will of the people—why should we give administrators power to encourage, shape, and facilitate citizen power? And why should we give a select group of citizens who can or choose to participate the power to influence policy and programs for all citizens? As we do more participation and engagement work, we may be experiencing fewer not-in-my-backyard (NIMBY) movements but, alternatively, we see and experience the ways in which bureaucratic norms, rules, and regulations constrain and limit participation and engagement. Yet, as Kweit and Kweit (2004) say:

> Although the reliance on the bureaucratic norms of expertise, efficiency and rules and regulations may produce good policy as judged by technical criteria, it may not result in policy that citizens evaluate as good. . . . Although it may be contrary to bureaucratic norms and may appear to impede service delivery, citizens' beliefs about participation can contribute to citizens' perceptions of governmental performance. The lesson for officials, generally and not just after disasters, is that citizens must feel that they are involved, for it is the citizens who ultimately determine what makes up good policy. (p. 369)

The dilemmas of citizen participation (see Roberts, 2004, for a more detailed discussion) and engagement need to be worked through in this second stage of transformation. Because the intersections of the roles and responsibilities of citizens and their governments will always be wicked situations, every context will call for a different kind of "fix." Administrators are required to manage less and *serve* and *facilitate* the public good more, resurrecting the idea of public service. We will need a tool chest of skills and techniques we have not yet developed; we will need to train, educate, and socialize public administrators differently (Callahan & Yang, 2005). Most importantly, we will need to focus not narrowly on tools and techniques but, instead, keep our eyes on the normative questions involved in our work—it is not just *how* we serve but, equally important, *why and what* we serve and *who* benefits.

Note

Much of this chapter is excerpted and/or revised from earlier work, in particular: King, Stivers, and collaborators (1998), King, Feltey, and Susel (1998), King (1999), Beckett and King (2002), and King and Zanetti (2005).

References

Barber, B. (1984). *Strong democracy: Participatory politics for a new age.* Berkeley: University of California Press.

Beckett, J., & King, C. S. (2002). The challenge to improve citizen participation in public budgeting: A discussion. *Journal of Public Budgeting, Accounting & Financial Management, 14,* 463–486.

Bennett, L. W. (1998). The uncivic culture: Communication, identity, and the rise of lifestyle politics. *Political Science & Politics, 31,* 741–761.

Berkshire, M. (2003). In search of a new landfill site. In B. Eckstein & J. A. Throgmorton (Eds.), *Story and sustainability: Planning, practice and possibility in American cities* (pp. 167–184). Cambridge, MA: MIT Press.

Bogason, P., Kensen, S., & Miller, H. (2004). Introduction: Extra-formal democracy. In P. Bogason, S. Kensen, & H. Miller (Eds.), *Tampering with traditions: The unrealized authority of democratic agency.* Lanham, MD: Lexington Books.

Box, R. C. (1998). *Citizen governance: Leading American communities into the 21st century.* Thousand Oaks, CA: Sage.

Callahan, K. (2002). The utilization and effectiveness of citizen advisory committees in the budget process of local governments. *Journal of Public Budgeting, Accounting & Financial Management, 14,* 295–319.

Callahan, K., & Yang, K. (2005). Training and professional development for civically engaged communities. *Innovation Journal, 10*(1), 1–16. Retrieved March 13, 2006, from www.innovation.cc/volumes-issues/callahan-yang.pdf.

Cooke, J. (Ed.). (1961). *The federalist papers.* Middletown, CT: Wesleyan University Press.

Crick, B. (2002). *Democracy: A very short introduction.* New York: Oxford University Press.

Denhardt, J. V., & Denhardt, R. B. (2003). *The new public service: Serving, not steering.* Armonk, NY: M.E. Sharpe.

Ebdon, C. (2002). Beyond the public hearing: Citizen participation in the local government budget process. *Journal of Public Budgeting, Accounting & Financial Management, 14,* 273–294.

Epstein, P., Coates, P. M., Wray, L. D., & Swain, D. (2005). *Results that matter: Improving communities by engaging citizens, measuring performance and getting things done.* San Francisco: Jossey-Bass.

Fischer, F. (1993). Citizen participation and the democratization of policy expertise: From theoretical inquiry to practice cases. *Policy Sciences, 26,* 165–187.

Fishkin, J. S. (1995). *We the people: Public opinion and democracy.* New Haven, CT: Yale University Press.

Frederickson, H. G. (1980). *New public administration.* Tuscaloosa: University of Alabama Press.

Frederickson, H. G. (1997). *The spirit of public administration.* San Francisco: Jossey-Bass.

Fromm, E. (1979). *To have or to be?* London: Abacus.

Gawthrop, L. C. (1984). Civis, civitas, and civilitas: A new focus for the year 2000. *Public Administration Review, 44,* 101–106.

Gawthrop, L. C. (1998). *Public service and democracy: Ethical imperatives for the 21st century.* New York: Chatham House.

Glassner, B. (2000). *The culture of fear: Why Americans are afraid of the wrong things.* New York: Harpercollins.

Heying, C. (1999). Autonomy vs. solidarity: Liberal, totalitarian, and communitarian traditions. *Administrative Theory & Praxis, 21,* 39–50.

Innes, J. E., & Booher, D. E. (2004). Reframing public administration: Strategies for the 21st century. *Planning Theory & Practice 5,* 419–436.

Jones, B. (1981). Party and bureaucracy: The influence of intermediary groups on urban public service delivery. *American Political Science Review, 75,* 688–700.

Kearny, R. J., & Sinha, C. (1988). Professional and bureaucratic responsiveness: Conflict or compatibility? *Public Administration Review, 48,* 571–579.

Kimball, R. (2000). Tocqueville today. Retrieved July 20, 2006, from The New Criterion, 19(3), http://www.newcriterion.com/archive/19/nov00/tocque.htm.

King, C. S. (1999). Imagining active citizenship and administration. Paper presented at the annual meeting of the American Political Science Association, Atlanta, GA.

King, C. S., Feltey, K. M., & Susel, B. O. (1998). The question of participation: Toward authentic participation in public decisions. *Public Administration Review, 58,* 317–326.

King, C. S., Stivers, C., & collaborators (1998). *Government is us: Public administration in an anti-government era.* Thousand Oaks, CA: Sage.

King, C. S., & Zanetti, L. A. (2005). *Transformational public service: Portraits of theory in practice.* Armonk, NY: M.E. Sharpe.

Kweit, M. G., & Kweit, R. W. (2004). Citizen participation and citizen evaluation in disaster recovery. *American Review of Public Administration, 34,* 354–373.

Lukensmeyer, C. J., & Brigham, S. (2002). Taking democracy to scale: Creating a town hall meeting for the twenty-first century. *National Civic Review, 91,* 351–366.

Marini, F. (1971). *Toward a new public administration: The Minnowbrook perspective.* Scranton, PA: Chandler.

McGregor, E. B. (1984). The great paradox of democratic citizenship and public personnel administration. *Public Administration Review, 44,* 126–131.

McNair, R. H., Caldwell, R., & Pollane, L. (1983). Citizen participation in public bureaucracies: Foul-weather friends. *Administration & Society, 14,* 507–523.

McSwite, O. C. (1997). *Legitimacy in public administration: A discourse analysis.* Thousand Oaks, CA: Sage.

Mill, J. S. (1972). *Utilitarianism, on liberty, and considerations on representative government* (H. B. Acton, Ed.). London UK: Dent/Everyman's Library.

Mladenka, K. R. (1981). Citizen demands and urban services: The distribution of bureaucratic response in Chicago and Houston. *American Journal of Political Science, 25*, 693–714.

Moore, M. (2000). *Creating public value: Strategic management in government.* Cambridge, MA: Harvard University Press.

Morone, R. (1990, January 29). Who's in control? Many don't know or care. *Washington Post*, pp. A1, A6–A7.

Mosher, F. C. (1982). *Democracy and the public service.* New York: Oxford University Press.

Osborne, D., & Hutchinson, P. (2004). *The price of government: Getting the results we need in an age of permanent fiscal crisis.* New York: Basic Books.

Popovich, M. (1998). *Creating high performance government organizations.* San Francisco: Jossey-Bass.

Portney, K. E. (2003). *Taking sustainable cities seriously: Economic development, quality of life, and the environment in American cities.* Cambridge, MA: MIT Press.

Preble, G. (2000, October 31). Amendments stripped the states of their influence. *Olympian*, p. 9.

Putnam, R. D. (1995). Bowling alone, revisited. *Responsive Community, 5*, 18–33.

Rimmerman, C. A. (1997). *The new citizenship: Unconventional politics, activism, and service.* Boulder, CO: Westview.

Roberts, N. (2004). Public deliberation in an age of direct citizen participation. *American Review of Public Administration, 34*, 315–353.

Skowronek, S. (1982). *Building a new American state: The expansion of national administrative capacities, 1877–1920.* Cambridge, UK: Cambridge University Press.

Stewart, T. R., Dennis, R. L., & Ely, D. W. (1984). Citizen participation and judgment in policy analysis: A case study of urban air quality. *Policy Science, 17*, 67–87.

Stivers, C. (1990). The public agency as polis: Active citizenship in the administrative state. *Administration & Society, 22*, 86–105.

Stivers, C. (2000). *Bureau men, settlement women: Constructing public administration in the Progressive Era.* Lawrence: University Press of Kansas.

Thomas, J. C. (1995). *Public participation in public decisions.* San Francisco: Jossey-Bass.

Timney, M. (1996, July). *Overcoming NIMBY: Using citizen participation effectively.* Paper presented at the fifty-seventh meeting of the American Society for Public Administration, Atlanta, GA.

Tocqueville, A. de. (1945). *Democracy in America* (2 vols.). New York: Vintage. (Original work published 1835)

Waldo, D. (1948). *The administrative state.* New York: Ronald Press.

Wang, X. (2001). Assessing public participation in U.S. cities. *Public Performance & Management Review, 24*, 322–336.

Wiebe, R. (1967). *The search for order: 1877–1920.* New York: Hill & Wang.

Wilson, W. (1887). The study of administration. *Political Science Quarterly, 2*, 197–222.

Yang, K., & Callahan, K. (2005). Assessing citizen involvement efforts by local governments. *Public Performance & Management Review, 29*, 191–216.

Democracy, Public Participation, and Budgeting

Mutually Exclusive or Just Exhausting?

Aimee L. Franklin and Carol Ebdon

Public administrators attempt to reconcile many values, such as efficiency, effectiveness, equity, and representation. The budgeting process is an arena where the balancing act between multiple values plays out very clearly. Consider, for example, standards concerning the safety of the water we drink. Scientists may determine a reasonable level of arsenic in our drinking water given guidelines on acceptable levels of risk, engineers may know the most cost-efficient methods for treating contaminated water, and population density studies can determine where to site a water treatment plant. But what if citizens do not like these expert answers because they will increase their taxes, or area residents object to the location of water treatment plants? Ultimately it is the elected officials that have to decide what the city will do when expert recommendations and citizen desires conflict.

The American form of democracy elects people to represent the interests of their constituents, so why is participation necessary? A key reason is that elections do not give guidance on specific policy issues. Participation provides a direct line of communication between elected officials and the public regarding allocation of public resources, such as addressing arsenic in the drinking water. In addition to providing a means for illuminating contradictory preferences, the budget process serves a variety of other purposes: it is a political process that determines winners and losers based on who pays and who receives government goods and services; it is a technical process concerned with formats, presentation, and calculations to balance revenues and expenditures; it is a planning process that aligns resources to move toward a desired future; it is an evaluation process that determines what results have been achieved from public expenditures and holds public officials responsible for results.

Each of the purposes of budgeting can be enhanced by participation. For example, the planning and evaluation purposes benefit from consideration of a wider range of interests than those of government officials, and increased input may result in decisions more closely aligned with the public interest. However, soliciting input can be costly in terms of time and effort. It can also make a political process even more highly charged by increasing the transparency of who is winning and who is losing. Meaningful participation is also difficult because of the technical nature of the budget presentation; many people feel intimidated by columns of numbers stated in terms that are hard to grasp. How do we assess the soundness of a national defense budget of $405 billion (Executive Office of the President, 2004, p. 379), when our annual household budget may be closer to $50,000? Who should participate in the decision to spend $405 billion, and how do we ensure that participants' views are representative? What will it take to guarantee that budgetary decisions are democratic?

While it may not be possible to determine the "right" level of participation in budgeting, that is, the level necessary to uphold democracy, we can probably agree that democracy, participation, and budgeting should not be mutually exclusive. We can probably also agree that the efforts necessary to integrate democracy, public participation, and budgeting decisions will, in all likelihood, be exhausting.

In this chapter we consider the connections between democracy, participation, and budgeting. Our purpose is to engage the issue of the effectiveness of citizen participation in budgeting by illustrating the concepts and exploring common issues and barriers. We will then reflect on what we have learned and offer a framework of considerations that can be used to structure participation that is responsive to varying environments, so that the principles of democracy are enhanced through budgetary decision-making.

The chapter starts by considering how participation enhances democracy in its American form. The second section outlines the traditional budget process. Using this base of knowledge, the third section details the normative underpinnings of participation by describing the potential benefits when this input is actively considered in the budget process. There are a variety of participants when this input is gathered; the stakeholders and their representativeness and expectations are the topics of the fourth section. The mechanics of gathering input from the participants are provided in the fifth section. In the sixth section, we explore what can limit effective participation and then make recommendations for overcoming these barriers in the final section. We conclude that effective budget participation can enhance democracy and that there are tools available to achieve this. The question remains: can we do this, and institutionalize it, so that it becomes a normal and vital part of democracy without exhausting everyone involved?

How Participation Enhances Democracy

Over the years, there has been an ebb and flow in the call for public participation in the budgeting process (Ebdon & Franklin, 2006). There have been many recent advocates of an expanded role for citizens in governance (Box, 1998; King, Feltey, & Susel, 1998; King, Stivers, & collaborators, 1998; Schachter, 1997; Thomas, 1995). Three common reasons are given for budget participation. First, it is a way for people to more clearly understand how public funds are allocated. Second, it provides an opportunity for individuals and groups to make their preferences known. Third, it enhances the ability of citizens to review whether officials are acting in the public interest. These reasons relate to the values that undergird the American form of democracy. Just what are these values and how can public participation in budgeting help foster democracy? To better understand the need for participation in resource allocation, we first consider some democratic characteristics and how they are fostered through participation.

The United States has been described as a society that values things such as individual freedom, equality, progress, efficiency, practicality, and humanitarianism (Williams, in Anderson, 2005, p. 40). These values dominated discussions during the founding of the nation and led to the democracy we have today. Table 5.1 describes some of the key characteristics valued in the American form of democracy in the left hand column. The right hand column then describes how citizen participation in budgeting can help to uphold these characteristics.

The first characteristic of democracy is the opportunity to participate in the decision-making process. This can be done through passive participation, such as voting in regular elections, or through active participation, such as serving on a citizens' advisory committee that provides direct input to elected officials. Unfortunately, elections of representatives do not indicate preferences on a range of issues. Active participation can make elected officials aware of constituent preferences when resources are being allocated. For example, a candidate may run on a platform of saving the environment. After election, what is her mandate for spending when citizens value a safe community as well as a healthy environment? Gathering direct input through her constituents can help to sort out preferences.

Serving the public interest by being good stewards of public funds is a

Table 5.1

Democratic Characteristics & the Contribution of Citizen Participation

Characteristics of Democracy	How Citizen Participation Can Help
1. Voter participation in regular elections. One person, one vote and majority rule = passive participation	Provides opportunities for active participation
2. Elected officials serve the public interest and are public stewards (financial and the public trust)	Ensures accountability for public assets, monitors waste/fraud/abuse
3. Independent branches of government with checks and balances	Input gathered by different actors who respond to different stakeholders
4. Individual preferences and rights are balanced against collective needs/desires	Confirms willingness to pay for a specific allocation of resources
5. Government provides services and protection for all, but especially for the less fortunate	Assures equal treatment through a transparent process
6. No taxation without representation	Permeability when taxpayers are encouraged to state their preferences and willingness to pay

democratic characteristic that receives great emphasis in the United States. In part, the attention reflects concerns brought about by media reports of public officials who abuse their positions and misuse public funds. It also reflects calls to redress dramatic declines in citizens' trust in government. Participation clarifies preferences of a wider, more representative range of constituents, and can also overcome the need to use election results as a proxy for the public interest in times of low voter turnout. Citizen input enhances accountability by shining light on how government resources are being used. Many budgets include financial details regarding spending levels in prior as well as upcoming fiscal years, allowing for better-informed citizens and the ability to assess trends in resource allocation and costs of services.

The Constitution was designed around another democratic characteristic, the separation of powers between branches of governments, with checks and balances on the powers of each branch. Actors in each branch may receive input from different stakeholders through varying methods, which can enhance policy deliberation and decision-making.

We also value a balance between the needs of individuals and that of the collective society. These interests can be determined through citizen participation, where stakeholders (individuals as well as groups) can state prefer-

Figure 5.1   **Characteristics of Democracy**

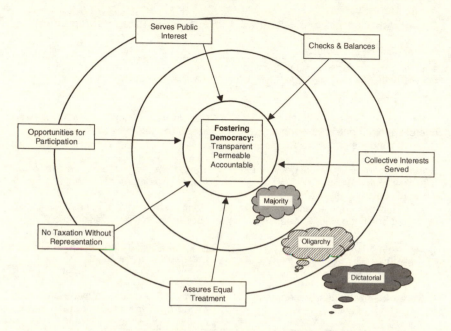

ences at both the micro and macro political levels. Citizens may wish to have potholes in their street filled quickly, but at the macro level they may be unwilling to raise taxes for this purpose. Getting participants to consider collective or macro-level issues, such as the aggregated costs of fulfilling everyone's individual desires, can be challenging, but is an important activity that is valued in a democracy that seeks to serve both the individual and society. After all, politics "is the way a democratic society resolves such differences" (Anderson, 2005, p. 5), and there are few more political processes than budgeting!

In addition, democracy seeks to assure equal treatment for all and to provide a social safety net for the less fortunate. When we gather budget input, unserved and emergent needs can be uncovered. For example, in Norman, Oklahoma, a grassroots effort to build a skate park for sports enthusiasts with no place to practice resulted in a new facility constructed at an existing city park.

Lastly, we remember the rallying cry of our Founding Fathers: "No taxation without representation." The tax revolts of recent decades are contemporary examples of an enduring concern with taxation levels. While voting assures representation, citizen participation is a better mechanism for assessing what level of taxation is acceptable since it provides a direct line of communication between elected officials and constituents regarding how much people are willing to pay for their government and by what means.

In reviewing this list of democratic characteristics, it becomes apparent that democracy is fostered when the structure and operations of government are transparent, when opportunities and mechanisms exist for stakeholders to permeate the system, and when accountability is assured. As shown in Figure 5.1, public input can move us from dictatorial or oligarchical decision-making by a few, which often results in the interests of the elite being over-stated (Schattschneider, 1960, p. 35), to decision-making that involves a group of participants that are more representative and reflect broader preferences. To foster democracy, we need to move toward the center of the bull's-eye. Citizen participation provides a means to move from the outer to the inner circle on each of the democratic characteristics.

The ideal relationship between democracy and direct public participation then is clear—or is it? As discussed in the Introduction to this book, there is a basic tension underscoring the American system of governance. As a society, we have not identified the dividing line between the decisions that we believe should be delegated to our elected representatives and the decisions in which we believe individual citizens should participate. It is not surprising that there are pervasive disagreements about the need for and the proper form of citizen participation in the public budgeting process.

The Traditional Budget Process

The city of Omaha, Nebraska, follows budgetary practices similar to those of many other local governments, and will be used here for illustrative purposes. The administration spends several months preparing a recommended budget. The finance department develops a revenue forecast and compares it to the amount necessary to provide services at the same level next year. Based on this information, and his/her priorities, the mayor sets overall guidelines for departments to use in crafting their proposals. Staff from the finance department and mayor's office review the requests and present options and recommendations to the mayor. The mayor makes final decisions on how the budget will be balanced, which may include changes in tax rates or user fees, and could result in an increased budget for one department for a new program while another department's budget is reduced.

The city council then has several weeks to review the proposed budget. This process includes a series of open meetings where council members question department representatives, as well as a public hearing for citizens to speak about the budget. Council members are also contacted directly during this period by individuals and groups to express their budget preferences.

The city council can make adjustments to the budget, but must legally adopt it by a specific date.

Public attention to the budget is typically greater in years when tax increases and/or major service level reductions are proposed. For example, in the midst of a national recession, budget balancing options for 2004 centered on either substantial service cuts such as closing a library branch, or labor union concessions that would require paybacks in future years. Public meetings drew considerable turnout, including concerned library patrons and proponents of other city services, as well as employee groups. The final budget included some layoffs and minor service cuts, but all libraries remained open, with union contract revisions saving the day.

The most recently adopted budget, on the other hand, proposed restoring some services in 2006. A tax on telephone usage was increased, but this tax had not been raised in ten years and the impact would be slight for the average residential customer. Turnout at the public hearing included only nine speakers. Public discussion revolved primarily around continued funding for a public safety auditor, and the need for additional police cruisers. The city council made several marginal adjustments that eliminated the public safety auditor, increased funding for police cars, added building and housing inspectors, and added support for a local art museum.

This scenario is typical: budget preparation by staff, consideration and discussion during public hearings, and approval by the legislative body. Public administrators and elected officials define priorities such as how much funding is necessary for law enforcement, and they make the key expenditure decisions that determine which services will be provided at what level and to whom. Revenue decisions impact who will pay for the services (for example, different groups of people may pay property tax versus sales tax).

Budget decisions have direct impacts on the lives of residents and the future of the community. To a certain extent, though, budgetary practices treat the process as a technical matter to be handled largely by professional staff, with final approval by elected officials. The high level of technical complexity can result in low public involvement. The public is often involved, if at all, only as a formality at the end of the traditional budget process. Cities are required to hold a public hearing on the proposed budget before final action in forty states, with forty-two states requiring public hearings by counties (Berner & Smith, 2004, pp. 4–7). However, this method has drawbacks. A public hearing usually occurs late in the process, minimizing the potential for input to affect budget outcomes. In addition, these forums allow only for one-sided communication rather than dialogue between citizens and public officials. Speakers at public hearings also tend to be those who have very strong feelings about a particular budget issue, and they may not be representative of the general public (Ebdon, 2002a; Thomas, 1995).

The vitality of democratic principles is diminished with the low level of input in the typical process. Can citizens have a significant influence in shaping public programs and policies through involvement in creation of public budgets? What might be the benefits of public involvement? The next section answers these questions based on existing theories and research.

Normative Underpinnings of Participation: Potential Benefits

Existing literature suggests a number of benefits from encouraging participation in the budget process (see Ebdon & Franklin, 2006). In this section, we examine these benefits, such as informing, educating, gathering input, and building social capital. Ultimately, the key benefit is democratic decision-making in which results are supported by all who are affected.

Participation is often viewed as a way to inform the public about the budget and, by doing so, to enhance trust through increased transparency. Berman (1997, p. 110) concluded that citizens in cities that foster participation are less cynical about local government. The use of community neighborhood boards in the city of Dayton, Ohio, has been cited as a reason for voter approval of every tax referendum over a twenty year period (Gurwitt, 1992, p. 50). Wang (2001, p. 333) found that managers generally perceive a positive relationship between participation and increased public trust.

Another potential benefit is educating citizens about government operations and programmatic costs. Public budgets are often complicated (Bland & Rubin, 1997; Kahn, 1997). A city government may have over one hundred separate funds, each for a specific purpose, with limited ability to move money between funds; this constrains budget decisions and it is often not understood by constituents. Budget participants have noted the benefits of processes that help educate citizens in these intricacies (Ebdon, 2002a, p. 286; Franklin & Ebdon, 2004, p. 223). Officials have also demonstrated success working with citizens to better communicate the need for funding priority areas with which the public did not initially agree (Watson, Juster, & Johnson, 1991, p. 236).

Effectively structured participation is a means for gathering information that can be useful for decision-makers. Franklin and Ebdon (2004, p. 225) find that citizen input assists the city council in performing its responsibility to represent constituents and to provide long-term vision and policy guidance. Public officials have noted that citizen input has affected their budget decisions (Ebdon, 2002a, p. 287; Franklin & Carberry-George, 1999, p. 41;

Roberts, 1997, p. 128; Simonsen & Robbins, 2000; Watson, Juster, & Johnson, 1991, p. 237), although input does not always have a direct impact on resource allocation (Franklin & Ebdon, 2004, p. 183).

Last, a long-term benefit that can be derived from participation is community building. One study found that the public believed that city agencies were more responsive in jurisdictions that utilized more participation (Halvorsen, 2003, p. 538). Participation is seen by some as a duty for citizens and a way to enhance a sense of community (Box, 1998; King, Stivers, & collaborators, 1998).

Democratic participation processes give everyone the opportunity to be heard and provide a basis for understanding the choices, hopefully resulting in decisions supported not just by clients but by citizens overall. When feedback is provided showing that the input was considered, participants are more satisfied with their involvement (King, Feltey, & Susel, 1998). How do we structure participation so that it has the highest likelihood of being effective, and meets varying needs and expectations? To answer this we turn to a description of the technical aspects of fostering participation that engages a wide range of interests.

Budgetary Stakeholders: Participants, Representation, Expectations

This section outlines the various actors in the budget process, the roles they play, and their expectations for participation. The challenges associated with ensuring that input is representative and not dominated by self-interested participants' views is discussed, based on literature regarding the importance of representation and participant expectations.

Four types of stakeholders participate in the budget process: (1) decision-makers, who are normally elected officials; (2) professional administrators, who are responsible for preparing and implementing the budget as well as advising the decision-makers; (3) citizens, who are impacted by the budgetary decisions; and (4) clients or their representatives, who seek to influence decisions. Elected officials and administrators are internal stakeholders, and are obligated to participate based on their official position. Citizens and clients are external stakeholders, and are voluntarily involved to advance the public interest and/or their own personal interests.

Roles played by internal and external stakeholders vary, as do their expectations for, and from, public participation. Elected officials may consider themselves as representatives who promote their constituents' preferences, or as knowledgeable elders, doing what is best for the community as a whole, or as businesspeople making rational decisions based on efficiency. All of these roles were evident in case studies of two midwestern cities (Franklin & Ebdon, 2004, p. 225).

Professional administrators are responsible for the technical aspects of budget development, implementation, and evaluation. They also serve an advisory role when analyzing and presenting policy alternatives to elected officials. Administrators are often responsible for creating and managing participation opportunities and sharing the results with elected officials.

External stakeholders may see participation as a civic obligation and offer budgetary input based on their concern for the public good. Participants may also seek involvement to promote their own self-interest. In traditional participatory methods, input is typically limited to one particular budget issue, with participants disregarding the consequences of their preferences on other areas of the budget or other subsets of the population. For example, the mayor of Topeka, Kansas, reduced funding to social service agencies by one-third in her 2001 proposed budget. Over one hundred people attended the six-hour public hearing. Virtually all of the speakers represented agencies arguing to restore their funding levels, without suggesting how this could be done while still balancing the budget (Ebdon & Franklin, 2004, p. 45).

The desire for and expectations regarding participation in budgeting decisions can vary greatly. The political environment can be a factor here. Cities with council-manager forms of government have been found to be more likely to be participatory (Ebdon, 2002a, p. 290; Kweit & Kweit, 1981), and participation is found more often in larger, more heterogeneous cities (Ebdon 2000a, p. 390; O'Toole, Marshall, & Grewe 1996, p. 53; Wang, 2001, p. 332). Political culture may also be important; one study found more participation in northern cities with a "moralistic" culture (Ebdon, 2000a, p. 390). State legal requirements can also affect participation opportunities; some communities focus solely on meeting the minimum requirements (Berner & Smith, 2004, p. 7; Orosz, 2002, p. 431).

Those who speak at public hearings are generally not perceived as being representative of the population. For more elaborate participation methods like simulations, it is not easy to find a representative group of citizens willing to put forth the necessary time and effort (Ebdon, 2002a, p. 291; Ebdon & Franklin, 2004, p. 47). A perception that input is received from a nonrepresentative group may weaken the level of influence. For example, the mayor of Topeka, Kansas, utilized focus groups in budget preparation one year; the city council ignored the results, because they believed the mayor had hand-picked participants who would support her priorities (Franklin & Ebdon, 2004, p. 221). Influence can also vary among groups; one study found that a citizen advisory committee was perceived to have greater influence in

city budget decisions than the business community and local nonprofit organizations (Franklin & Ebdon, 2004, pp. 223–224).

For these reasons, who participates can be very important. Officials should
pay attention to who will identify and how they will invite external stakeholders to participate. Successful methods have generally been those that are
open to large numbers of people (Kathlene & Martin, 1991, p. 53; Thomas,
1995), and include participants who are representative of the community
(Crosby, Kelly, & Schaefer, 1986, p. 171; Johnson, 1998, p. 17; Watson,
Juster, & Johnson, 1991, p. 237).

What is expected from participation? As noted earlier, there are several
potential benefits from budget participation, but stakeholders may differ on
the goals and expected outcomes of participation. Elected officials and administrators in one case may be primarily interested in educating citizens on
the trade-offs required to balance a budget. In another case, internal stakeholders may want to obtain input regarding public preferences and willingness to pay for services. External stakeholders may see participation as a
learning process and/or be more interested in affecting resource allocation
decisions. Participation goals and expectations are frequently not clearly stated
in advance, but they should be to enhance the effectiveness of participation
(Crosby, Kelley, & Schaefer, 1986, p. 175; Ebdon & Franklin, 2006; Kathlene
& Martin, 1991, p. 61; Rosener, 1978, p. 462; Simonsen & Robbins, 2000;
Thomas, 1995).

Fostering participation from each of the four different types of stakeholders can be critical to successful participation, or participation that makes
democratic governments more effective. Stakeholders play varying roles,
which are structured to assure decisions that are permeable, transparent, and
accountable. The expectations held by each group can also be dramatically
different. Rather than viewing this disconnect as negative, we need to develop mechanisms to uncover a wide range of preferences to enliven the
discussion about how to best serve the public interest. Purposeful opportunities for participation can create a marketplace of ideas (Lindblom &
Woodhouse, 1993, p. 126), where it is more likely that sound decisions can
be made by government officials on behalf of the collective interests of the
society. How do we design participation opportunities around the roles and
expectations of the stakeholders, to maximize the potential for effective outcomes? The next section identifies important elements.

The Mechanics of Participation

A variety of mechanisms have been used to gather input in the budgeting
process, each with strengths and weaknesses. Participatory methods can be

Figure 5.2   **Continuum of Participation Mechanisms**

Budget information printed and available to citizens, public hearings	Focus groups, simulations, advisory committees	Multiple participation mechanisms employed
Easy	*Access*	Difficult
Low	*Complexity*	High
One-way	*Input Desired*	Two-way

arranged along a continuum based on ease of access, complexity of involvement, and the type of input desired. The easiest methods, shown on the left end of the continuum in Figure 5.2, allow one-way communication: providing information to citizens about the budget, and public comment to officials at public meetings. For these methods, access is easy, involvement is not complex, and there is no expectation of input; resource costs are low, but so are the resulting levels of useful input.

In the middle of the continuum are methods such as focus groups, simulations, and advisory committees in which input is more defined and focused. It is more difficult to assure access to these methods because of the longer time commitment required by participants. Complexity also increases as participants are exposed to information about various budgetary issues that may include financial details and indicators of performance. The type of input desired can range from voting on a range of issues with no consideration of the "cost" of the decision, to elaborate methods where participants prioritize their choices within limited amounts of funding.

At the right end of the continuum are multiple input mechanisms. Opportunities are offered to gather input from large numbers of participants and to make sure that the input is representative of all constituents. This approach has the advantage of allowing different groups and individuals to provide input in different ways (Ebdon & Franklin, 2006). More complex participation efforts may facilitate greater access, but they also entail greater resources, and aggregating input can be a challenge with multiple and conflicting stated preferences.

Making information publicly available is a good way to educate citizens about the budget and can spur interested individuals into becoming involved in budget deliberations. Burlington, Iowa, publishes a one-page newspaper advertisement with basic information about the proposed city budget. Other informational methods can include citizens' guides or budget summaries, posting the budget on government websites, use of public access television, and even presentations at citizen academies (Lun, 2004, p. 35). Budget documents may include pie charts that clearly demonstrate where funding comes from and the major functional areas to which resources are allocated, as well as other visual methods to communicate budget information (Marlowe, 2005). States often mandate information requirements for local governments; for example, published budgets or summaries must be available to the public in cities in twenty-five states, and in counties in twenty-nine states (Berner & Smith, 2004, pp. 4–11).

Citizen surveys are often used to gather input regarding budget preferences. Surveys may be more representative than other methods and can be repeated over time to reveal trends (Miller & Miller, 1991; Webb & Hatry, 1973). However, they may not reflect the intensity of respondents' opinions (Thomas, 1995), they can be costly to administer, they may be of doubtful value when there is insufficient information for informed decisions, and they require careful design in the writing of questions (Hatry & Blair, 1976, p. 137). A case study of surveys in Auburn, Alabama, showed the benefit of citizen surveys in city budget preparation. Respondents were presented each year with a list of city services and asked for their highest budget priority. A long-term emphasis on streets in the survey results appeared to affect officials' decisions to increase spending in this area. Elected officials also became aware that public views were not necessarily aligned with their own; as a result, the city enhanced efforts to publicize the need for a new park and an airport expansion project (Watson, Juster, & Johnson, 1991, p. 235).

As mentioned previously, public meetings are among the most commonly used budget input methods. Large numbers of people can participate and meetings can be a forum for sharing information and educating people about issues. Public meetings can show the strength of opinion about specific issues, and are not closed to anyone (Adams, 2004, p. 47). Unfortunately, attendance is often low and participants may be self-interested rather than representative of community preferences, may not have the knowledge to provide effective input, and are forced to comment on a reality that has already been constructed by city officials (Thomas, 1995). Public hearings are also not viewed as good methods of gathering sincere preferences of the public and its willingness to pay for services (Glaser & Denhardt, 1999, p. 307). In addition, many governments have a small group of citizens who show up regularly at budget hearings with the same complaints and no longer have credibility with elected officials (Ebdon, 2002a, p. 292).

There are examples of public forum usage in times of fiscal stress where citizens have helped develop budget solutions. The Rosemont, Minnesota, school district experienced a 38 percent reduction in state aid and needed to make significant budget cuts. Decisions were made through a thorough, public deliberation process, with suggestions solicited from employees, students, and the public over a four-month period. The ideas were reviewed and analyzed, then presented to public meetings held in ten different locations, where 2,000 participants discussed the options. The superintendent reviewed all of the input before making her recommendations, which were approved unanimously by the board of education (Roberts, 1997, p. 127).

Structured meetings can be designed in other ways to gather input. Focus groups, which are invited meetings with small groups of people purposefully chosen, provide opportunities to explore preferences and to interpret reactions to proposals (Thomas, 1995), but focus group participants may not be representative and people with strong opinions may unduly influence the input (Ebdon & Franklin, 2006). A number of new group-process techniques have been developed in recent years. Practitioners now make use of many new quasi-legislative and quasi-judicial governance processes, including deliberative democracy, e-democracy, public conversations, participatory budgeting, citizen juries, study circles, collaborative policy making, and alternative dispute resolution (Bingham, Nabatchi, & O'Leary, 2005, p. 554). These techniques can enhance active participation in budgeting.

Citizen advisory committees are another small-group participation mechanism that has been used to review the proposed budget, or is used earlier in the process during budget preparation. Committees are also commonly used for specific parts of the budget, such as the Capital Improvement Program, or Community Development Block Grant fund allocation (Ebdon, 2002b, p. 36). Committee participants often develop expertise about the budget process and can be purposefully selected to represent different sections of the community, but committees can require more time and effort to administer and participants can become disenfranchised if they perceive that their input is not considered (Ebdon, 2003, p. 174; Thomas, 1995). One study found that advisory committees were perceived to be effective when the committee had clear goals and objectives and appointments were made in a democratic manner (Callahan, 2002, p. 315). The city of Burlington, Iowa, uses an eleven-member Citizen's Budget Education Committee whose purpose is to "recommend an educational process that achieves maximum coverage to all social economic groups in the community" (City of Burlington, 2001, p. 1). The committee, which represents a variety of stakeholder groups, recommends informational methods to inform citizens of budget issues and choices; members also informally "spread the word" through their community contacts.

In budget simulations, participants are forced to make trade-offs to balance the budget. Simulations require a substantial amount of time to develop and require a certain level of knowledge or education among the participants prior to the exercise. It is common that participants will be asked to focus on just a few key issues, leading to an environment perceived as being artificial. The city of Wichita, Kansas, has used budget simulation exercises with neighborhood leaders. During the 2001 budget process, for example, staff presented cost and performance data on thirty-four different activities in six functional area groupings. Each group of participants could add or reduce funding for individual activities, but any changes had to be balanced by revenue increases or other spending adjustments. Participants identified several priority areas, such as at-risk youth programs, code enforcement, and infrastructure maintenance. Most groups chose to increase the tax rate to fund additional spending rather than reducing other services, an outcome that was not expected by city officials (Ebdon & Franklin, 2004, p. 44).

There are shortcomings evident in each form of participation. One way to overcome this is to use multiple mechanisms to leverage the strengths of each and offset the weaknesses. Eugene, Oregon, used an eighteen-month multistage process to deal with significant budget issues. Through a combination of budget balancing exercises, surveys, and public meetings, decision-makers were able to discern preferences and to estimate willingness to pay for different options. The city council then developed three strategies and went back to the public for feedback. This process ultimately resulted in savings of approximately $5.4 million, with reductions in seventy-one programs and fee increases in some areas (Simonsen & Robbins, 2000).

New technology can also enhance citizen input. For example, an online survey of state budget issues in Nebraska utilized patented Internet research techniques. This method allowed for pre- and post-"testing" of participants' knowledge levels, solicitation of preferences and values, and video streaming of educational information and interviews with budget experts. Results showed that the website helped to overcome an initial lack of knowledge of the state budget by a large portion of respondents, appeared to serve some educational purpose, and provided input to state legislators regarding public priorities (Ebdon, 2002b). These types of exercises can reach larger numbers of people at lower costs than mail or telephone surveys. Fairly complex online budget simulations have also been developed (for example, Budget Utah, at www.governor.state.ut.us/budget/fy2000).

This section has pointed out a number of differences between input mechanisms, including: when the participation occurs in the budget process; whether the opportunity is available to large groups; the extent to which participants are representative of the community; and whether communication is primarily one-way versus two-way dialogue. Scholars advocate two-way communication early in the budget process, with sufficient time for deliberation,

broad representation, input solicited in a way that reveals sincere preferences, and officials that consider citizen input in decision-making (Ebdon &
Franklin, 2006; Franklin & Ebdon, 2005, p. 181).

Previous sections have examined how participation can support the characteristics of democracy, described stakeholders and issues related to representation and expectations, and considered the mechanics of participation.
In the next section, we move from the normative ideas of what should be
done to the reality of how difficult and even exhausting this process can be.
Proactively addressing these issues may be key to overcoming barriers to
effective participation.

Exploring the Potential for Effective Participation: Issues and Barriers

Empirical evidence suggests that participation in the budget process is relatively minimal and that few identifiable changes in the budget can be directly
attributed to citizen input. This reduces the perceived effectiveness of the
participatory process and does not enhance democracy. This section explores
common issues and barriers to effective participation. Barriers can be overcome through careful assessment of the local context combined with thought-
ful consideration of factors thought to be directly related to participation
outcomes.

One issue relates to the locus of responsibility for gathering input and the
sharing of decision-making. Ideally, in our form of democracy, the responsibility for fostering citizen participation is shared between elected officials
and public administrators. However, one or both of these groups may be
reluctant. For example, finance officers have been found to desire participation, but they think it is the responsibility of the elected officials to initiate it
(Miller & Evers, 2002, p. 257). Professional administrators may also have
concerns about sharing decision-making on complex issues with the public
(O'Toole & Marshall, 1988, p. 54; Thomas, 1995). Administrators and elected
officials may feel that citizens already have sufficient access (Franklin &
Ebdon, 2004, p. 224), that the increased input makes their jobs even harder
(Bland & Rubin, 1997; Thompson & Jones, 1986, p. 569), or that the budget
is too complex for useful public input (Ebdon, 2002a, p. 287). If opportunities are too limited, the decisions may be perceived as dictatorial when made
only by the council or elitist or oligopolistic if only a few influential "citizens" have input.

Another barrier can arise if there is a lack of public willingness to participate. Research shows that some individuals are not at all interested in budget
participation, others want to play an active role, and still others might be able

to be talked into it (Miller & Evers, 2002, p. 265). It is difficult to achieve input that is representative of the community when large numbers of people do not have the time or interest, or perceive that their opinions are not wanted anyway (Ebdon, 2002a, p. 287). When this happens, it is difficult to consider the interests of the community since reluctant actors may be self-interested, tuning into station WIFM (What's in it for me?).

A related issue is having an appropriate number of participants. Research shows that the number of stakeholders providing input can be increased if there are many opportunities to provide input held around the community and if special efforts are made to invite citizens to attend (Franklin & Ebdon, 2005, p. 180). We know a public budget expert who argues that he pays taxes to too many jurisdictions (federal, state, city, county, school district, etc.) to be able to have enough time or knowledge about their budgets to participate. If this argument represents the views of many citizens, the number of people participating will be low.

Research shows that participation levels are influenced by the types of input mechanisms used. Utilization of the various mechanisms varies dramatically. Public hearings are widely used, as are attempts to provide budget information to the public (Ebdon, 2000a, p. 388; Ebdon, 2002b, p. 388; O'Toole, Marshall, & Grewe, 1996, p. 27). Results of a 1996 survey showed that only 18 percent of responding council-manager cities held community meetings for budget development input, and 32 percent used citizens' groups to make formal recommendations to the city council during budget consideration (Ebdon, 2000a, p. 387). In another survey, 46.2 percent of responding city chief administrative officers reported active involvement by citizens in the budget process; this rate was much lower than the level of activity reported in other functions, such as zoning, parks, and public safety (Wang, 2001, p. 331).

A last issue in designing effective participation is the timing of the input. Budget participation appears to be limited primarily to traditional formats that occur late in the budget process. When input is gathered at a public hearing, it is often too late to change preliminary budget decisions. The likelihood of input impacting decision-making is raised if the input is gathered much earlier, such as during the city's strategic planning process.

There are many issues to consider when designing public participation in budgetary decision-making: the perception of dictatorial decision-making; inclusion of a wide range of interests; appropriate number of participants; choice of mechanisms used; and timing of the input. In the next section, we present a framework to assess how various combinations of choices can align democratic goals and budgetary inputs to make participation optimally effective.

Figure 5.3   **Matching Participation to Democratic Goals and Budgetary Inputs**

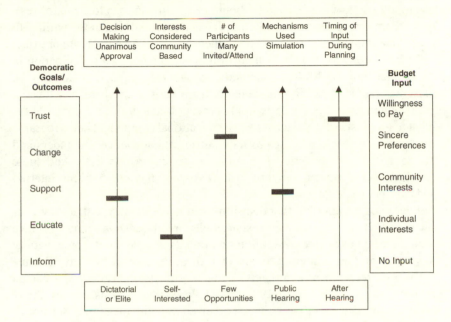

Recommendations for Structuring Participation

Structuring participatory methods to achieve desired outcomes can be difficult, particularly if the stakeholders are not sure of the goals of the process. A number of useful methods are available that can be adapted for use by individual jurisdictions, but because each government faces a unique environment and different issues, there are no cookie-cutter approaches that can be implemented with little effort. It can take considerable time and effort to design the appropriate methods, and often this process can be financially costly (Roberts, 1997, p. 129).

In Figure 5.3, we suggest the range of issues to consider and adjust given the situational context in which budget participation will occur. In this framework, it is possible to consider how citizen participation can be structured to help participants change channels from WIFM and tune into a channel that better enhances democracy. Using the metaphor of a radio tuner, we can adjust the different issues based on local preferences and constraints to overcome common barriers. Just as adjusting controls alters the sound of a stereo, adjusting the participatory settings can alter democratic outcomes.

What are some suggestions for adjusting these settings? Careful planning should go into determining the range of participants. More effective outcomes have been achieved with representative participants reflective of the community as a whole. Officials should extend invitations to a mix of residents from diverse backgrounds, but most importantly to those willing to focus on community-wide concerns rather than their own pet issue or gripe.

There is not one "best" mechanism for obtaining citizen participation in the budget process. Multiple methods of gathering input may actually be most successful in gaining the benefits from various mechanisms. Ideally, participation should begin early in the process to maximize the potential for input to be considered in decisions. An educational component helps to frame the discussion so that participants have sufficient knowledge and understand the necessity of considering issues facing the city as a whole. And some activities should be structured to foster two-way dialogue between internal and external stakeholders.

Finally, it is important that decision-makers communicate that they considered all input even though resource allocation decisions may not have been modified as a direct result. Public officials receive input from a variety of sources and most attempt to consider all of the information they receive regarding preferences. Ultimately, budgetary decisions reflect aggregated priorities (McIver & Ostrom, 1976, p. 93). When this happens, approval may not be unanimous, but it will not be perceived as being made by a dictator or a privileged elite.

Seldom will we have the time, resources, or level of stakeholder commitment at the optimal setting (all levers moved to the top of the diagram). For some jurisdictions, this may not even be the desired level given the expected goals/outcomes. The participation process can be conceptualized as a series of choices that interact with other choices to affect the overall level of outcomes. By using this framework to diagnose the situation that exists and then assess what is feasible among many choices, we can leverage outcomes in an effective participation process.

Conclusions

While citizen participation efforts have been judged effective in some budget processes, there is little evidence of institutionalization of these methods, beyond the traditional public hearing. Governments may try a focus group, survey, or advisory committee once or twice with some success, but then not continue the practice, or may continue to experiment with other methods (Ebdon & Franklin, 2004, p. 224). The lack of institutionalization may be due to the recency of some of these attempts and the ongoing efforts to improve the process, as well as the problematic barriers cited above. We suggest that by using the framework outlined above, the likelihood that participation will be perceived as being beneficial in terms of allocating resources and enhancing democracy can be increased.

Given the complexities of and barriers to instituting effective budget participation, is it worth pursuing? We think so. Public budgeting has undergone tremendous changes over the past century. Attention has shifted from a strict focus on financial accountability, to efforts to measure efficiency, to a linkage with broader planning concepts, to current reforms that attempt to develop goals and performance standards for utilization in allocating resources. These changes reflect changes in primary values over time. However, governments have adapted and continue to use elements of each of these reforms to meet the needs of their organization and community (Rubin, 1990, p. 186). The same can be true of efforts to enhance citizen participation in the budgeting process, and we suggest a framework of important issues to consider in order to do this.

We constantly hear individuals complain that their taxes are too high, but in the next breath express displeasure because their child's public school class size is too large, or local streets are not maintained well enough. The tax limitation efforts that began in the late 1970s have not apparently reduced this level of dissatisfaction. Citizens do not have a good understanding of how much they actually pay for government, the costs of government services, or the impacts of varying financing methods. We believe that citizen participation is absolutely crucial as a way to begin to educate citizens, work toward consensus-building about government realities and priorities, and along the way enhance democracy and community.

We have pointed out a number of factors that are important in structuring citizen participation. First, officials should consider their goals and the potential goals of, and benefits to, the participants. These efforts can have tremendous payoffs, but stakeholders need to be realistic and not expect unreasonable outcomes. The lack of institutionalization of participatory practices may be related to not having clear goals or reasonable expectations up front. Institutionalization can be important for fostering clear roles and relationships between the different stakeholders that will lead to commonly held expectations about the input process. When this happens, trust between the stakeholders should increase and democracy should be enhanced.

Citizen participation will not resolve the tension involved in making budgetary trade-offs. The balancing act between different priorities and values will continue, and perhaps be more challenging with increased input. Ultimately, citizens in some places may be happier with governments where elected officials make budget decisions without much external input. However, we believe that public officials and citizens with a strong sense of civic duty and a willingness to commit to effective participation will have a greater likelihood of success in creating change and exercising influence. For this to happen, participation opportunities need to go beyond the standard public hearing and be carefully designed with clear objectives. When writing about participatory equality, one group of authors argues that for participation to be meaningful citizens must speak loud and clear and public officials must hear what citizens want and make sure that they are equally responsive to the preferences of all citizens' voices in politics (Verba, Schlozman, & Brady, 1995, pp. 532–533). Let us work toward clear, loud, and equal public voices in the budget process.

References

Adams, B. (2004). Public meetings and the democratic process. *Public Administration Review, 64*, 43–54.

Anderson, J. E. (2005). *Public policymaking: An introduction* (6th ed). Boston: Houghton Mifflin.

Berman, E. M. (1997). Dealing with cynical citizens. *Public Administration Review, 57*, 105–112.

Berner, M., & Smith, S. (2004). The state of the states: A review of state requirements for citizen participation in the local government budget process. *State and Local Government Review, 36*, 140–150.

Bingham, L. B., Nabatchi, T., & O'Leary, R. (2005). The new governance: Practices and processes for stakeholder and citizen participation in the work of government. *Public Administration Review, 65*, 547–558.

Bland, R. L., & Rubin, I. S. (1997). *Budgeting: A guide for local governments.* Washington, DC: International City/County Management Association.

Box, R. C. (1998). *Citizen governance: Leading American communities into the 21st century.* Thousand Oaks, CA: Sage.

Callahan, K. (2002). The utilization and effectiveness of citizen advisory committees in the budget process of local governments. *Journal of Public Budgeting, Accounting & Financial Management, 14*, 295–319.

City of Burlington. (2001). Citizen budget education committee. Burlington, Iowa.

Crosby, N., Kelly, J. M., & Schaefer, P. (1986). Citizens panels: A new approach to citizen participation. *Public Administration Review, 46*, 170–178.

Ebdon, C. (2000a). The relationship between citizen involvement in the budget process and city structure and culture. *Public Productivity & Management Review, 23*, 383–393.

Ebdon, C. (2000b). The effects of voter control on budget outcomes. *Journal of Public Budgeting, Accounting & Financial Management, 12*, 22–42.

Ebdon, C. (2002a). Beyond the public hearing: Citizen participation in the local government budget process. *Journal of Public Budgeting, Accounting & Financial Management, 14*, 273–294.

Ebdon, C. (2002b, October). Interactive surveys as tools to combine citizen education and preference revelation. Paper presented at the meeting of the Association for Budgeting and Financial Management, Kansas City, MO.

Ebdon, C. (2003). Citizen participation in the budget process: Exit, voice and loyalty.

In J. Rabin (Ed.), *Encyclopedia of public administration and public policy* (pp. 173–176). New York: Marcel Dekker.

Ebdon, C., & Franklin, A. (2004). Searching for a role for citizens in the budget process. *Public Budgeting and Finance, 24*, 32–49.

Ebdon, C., & Franklin, A. (2006, in press). Citizen participation in budgeting theory. *Public Administration Review, 66.*

Executive Office of the President. (2004). Table B-80, Federal receipts and outlays, major category and surplus or deficit, fiscal years 1940–2005, in *The economic report of the president, 2004.* Washington, DC: United States Government Printing Office.

Franklin, A., & Carberry-George, B. (1999). Analyzing how local governments establish service priorities. *Public Budgeting & Finance, 19*, 31–46.

Franklin, A., & Ebdon, C. (2004). Aligning priorities in local budgeting processes. *Journal of Public Budgeting, Accounting & Financial Management, 16*, 210–227.

Franklin, A., & Ebdon, C. (2005). Citizen participation in city resource allocation: Comparing theory and practice. *American Review of Public Administration, 35,* 168–185.

Glaser, M. A., & Denhardt, R. B. (1999). When citizen expectations conflict with budgetary reality: Discontinuity between the public's demand for services and its willingness to pay taxes. *Journal of Public Budgeting, Accounting & Financial Management, 11*, 276–310.

Gurwitt, R. (1992, December). A government that runs on citizen power. *Governing, 6*, 48–54.

Halvorsen, K. E. (2003). Assessing the effects of public participation. *Public Administration Review, 63*, 535–543.

Hatry, H. P., & Blair, L. H. (1976). Citizen surveys for local governments: A copout, manipulative tool, or a policy guidance and analysis aid? In T. N. Clark (Ed.), *Citizen preferences and urban public policy* (pp. 129–140). Beverly Hills, CA: Sage.

Johnson, E. R. (1998). Recommended budget practices: Incorporating stakeholders into the process. *Government Finance Review, 14*(4), 15–18.

Kahn, J. (1997). *Budgeting democracy.* Ithaca, NY: Cornell University Press.

Kathlene, L., & Martin, J. A. (1991). Enhancing citizen participation: Panel designs, perspectives, and policy formation. *Journal of Policy Analysis and Management, 10*, 46–63.

King, C. S., Feltey, K. M., & Susel, B. O. (1998). The question of participation: Toward authentic public participation in public administration. *Public Administration Review, 58*, 317–326.

King, C. S., Stivers, C., & collaborators. (1998). *Government is us.* Thousand Oaks, CA: Sage.

Kweit, M. G., & Kweit, R. W. (1981). *Implementing citizen participation in a bureaucratic society.* New York: Praeger.

Lindblom, C., & Woodhouse, E. (1993). *The policy-making process* (3rd ed.). Englewood Cliffs, NJ: Prentice Hall.

Lun, N. (2004). Local government finance and budgeting 101: Encouraging meaningful citizen participation through education. *Government Finance Review, 20*(2), 33–38.

Marlowe, J. (2005). *The budget as a communication tool.* Washington, DC: International City/County Management Association (IQ Report).

McIver, J. P., & Ostrom, E. (1976). Using budget pies to reveal preferences: Validation of a survey instrument. In T. N. Clark (Ed.), *Citizen preferences and urban public policy* (pp. 87–110). Beverly Hills, CA: Sage.

Miller, G. J., & Evers, L. (2002). Budgeting structures and citizen participation. *Journal of Public Budgeting, Accounting & Financial Management, 14*, 233–272.

Miller, T. I., & Miller, M. A. (1991). *Citizen surveys: How to do them, how to use them, what they mean.* Washington, DC: International City Management Association.

Orosz, J. F. (2002). Views from the field: Creating a place for authentic citizen participation in budgeting. *Journal of Public Budgeting, Accounting & Financial Management, 14*, 423–444.

O'Toole, D. E., & Marshall, J. (1988). Citizen participation through budgeting. *The Bureaucrat, 17*(2), 51–55.

O'Toole, D. E., Marshall, J., & Grewe, T. (1996). Current local government budgeting practices. *Government Finance Review, 12*(6), 25–29.

Roberts, N. (1997). Public deliberation: An alternative approach to crafting policy and setting direction. *Public Administration Review, 57*, 124–132.

Rosener, J. B. (1978). Citizen participation: Can we measure its effectiveness? *Public Administration Review, 38*, 457–463.

Rubin, I. S. (1990). Budget theory and budget practice: How good the fit? *Public Administration Review, 50*, 179–189.

Schachter, H. L. (1997). *Reinventing government or reinventing ourselves.* Albany: State University of New York Press.

Schattschneider, E. E. (1960). *The semi-sovereign people.* New York: Holt, Rinehart & Winston.

Simonsen, W., & Robbins, M. D. (2000). *Citizen participation in resource allocation.* Boulder, CO: Westview.

Thomas, J. C. (1995). *Public participation in public decisions.* San Francisco: Jossey-Bass.

Thompson, F., & Jones, L. R. (1986). Controllership in the public sector. *Journal of Policy Analysis and Management, 5*(3), 547–571.

Wang, X. (2001). Assessing public participation in U.S. cities. *Public Performance & Management Review, 24*, 322–336.

Watson, D. J., Juster, R. J., & Johnson, G. W. (1991). Institutionalized use of citizen surveys in the budgetary and policy-making processes: A small-city case study. *Public Administration Review, 51*, 232–239.

Webb, K. W., & Hatry, H. P. (1973). *Obtaining citizen feedback: The application of citizen surveys to local governments.* Washington, DC: Urban Institute.

Verba, S., Schlozman, K. L., & Brady, H. E. (1995). *Voice and equality: Civic voluntarism in American politics.* Cambridge, MA: Harvard University Press.

Citizen Participation in Performance Measurement

Alfred T. Ho

For the past two decades, many governments have paid growing attention to a tool that has been around for almost a century—performance measurement. With the advancement of information technologies, the ease of data analysis, and the popular concept of "results-oriented government," performance measurement has become more sophisticated and is now commonly used in today's public management. While collection of input, workload, and cost-efficiency measures was the focus for many decades and has remained an indispensable part of the exercise, more effort is now placed on measuring outcomes and results and exploring the links between performance measurement and management. Collecting and reporting data are no longer sufficient. Government officials are now expected to use the information intelligently to align performance goals and activities and demonstrate results and progress. Nonetheless, the major clientele utilizing performance information has largely remained the same—program managers, budget analysts, and the elected officials of the government. The public and external stakeholders are seldom involved in defining, selecting, and using performance measures.

The purpose of this chapter is to explore the possible role of citizens in performance measurement and to discuss why they should be involved more and how they should be engaged in the process. The chapter argues that performance measurement may lose part of its potential relevancy and significance in the political decision-making process if the public is not involved. Even though there are many technical and political hurdles to engaging citizens in performance measurement, public managers also have a professional and ethical duty to expand the scope of users of performance measurement so that the tool can indeed be used to hold government more accountable to the public.

Performance Measurement in Government

Performance measurement refers to the usage of quantifiable indicators to measure the output, efficiency, and results of public services. Even though the practice has caught the attention of many policy makers and managers over the past two decades, it is hardly a recent innovation. As early as the turn of the twentieth century, the New York Bureau of Municipal Research had already proposed tracking the cost and output of public programs so that managers could conduct unit-cost analysis to improve efficiency and prevent fraud and corruption (New York Bureau of Municipal Research, 1918; Ridley & Simon, 1938). The practice was gradually adopted by state and local governments that were more progressive in reforming their managerial practices, and later, by the U.S. federal government in the 1950s when some of the early reformers from the New York Bureau of Municipal Research, such as Frederick Cleveland, went to the federal government to help implement budgetary reforms (Kahn, 1997).

For the past few decades, the practice of performance measurement has continued to evolve, becoming broader in scope and more sophisticated. For example, the types of measures that government agencies keep track of have expanded from cost-efficiency data to output, workload, intermediate outcome, outcome, and explanatory data (Ho & Ni, 2005). Agencies that adopt performance measurement have also expanded, from more technical departments such as public works and police, to human-service-oriented departments, such as education, welfare, and community development. Many reforms have also been introduced to integrate performance measurement into public decision-making, particularly the budgetary process. For example, the "planning-programming-budgeting system" (PPBS) in the late 1960s attempted to introduce the measurement of program output, efficiency, and effectiveness to guide policy making and program budgeting. Later reforms, such as "zero-base budgeting" (ZBB) in the 1970s and "management-by-objectives" (MBO) in the 1980s followed the same emphasis and tried to use performance information to rationalize budgetary and program decision-making (U.S. GAO, 1997).

In the 1990s, the performance measurement movement reached another peak of development. Because of the antigovernment movement and the tax revolts of the 1980s, many politicians looked for ways to change the image of government bureaucracy and rebuild public trust in their capacity to deliver public services efficiently and effectively (Nye, Zelikow, & King, 1997). It was in this context that Osborne and Gaebler (1993) published their landmark work, *Reinventing Government*, in which they pushed for new ways to manage government operations, such as the idea of "competitive government" through contracting-out and "mission-driven government," which focuses more on goals, not rules. They also recommended "results-oriented government," in which government should measure and reward policy outcomes.

> Traditional bureaucratic governments . . . focus on inputs, not outcomes. They fund schools based on how many children enroll; welfare based on how many poor people are eligible; police departments based on police estimates of manpower needed to fight crime. They pay little attention to outcomes—to results. . . . Entrepreneurial governments seek to change these rewards and incentives. Public entrepreneurs know that when institutions are funded according to inputs, they have little reason to strive for better performance. But when they are funded according to outcomes, they become obsessive about performance. (Osborne & Gaebler, 1993, p. 139)

The idea of "results-oriented government" was quickly disseminated among federal, state, and local governments. At the federal level, the Clinton administration introduced the National Performance Review and Congress passed the Government Performance and Results Act to require agencies to establish goals and measure outcomes. At the state and local level, many governments introduced their own versions of performance measurement reforms that emphasized public accountability to taxpayers. More public officials began to ask questions like the following:

- Are my performance measures aligned with the goals and performance targets of programs?
- How can the budget office use performance information to evaluate program results more effectively, ensuring that tax money is put to the best use?
- How can program managers use performance measures to motivate line staff to make continuous improvements to program delivery?
- How can policy makers and managers use performance information to evaluate the current status of program delivery and establish strategic goals for programs?

Beyond Performance Management

There is evidence to show that the new emphasis of performance measurement has made a difference in the way government is managed. At the federal government, for example, program managers are found to pay closer attention to program results and public accountability (U.S. GAO, 2004). Studies of state and local government reforms have also confirmed similar effects and show that performance measurement can help improve communication between the budget office and departments and between the executive branch and the legislative branch, as well as strengthen the culture of public accountability (Ho, 2006a; Melkers & Willoughby, 2001).

However, the impact to date seems to have been limited to the executive process of decision-making. Even though performance information is advocated as a way to influence how legislators make policy and budgetary decisions so that appropriation decisions can be rationalized to maximize program efficiency and effectiveness, empirical evidence has generally shown that many legislators pay limited attention to performance information (Jordan & Hackbart, 1999; Joyce, 1993). Special interests, partisan influence, and political maneuvering seem to remain the primary driving force behind budgeting and other policy decisions. Hence, until performance information has greater political weight—that is, when the information means something to voters and major stakeholders who will use it to hold politicians accountable for results—the political reality that performance information has limited influence in the legislative phase of government is unlikely to change.

For advocates of performance measurement, this has been a disappointing finding. Although many data and reports are being generated each year by the government bureaucracy, the information has not been fully used, which means time and resources have been wasted in the data collection and analysis process. Also, one has to question whether managers have been measuring the "right" thing. If major stakeholders are not interested in the information, which is supposed to show the "results" that matter, the whole purpose of "results-oriented management" may be an empty promise.

The lack of citizen participation may also create implementation hurdles in performance-oriented reforms even within the executive branch of government. Past studies have shown that if a government engages citizens more in performance measurement, its officials are more likely to use performance information to make managerial changes, including setting strategic goals, improving internal and external communication, and reinforcing the customer focus of government (Ho, 2006a). They are also more likely to establish performance targets for departments and discuss performance results in meetings to hold department officials accountable for results (Ho, 2006b). Hence, insufficient effort to engage policy stakeholders and the public not only limits the impact of performance measurement on the legislature, but also reduces the incentive for managers to follow through and use the information to make a difference in program management.

Role of Citizens in Performance Measurement

Perhaps these are some of the reasons why in recent years several professional organizations have started to advocate the role of citizens in performance measurement. For example, in the guidelines for reporting "service effort and accomplishments" (SEA) released in 2003, the Governmental Accounting Standards Board (GASB) recommends the following practices (GASB, 2003, pp. 6–8):

> The [performance measurement] report should include a discussion of involvement of citizens, elected officials, management, and employees in the process of establishing goals and objectives for the organization. . . . Citizen and customer perceptions of the quality and results of major and critical programs and services should be reported when appropriate.

Many local governments and community organizations have also started to involve citizens. For example, the Jacksonville Community Council has worked with local officials and community leaders to produce an annual quality-of-life report that evaluates the performance and needs of health and human services according to a strategic vision and specific goals, and the experience has been highly constructive for the community. The Fund for the City of New York has involved citizens in focus-group discussions and monitoring and measurement efforts to deal with street-level problems, such as graffiti, garbage collection, and potholes in roadways, and the effort has made some impact on how New York City manages its neighborhood services. The Sustainable Seattle group has organized continuous dialogues among local residents and officials to analyze community indicators and rethink neighborhood issues. Several Iowa municipalities have also launched an initiative called "citizen-initiated performance assessment," in which citizens help elected officials and managers develop, select, and use performance indicators to improve the quality of public services (Ho & Coates, 2004).

Reviewing some of these successful experiences of different communities that engage citizens in performance measurement, Epstein, Coates, and Wray (2005) in their recent book, *Results That Matter*, summarize five roles that citizens may play:

- Citizens as customers and stakeholders
- Citizens as advocates
- Citizens as issue framers
- Citizens as collaborators
- Citizens as evaluators

Challenges in Engaging Citizens

One may agree normatively that citizens should be more involved. However, public administrators face many practical challenges in their attempt to engage citizens meaningfully and effectively in the exercise of performance measurement. Theories of public choice have long established that citizens are rational decision-makers and have little incentive to participate in public decision-making when the benefits of participation are spread across a community but the costs of participation, both monetary and non-monetary, are individualized and can be very high. Political apathy is especially common in a well-governed community in which citizens are satisfied and see no looming crisis that should prompt their immediate participation in public affairs.

Citizen participation in performance measurement is even more difficult when compared to other forms of public participation, such as voting, because of the following reasons:

- Performance measurement involves technical details and data questions. Ordinary citizens may not feel interested in understanding the methodological and technical questions involved.
- Performance measurement is a routine exercise that tries to track data over time to monitor progress and evaluate results. It is not a single event that has a clear beginning and end.
- Performance measurement does not necessarily dictate policy outcomes. Performance measures are simply information that allows more meaningful and informed dialogues about policy and program decisions. How the information should be used and what policy options should be proposed and chosen are often beyond the scope of performance measurement. Citizens who expect to use performance measurement to dictate how elected officials should govern may feel disappointed and may not be interested in participating.
- Even if elected officials and managers are serious about performance measurement and are committed to use public input and performance information to make a difference in policy making and program management, citizens are unlikely to see concrete results from their input until years later. This again may discourage citizen participants to commit their time and effort to the exercise.

How to Engage Citizen Participants: The Experiences of the Iowa Citizen-Initiated Performance Assessment Project

These inherent challenges are real and significant and can easily deter government officials and citizens from public engagement in performance measurement. Overcoming these hurdles requires diligent and innovative effort in rethinking and reorganizing the performance measurement routines. In

2001–4, a number of Iowa cities experimented with "citizen-initiated performance assessment" (CIPA), in which citizens joined with elected officials and managers to develop and use performance measures and help government evaluate various municipal services, such as nuisance control, garbage disposal, snow removal, police and fire protection, and transportation (Ho & Coates, 2004). Based on the three-year project experience, several practical lessons about citizen engagement have emerged.

1. Traditional Mechanisms of Citizen Participation

Citizen committees, public hearings or town hall meetings, and focus-group discussions are still useful tools to engage citizens in discussing performance of government programs and services. There is nothing more effective than face-to-face interactions between citizens and public officials, helping break down stereotypes and mistrust and showing each other they can be sincere and equal participants in making government more effective in meeting the needs of a community.

However, these mechanisms have significant limitations. For example, they allow only a small number of citizens to engage in in-depth dialogues and exchanges of ideas. The frequency and length of discussion are also constrained by the physical location of the meeting place and the time schedules of the participants. Finally, citizens who volunteer to participate in these meetings tend to be community activists or citizens who can afford the time. As a result, they may not be highly representative of the demographic profile of a community.

2. Usage of Surveys and Response Cards

Citizen surveys are another viable mechanism to solicit public input about the quality and performance of public programs. Many local governments have annual or biennial citizen surveys to evaluate citizen satisfaction with and perception of community priorities. Many governments also have user response cards for specific services. Instead of surveying a whole community where not many may be users of particular services, user response cards are targeted surveys of particular user groups to evaluate specifically how users perceive the quality of services. The tool is applicable for many local services, such as library, public works, water and sewage services, and other customer services. In Iowa, for example, some communities use response cards to evaluate the responsiveness and professionalism of fire and medical emergency staff. If these citizen and user surveys are conducted with the appropriate sampling methodology, usually by random phone or mail surveys of the community or the specific user group, the data can give managers and policy makers valuable input about the performance of the government from a representative sample of citizens. If the data are tracked consistently over time, they can also provide a trend analysis of program performance so that policy makers can evaluate whether steady improvement has been accomplished.

Like the above mechanisms, citizen surveys and response cards also have their limitations. First, the validity of the instruments depends on the sampling methodology. If the sampling frame is not representative, possibly because of out-of-date addresses or phone numbers, non-listing of certain residents, or using only a selected segment of the population, policy makers may get biased results that may misinform decision-making. Second, the response rate can be a major concern. Many citizens are tired of answering phone and mail surveys. The response rate problem can be worse in communities with many low-income families and minority population, as these groups tend to have lower response rates to government surveys. To compensate for these problems and to make the survey results more reliable and representative, government officials usually have to invest more time and resources to circulate follow-up surveys and must use different incentives to induce better responses. However, these mechanisms can be expensive, and not many communities have the fiscal capacity or the willingness to invest in them.

Moreover, surveys suffer from the fact that the public feedback is constrained heavily by the structure and wording of the survey instruments. Unlike committee work or focus-group discussion, in which citizens have more freedom to express their opinions and concerns, survey respondents have to respond to specific questions and select specific answers in multiple choice questions. If the questions and answers are framed in a biased way or if certain questions are not asked to avoid potential political embarrassment, the true public perception of public program performance may not be revealed.

Finally, there is a constraint about how frequently a survey can be conducted, and when a survey can be sent out. Too many surveys will create survey fatigue and low response rates. Surveys sent at the wrong time, such as before holidays, may also yield a low response rate. Also, because of the length and complexity concerns, a government cannot give too much information prior to asking a question and can only ask a limited number of questions in a survey. A mail survey is also more constrained in structure than a phone survey and survey questions cannot be tailored easily by user responses. Hence, though surveys are good instruments to get at public perception of program performance, they have many technical and cost constraints of which managers should be aware.

3. Usage of the Internet

Information technologies and the World-Wide Web open up new possibilities to solicit public input and evaluate the performance of public programs more conveniently and easily. Instead of coming to a physical location or filling out a paper survey, citizens can now visit a specific website to file complaints or service requests, report their satisfaction level with government services, and conduct synchronous or asynchronous discussions with officials and other fellow citizens to find solutions to improve government performance.

The advantages of the Internet over traditional means of public engagement are not only that it is more convenient and less constrained by time and physical location, but also that the content can be flexibly tailored to the needs and interests of the users and can allow many interactive features to help the public make more informed decisions. For example, when a citizen is asked to evaluate the performance of the police department online, he or she may be presented with some performance statistics, such as the crime rates and the average response times to different types of crimes and in different neighborhoods of a community, side by side with the survey. After the survey, the respondent can be asked to give open-ended comments on how the department may improve its services, whether the respondent is interested in learning more about various volunteering opportunities, and whether he or she is willing to participate in some of the programs and connect with other citizen volunteers.

However, there are also significant limitations to using the Web. First, even though the Internet has become more widely accessible and commonly used, there is still a concern about the "digital divide" problem among racial minorities, the elderly, and the poor. Second, how to get residents to learn about the city government website and visit it can be a major challenge. Third, because Internet surveys can be done so easily and cheaply, ensuring that no one can easily "game" the system and try to provide multiple entries to bias the results can be a technical challenge. These limitations suggest that while the Internet can offer a lot to enhance public participation, it is still at a developing stage and so should be complemented with other forms of participating channels to get a more balanced and representative view of government performance.

4. Usage of Administrative Data

Finally, a government may tap into its internal database and evaluation instruments to get objective public input about program performance. For example, the number of program users or members and the number of volunteers and donations that support a program may indirectly reflect the performance and user satisfaction with the program. The number of service requests and complaints and types of service requests may show what areas are poorly rated by the public and need improvement. Data such as response times and scientific or standardized test results may also complement the survey-based data to facilitate evaluation of the performance of public programs.

For the past few decades, many professional organizations and government agencies have invested significant resources in developing and standardizing methodologies for generating and collecting various kinds of administrative data. For example, crime statistics and response times for the police department and many user statistics for library services are now commonly available in many local governments because of these efforts by the federal government and professional organizations. These accomplishments should be applauded and maintained. However, public managers should also recognize that these administrative data have some limitations and cannot replace direct public input. First, collecting these data may require significant investment of time and resources. Managers should strike a balance between the benefits and costs of getting the data and should be aware of the opportunity cost implications for service delivery. Second, some of the data, such as scientific data about water quality and usage, can be highly technical. How to communicate the data and analytical results effectively to policy makers and the public is an important but often overlooked step. Finally, managers need to remember that "perception is reality" in the political decision-making process. One or two tragedies in a community, an unexpected event such as a natural disaster, and changes in the political and economic atmosphere may completely change the political significance and interpretation of these "objective" data. Even if the data themselves have not changed much over time, policy makers and managers may still need to make policy and program changes to cater to the changing expectations and demands of the public. Hence, the usage of administrative data should also be complemented with other forms of public input to give a full picture of the public's evaluation of government performance.

Conclusion

For the past few decades, the practice of performance measurement in the public sector has become more widespread and sophisticated. Many useful and detailed data are collected and reported internally by federal, state, and local governments each year. As the data-collection effort matures, policy makers and managers today are challenged to think more carefully about how to use and report the data more intelligently and effectively. One of the responses to this challenge, which has been a major emphasis in recent public administration reforms, is to focus on "performance management" or "results-oriented management" and think about how to align performance measurement with strategic planning, program evaluation, budgeting, and personnel decisions. Another response, which is equally important but has been overlooked by many practitioners, is how to engage the public and policy stakeholders more to develop and use the performance information so that the information becomes more relevant and significant in the political process.

The second response about public engagement is especially important in the current fiscal environment, in which the federal government has a serious problem of structural deficits and must ask state and local governments to take on additional responsibilities. This is occurring while many voters are not fully prepared to think about the tax implications of federal devolution, yet expect state and local governments to do more without paying more. Every state and local politician will eventually face this harsh reality and will have to consider which programs and services should be cut or what taxes will have to be raised. To help make these tough decisions, both voters and politicians are better off if they are more informed about the needs of the community and the service accomplishments and efforts of the government so that they can make informed and balanced decisions about revenue and spending choices. It is in this context that performance measurement can contribute much to meeting the future challenges of public administration, but its potential benefits can only be fully realized if it is used along with effective public engagement strategies.

Tremendous progress has been made in efforts to obtain performance measurement data for the past few decades. However, performance measurement in the twenty-first century has to move beyond the data focus and pay more attention to issues of performance management and governance—how different stakeholders and users can be more effectively involved to use the data. As this happens, it is inevitable that performance measurement may become less technically driven by professional managers, some of the measures may become less objective and scientific, and political pressure to manipulate the collection and interpretation of performance data may increase. These challenges, however, are some of the inherent social costs of democracies, in which information is always vulnerable to distortion by different political, social, and economic segments of society. Citizens should not be shielded from performance measurement and performance politics. After all, they are the owners of a democratic government and have the right to define the "results" and "performance" for which government managers should strive.

References

Epstein, P., Coates, P. M., & Wray, L. D. (2005). *Results that matter: Improving communities by engaging citizens, measuring performance, and getting things done.* San Francisco: Jossey-Bass.

Governmental Accounting Standards Board [GASB]. (2003). *Reporting performance information: Suggested criteria for effective communication.* Norwalk, CT.

Ho, A. T.-K. (2006a). Accounting for the value of performance measurement from the perspective of city mayors. *Journal of Public Administration Research & Theory, 16,* 217–237.

Ho, A. T.-K. (2006b, in press). Exploring the roles of citizens in performance measurement. *International Journal of Public Administration.*

Ho, A. T.-K., & Coates, P. (2004). Citizen-initiated performance assessment: The initial Iowa experience. *Public Performance & Management Review, 27,* 29–50.

Ho, A. T.-K., & Ni, A. (2005). Have cities shifted to outcome-oriented performance reporting? A content analysis of city budgets. *Public Budgeting & Finance, 25,* 61–83.

Jordan, M., & Hackbart, M. (1999). Performance budgeting and performance funding in the states: A status assessment. *Public Budgeting & Finance, 19,* 68–88.

Joyce, P. G. (1993). Using performance measures for federal budgeting: Proposals and prospects. *Public Budgeting & Finance, 13,* 3–17.

Kahn, J. (1997). *Budgeting democracy: State building and citizenship in America, 1890–1928.* Ithaca, NY: Cornell University Press.

Melkers, J. E., & Willoughby, K. G. (2001). Budgeters' views of state performance-budgeting systems: Distinctions across branches. *Public Administration Review, 61,* 54–64.

New York Bureau of Municipal Research. (1918). The citizen and the government— a statement of policy and method. *Municipal Research, 57,* 1–4.

Nye, J. S., Jr., Zelikow, J. D., & King, D. C. (Eds.). 1997. *Why people don't trust government.* Cambridge, MA: Harvard University Press.

Osborne, D., & Gaebler, T. (1993). *Reinventing government: How the entrepreneurial spirit is transforming the public sector.* New York: Plume.

Ridley, C. E., & Simon, H. A. (1938). *Measuring municipal activities: A survey of suggested criteria and reporting forms for appraising administration.* Chicago: International City Managers' Association.

U.S. General Accounting Office [GAO]. (1997). *Performance budgeting: Past initiatives offer insights for GPRA implementation.* GAO/AIMD-97–46. Washington, DC.

U.S. General Accounting Office [GAO]. (2004). *Results-oriented government: GPRA has established a solid foundation for achieving greater results.* GAO-04–38. Washington, DC.

Democracy and the "Republican Revival" in Administrative Law

Christine M. Reed

Joshua DeShaney was five years old when he was beaten so severely by his father that he suffered severe and permanent brain injury. His mother, who was divorced from Joshua's father and did not have custody of the boy, sued the government of Winnebago County, Wisconsin. The lawsuit alleged that the county government and its employees had failed to provide Joshua with adequate protective services, a failure that constituted a violation of Joshua's constitutional right to due process of law. The case went to the U.S. Supreme Court. Chief Justice Rehnquist, writing for the majority, made the following statement:

> But nothing in the language of the Due Process Clause (of the U.S. Constitution) requires the State to protect the life, liberty, and property of its citizens against invasion by private actors. The Clause is phrased as a limitation on the State's power to act, not as a guarantee of certain minimal levels of safety and security. . . . Its purpose was to protect the people from the State, not to ensure that the State protected them from each other. (*DeShaney v. Winnebago County*, 1989, p. 195)

The facts of the case showed a persistent pattern of suspicious injuries to the child, but the county Department of Social Services never removed the child from the custody of his father. Chief Justice Rehnquist expressed sympathy; however, he made a classic statement about the purpose of constitutional limits in a liberal democratic society: The Constitution exists to constrain the excesses of government and to provide individual citizens freedom from the arbitrary and capricious conduct by government employees. Individual autonomy is so important in a liberal democratic society that citizens fear federal or state government coercion. Liberal democracy also discourages the local *community* as a political entity from stepping in to protect its vulnerable members.

Administrative law functions within this constitutional system to ensure that federal and state government agencies act in a fair and reasonable manner. A noted public administration scholar observed that public administrators exercise all three constitutional powers: rulemaking (legislation), enforcement (executive), and adjudication of appeals (judicial) resulting from enforcement (Rosenbloom, 1983). A separation of powers within agencies is maintained in order to ensure that civil servants make rules, implement programs, and hear appeals subject to principles of representative democracy and due process of law. Administrative law constrains the discretion of public administrators in order to prevent arbitrary and capricious decisions, as well as protect the individual rights of citizens who are affected by government regulation and who depend on the government for social services.

A detailed description of the provisions of administrative law is beyond the scope of this chapter. Instead, this chapter focuses on the idea of administrative law and democracy. Until recently, many aspects of administrative law balanced professional expertise with the values of liberal democracy, particularly the theory of natural rights articulated by political philosopher John Locke in the eighteenth century. Locke argued that if individuals were living in a "state of nature" (that is, prior to the formation of government) they would agree to a social contract limiting the scope of government and securing the natural rights of all citizens. As Lakoff (1996, p. 226) explains, "Locke's insistence that rights were natural and that political power originated in an effort to protect these rights both rationalized and encouraged efforts to restrict the power claimed in the name of sovereignty."

In recent years, several distinguished legal scholars have tried to revive civic republican ideas that predate the natural rights/social contract theory of the eighteenth century. The civic republican tradition views the U.S. Constitution as a framework for collective self-government, rather than a set of rules to limit government power and protect individual rights. In addition, civic republicanism critiques the liberal democratic idea that government's role is to be a neutral arbiter of competing interest groups. Instead it calls for a more active and deliberative role for all branches of government. While civic republicanism calls for citizen engagement and concern for the common good over individual self-interest, it is distinguished from "communitarian" political theories that base interdependence among citizens of a community on *pre-political* commonalities, such as race, religion, or culture (Holohan, 2002, p. 8).

Think back to the Rehnquist Court's statement about the function of the Constitution in the *DeShaney* case. Imagine how a civic republican response to the same set of facts would differ from the Court's rationale. The likely reaction would be to lament the moral neutrality of the Court, in particular its insistence that the Constitution insulated the county social services agency from criticism by members of Joshua's community. The Wisconsin child welfare law (as in other states) authorized the agency to assume full legal authority for child protective services, thereby limiting the role of neighbors and concerned citizens to that of reporting suspicions to the county government. A republican critique of this case would argue that the legal system encouraged members of Joshua's community to passively attend to their own private concerns and turn their backs to the unfolding tragedy.

Administrative law imposes constraints on agencies to protect the rights of individuals (such as Joshua's father) potentially coerced by government intervention. The Administrative Procedure Act spells out the elements of a formal hearing if an agency's authorizing statute requires it. A "hearing on the record" has many of the features of a judicial trial: formal notice of the charge, the right to an adversarial hearing before an impartial administrative law judge, a written finding of law and facts explaining the basis for the decision, and the right to appeal that decision to the courts. In addition, the law provides individuals an opportunity to comment on proposed agency rules published in the *Federal Register* as a way to ensure that affected interests have the opportunity to participate (Rosenbloom, 2003, chap. 4).

These provisions are consistent with the values of liberal democracy because they ensure that agency rulemaking communicates information to citizens, allows individuals to participate by submitting comments, and is accountable to the public (Kerwin, 2003, chap. 2). If administrative law were amended to reflect the values of civic republicanism, there would be greater emphasis on deliberation about policy issues and substantive rules that reflect local wisdom about the common good. In the context of administrative law, this change would mean participation by units of local government in the design of federal and state agency rules affecting their small communities. As Seidenfeld writes (1992, p. 1534),

> By insisting that government actions reflect social consensus about the common good, civic republicanism facilitates the adoption of laws that respects the interests of minorities and other groups historically excluded from political power and that simultaneously comports with the polity's general sense of justice. This facilitation, however, can only occur if the decision-making process includes representatives of groups normally excluded from the political process or so frustrated by it that they have become apathetic or even alienated.

Reviving Democratic Practice in Agency Rulemaking

When scholars refer to the republican tradition, they often point to civic virtue in Revolutionary War leaders who sacrificed private comforts for the sake of the republic. Thomas Jefferson, who authored the Declaration of Independence, defined republican government as direct and constant control by citizens. His primary concern was to defend freedom through active participation in government by educated citizens (Bellah et al., 1985, p. 30). In the twenty-first century, this aspect of the republican tradition may seem quixotic. Most scholars agree that the ratification of the Constitution signaled the loss of small republican communities. The challenge for legal scholars who seek to revive civic republicanism is to develop a vision of community and self-government appropriate for today's complex society. The key is public decision-making based on deliberation about the common good, rather than on the accommodation of private interests.

Citizen self-government is the subject of other chapters in this book. In administrative law, changes that are consistent with civic republicanism could contribute to collective self-government. The agency rulemaking process limits public participation to comments on proposed rules developed in-house by scientific and technical advisors. This process hardly allows citizens to deliberate on the common good, and it has alienated many groups, including administrators from local governments in small communities. Their communities are impacted by federal regulations, but they sense that their perspectives are not recognized by policy makers in Washington, DC, as being informed about issues. Agency rule-writers tend to discount local, practical knowledge because they need "probative" data suitable for inclusion in the rulemaking record in case of a legal challenge.

One of the most frustrating aspects of rulemaking for local government officials from small communities is that it favors large organized interests with the resources and expertise to promote their agendas. Once a proposed rule is published in the *Federal Register*, it takes a concerted effort by interest groups and advocacy organizations to solicit comments from their membership. The availability of a new Internet portal (Regulations.gov) where members post comments directly on the website in response to e-mail "alerts" makes it even easier for interest groups to stage public comment campaigns (Emery & Emery, 2005, p. 8). This process leaves many groups and individual citizens with a sense of futility. Local officials from small communities are more likely to contact their congressional delegations if they are concerned about proposed rules than they are to attempt to exert influence in the rulemaking process.

One way to make the process more deliberative is to give marginalized groups an opportunity to participate in the *initial* formulation of rules

(Seidenfeld, 1992, p. 1560). The 1996 Small Business Regulatory Enforcement Fairness Act (SBREFA) requires federal agencies to consider the effects of rulemaking on small entities, including local governments, *prior to* the Notice of Proposed Rulemaking. Early consultation involves agency outreach and direct engagement with officials of small local governments. Since 1998, the Environmental Protection Agency (EPA) has funded a series of cooperative agreements and contracts extending the spirit of SBREFA beyond the agency stakeholder review panel required by that law. The EPA project creates "deliberative communities" among federal rule-writers and local governments. Until 2005, the contractor was the National Association of Schools of Public Affairs and Administration (NASPAA).[1]

Public administration faculty members from NASPAA member schools acted as facilitators of group dialogues with local officials, staff, and administrators in small communities about rules under development. They used discussion guides specific to each rule and written in such a way that laypersons could follow the scientific rationale for regulation in a particular area. The discussion guides framed the key issues identified by EPA rule-writers, and provided a structured way for local discussants to communicate their ideas back to EPA. The project, named the Small Communities Outreach Project for Environment Issues, operated in over 500 small communities and in twenty states on eight environmental rulemakings (NASPAA, 2005, p. 4).

Between 1998 and 2000 there were two rounds of small-group dialogues held in small communities in six states about an upcoming amendment to the rule regulating drinking water from underground sources. EPA's science advisory board had recommended requiring universal disinfection of all groundwater sources based on several major disease outbreaks in major cities attributed to contaminated drinking water. Career staff developed discussion guides explaining the scientific reasons for recommending universal disinfection, but they also posed a series of policy alternatives in summary form in the discussion guides. Local government staff responsible for operating drinking water systems attended these sessions and provided feedback to EPA.

> Certainly, as a result of the extensive early consultation process and analytic exercises required of EPA by various statutes and executive orders, the proposed Ground Water Rule (GWR) looks significantly different than it might have otherwise: EPA did not include a requirement for universal disinfection of groundwater as its Science Advisory Board had strongly urged them to do. Furthermore, the policy design underlying the proposed rule builds on existing state and local initiatives to protect well heads from nearby contamination and targets the most onerous requirements for source water monitoring to those areas of greatest hydro-geological sensitivity. (Collins et al., 2002, p. 92)

There were several notable features about this case study. First, local governments—small units in particular—are among the groups traditionally disadvantaged by rulemaking. Federal regulation typically disregards the special burdens on small entities, especially their lack of size needed to take advantage of economies of scale in regulatory compliance (Sargentich, 1997, p. 125.) In addition, local governments in small communities lack the financial and human resources needed to monitor and respond to an extensive federal rulemaking agenda. They rely on intermediaries, such as the "SCOPe" facilitators, to alert them to salient issues and to bridge the divide between their local knowledge and federal scientific data. Membership associations like the National League of Cities and its state affiliated organization could serve a similar function. At present, however, these membership organizations tend to track legislation rather than rulemakings.

A second notable feature of the Ground Water Rule project was its educational aspect. The discussion guides highlighted the public health risks of groundwater contamination. Local and state environmental professionals, in turn, educated EPA staff about the contextual knowledge required to design an ecologically rational rule. Different groundwater aquifers have varying sensitivities to contamination depending on the hydro-geology of the area. The chemistry of the groundwater supply also varies. The chemicals in disinfectants could trigger a chain reaction of unintended negative consequences when combined with minerals in certain groundwater sources, requiring further treatment of the water.

The third important feature was the timing—at the *pre-notice* or early consultation stage. Once a proposed rule becomes an official document, most of the key policy decisions are already settled. In fact, a major change would necessitate reopening the entire rulemaking proceeding. This requirement prevents the agency from publishing a final rule that differs substantially from what interested parties thought were in the contents of the proposed rules to which they filed their comments. The formality of the process, however, discourages deliberation about the common good. The SCOPe project allowed EPA officials to "think out loud" together with local officials before their decisions were cast in the official stone of a Notice of Proposed Rulemaking. This project is just one example of how deliberation can inform the rulemaking process. It also exemplifies how federal recognition of the unique perspectives of small local governments helps to overcome their sense of exclusion from the larger political community.

Reviving Democratic Practice in Agency Adjudication

The Administrative Procedure Act spells out the elements of a formal agency hearing and requires agencies to apply those provisions whenever their authorizing statutes call for them to make orders following a "hearing on the record." These provisions reflect the constitutional principle that government shall not deprive a person of life, liberty, or property without due process of law. In the context of administrative law, agencies rarely deprive individuals of their liberty rights. Criminal courts can deprive a person of liberty through imprisonment and life by means of a conviction for a capital crime with a sentence of death by execution. Administrative law can, however, impact people's lives by, for example, revoking licenses to practice law or medicine or terminating benefits to social services on which they depend.

Agency adjudication is, by its very nature, an adversarial process in which an individual feels aggrieved by action taken against him or her personally. Agency orders affect individuals instead of an entire community. Adjudication is also retrospective in its orientation, reviewing the previous actions of agency officials to determine if the basis for orders was arbitrary and capricious. The adversarial nature of an agency hearing protects individuals from the government by ensuring the right to be notified of the pending adverse action and to be heard before an impartial agency judge.

It is difficult to envision how republican values might flourish in agency adjudication. Democracy in the republican tradition assumes that citizens deliberate together and that members of the community have agreed to sacrifice certain private privileges for the sake of the common good. The republican tradition emphasizes common unity over the freedom of the individual to pursue private ends (Kemmis, 1990). Litigation based on an adversarial process would mean the breakdown of community. Put differently, republican communities ideally resolve conflicts as part of public deliberations before the need arises for litigation. Seidenfeld (1992, p. 1529) writes, "it is this transformative power of politics that enables a polity to reach consensus about the common good. Through the transformative power of politics, citizens are able to define the community norms that restrict the behavior of all community members, yet that all accept as just."

According to some public administration scholars, there is a national resurgence of civic environmentalism (Dewitt, 1994) and an ethic of civic responsibility (Weber, 2003) in protecting natural resources and public lands, as well as other policy arenas. A study of communities in the Pacific Northwest documented efforts by citizens to eliminate litigation between extractive industries (timber, fisheries, and so forth) and national environmental advocacy organizations in their communities. Residents of the communities concluded that the adversarial tactics used by these large organizations and their lawyers "were not only destroying any sense of community, they were not necessarily beneficial to long-term ecological and economic health either" (Weber, 2003, p. 47).

Federal administrative law provisions encouraged this situation by requiring agencies responsible for public lands and natural resources to balance competing interests, such as the extractive industries and environmental protection groups. According to Weber (2003, p. 47), "participants in Grass Roots Ecosystem Management believe that too often, current politics rewards a self-interested orientation and, correspondingly, reinforces winner-take-all or win-lose solutions for problems affecting the community, especially those deriving from judicial decisions." Many citizens in those communities distrusted the federal Bureau of Land Management and the U.S. Forest Service because they felt excluded from decision-making. They also documented cases in which multiple federal agencies working at cross purposes had actually damaged local ecosystems. They had no use for national organizations whose staff provoked environmental litigation. While federal agencies could not forfeit legal authority for public lands and national forests, they did agree to work through community-based advisory boards using collaborative, consensus-based decision forums. Major stakeholder groups, including industry, environmentalists, local tree farmers, and federal and state officials, also participated (Weber, 2003.) The whole point of these advisory boards was to avoid conflict and litigation, especially lawsuits initiated by national advocacy organizations against industries.

The practices and processes used to mitigate conflict are similar to those described for early consultation in rulemaking: collaboration, negotiation, and facilitation involving a broad array of citizens and stakeholders. Administrative law authorizes agency involvement in alternative dispute resolution practices by a 1996 amendment to the Administrative Procedure Act. The use of "quasi-legislative" processes as part of policy making and *enforcement* helps to involve citizens in what is normally a private and limited encounter between parties to a dispute. As seen in the case study of small communities of the Pacific Northwest, dispute resolution has come to mean deliberation among citizens and stakeholders about future growth and development. The common good encompasses economic growth as well as ecosystem health.

Other forms of alternative dispute resolution authorized by the Administrative Procedure Act are more quasi-judicial in the sense of limiting the scope of deliberations. Even then, these tools encourage citizen involvement and deliberation in search of the common good. These tools include early neutral assessment, mini-trials, and nonbinding arbitration. All alternative dispute resolution practices focus on common interests rather than protected rights. They seek to involve the parties to the dispute as participants in a dialogue, rather than as plaintiffs confronting defendants. Such practices build on a desire to protect what is good for the community as a whole.

Conflict resolution skills, practices, and processes can contribute to the quality of deliberation by assisting participants in expressing their preferences and reconciling differences in them. So too there is deliberation during quasi-judicial conflict resolution processes such as mediation and facilitation in policy implementation and enforcement as participants exchange viewpoints, rational arguments, and personal narratives to explain their positions and interests. (Bingham, Nabatchi, & O'Leary, 2005, p. 554)

Conflict resolution can occur at the community level with federal and state officials participating in public dialogues, or as an alternative to formal agency adjudication involving individual parties. One republic legal scholar has expressed the view that formal proceedings encourage "deliberative decision-making aimed at furthering public rather than private values" (Seidenfeld, 1992, p. 1554). He argues that career staff serving as administrative law judges are more insulated from political pressures than agency rule-writers, although he acknowledges that formal proceedings are not conducive to deliberation. Another limitation of making adjudication the locus of republican self-government is that administrative law judges are an insulated cadre of career civil servants. The judiciary also tends to separate citizens from the process of governing.

There may be a "dialogical community" *inside* the hearing room, but as Kahn (1989, p. 37) argues, "this means that between those within and those outside of that dialogical community there may be no common ground by which to evaluate disagreement." Amending the Administrative Procedure Act to authorize alternative dispute resolution will revive democratic practice in the form of collective self-government only if all of the parties involved (including those from government agencies) consider themselves to be *inside* the same dialogical community. The citizen advisory boards in the case of small communities in the Pacific Northwest acted as intermediaries between federal agencies and citizens at large. Career staff participated in dialogues involving historically situated communities, and *their* values were shaped by those deliberations as well as citizens and stakeholders.

The Role of State Administrative Law in Reviving Democratic Practice

All fifty states have separate administrative procedure acts governing public agencies that authorize rulemaking and adjudication processes similar to those at the federal level. Some states have adopted alternative dispute resolution and negotiated rulemaking provisions, which authorize state government officials to pursue informal, consensus-oriented processes (Bingham,

Nabatchi, & O'Leary, 2005, p. 551). State governments are closer to citizens than are federal agencies, yet there is little mention of their role in reviving the republican tradition. State government representatives served on citizen advisory boards in the Pacific Northwest communities and played an important role in pursuing the common good. There is an untapped potential for state agencies to play an important role in reviving republican self-government at the community level.

During the SCOPe project, state environmental agency staff played a key role in the facilitated discussions with local government officials. In many cases, local officials and citizens trusted state government career staff more than their federal counterparts. In Nebraska, for example, drinking water program staff participated in the focus groups and contributed to the deliberative nature of the meetings by explaining how various alternatives proposed by EPA would change existing state regulations. They provided a key educational component and offered the idea of assessing hydro-geological risk assessments in each state as an ecologically rational alternative to universal disinfection (Collins et al., 2002, p. 94.)

State government career staff members are in an excellent position to alert local government administrators and staff in small communities to salient issues in federal and state rulemakings. They tend to work side by side with local government staff in parallel areas of policy, and they serve as key intermediaries between local and federal governments because many federal rules "pass through" state government to the local level. Professional associations of state agency staff tend to monitor the federal rulemaking process more intensely than county and municipal associations that track federal and state legislation, but that focus only on the most salient federal rules.

Democracy and Administrative Law: A Final Assessment

Even with amendments to the basic framework of administrative law, federal and state agency rulemaking and adjudication will never approach the ideal of collective self-government in civic republicanism. What *is* more evident now than twenty years ago is resistance by units of local government to a "one-size-fits-all" approach to regulation of problems like drinking water contamination. Other evidence suggests that there is a "resurgence of *communitarian* sensitivity to the responsibility of local residents for taking care of their own problems" (Box, 1998, p. 6). The trend, in other words, is more than a reaction against federal or state control of the policy process. There has been an accompanying change in how local government officials collaborate with civic groups, as well as federal and state career staff, to address complex issues in more holistic ways. The case study of grassroots ecosystem management in the Pacific Northwest is one example, but there are many other stories to demonstrate this turn to the local level.

Civic republicanism will ultimately require a different normative model for bureaucracy in a democracy: one based on Jeffersonian values maximizing administrative accountability to the public at large, rather than the value of maximizing administrative efficiency associated with Alexander Hamilton or the balancing of administrative interest group demands urged by James Madison in the design of the Constitution. "Here the emphasis is upon maximizing accountability to the public *as a whole* [italics added] often at the expense of administrative efficiency or satisfying special interest groups" (Stillman, 1996, p. 386). The examples presented in this chapter illustrate how it is possible to expand the influence of local contextual knowledge over government expertise in addressing complex policy issues. The implications are both a greater inclusiveness in decision-making *and* a loosening of restrictions on agency processes allowing deliberation, rather than pressure group tactics, within administrative processes.

Note

1. In future years, administration of the project will likely move to a university.

References

Bellah, R. N., Madsen, R., Sullivan, W., Swidler, A., & Tipton, S. M. (1985). *Habits of the heart: Individualism and commitment in American life*. New York: Harper & Row.

Bingham, L. B., Nabatchi, T., & O'Leary, R. (2005). The new governance: Practices and processes for stakeholder and citizen participation in the work of government. *Public Administration Review*, *65*, 547–558.

Box, R. C. (1998). *Citizen governance: Leading American communities into the 21st century*. Thousand Oaks, CA: Sage.

Collins, K. J., Jacobson, K. M., Morris, J. C., Reed, C. M., & Rosenbloom, D. (2002). EPA, collaborative rule making and the small communities outreach project for environmental issues: Three-state experience. *Public Works Management & Policy*, *7*, 87–97.

DeShaney v. Winnebago County Department of Social Services. 489 U.S. 189 (1989).

DeWitt, J. (1994). *Civic environmentalism: Alternatives to regulation in states and communities*. Washington, DC: CQ Press.

Emery, F., & Emery, A. (2005). A modest proposal: Improving e-rulemaking by improving governments. *Administrative Law & Regulatory News*, *31*, 8–9.

Holohan, I. (2002). *Civic republicanism*. New York: Routledge.

Kahn, P. W. (1989). Community in contemporary constitutional theory. *Yale Law Journal*, *99*, 1–85.

Kemmis, D. (1990). *Community and the politics of place*. Norman: University of Oklahoma Press.

Kerwin, C. (2003). *Rulemaking: How government agencies write law and make policy.* Washington, DC: CQ Press.

Lakoff, S. (1996). *Democracy: History, theory, practice.* Boulder, CO: Westview.

National Association of Schools of Public Affairs and Administration [NASPAA]. (2005). *Small communities and e-rulemaking.* Washington, DC.

Rosenbloom, D. H. (1983). Public administration theory and separation of powers. *Public Administration Review, 43,* 219–227.

Rosenbloom, D. H. (2003). *Administrative law for public managers.* Boulder, CO: Westview.

Sargentich, T. O. (1997). The small business regulatory enforcement fairness act. *Administrative Law Review, 49,* 123–137.

Seidenfeld, M. (1992). A civic republican justification for the bureaucratic state. *Harvard Law Review, 105,* 1512–1576.

Stillman, R. J., II. (1996). The future of the American bureaucratic system. In R. J. Stillman II, *The American bureaucracy: The core of modern government* (Chap. 7). Chicago: Nelson-Hall.

Weber, E. P. (2003). *Bringing society back in: Grassroots ecosystem management, accountability, and sustainable communities.* Cambridge, MA: MIT Press.

En-gendering Democracy

A Feminist Perspective on the Body Politic

Janet R. Hutchinson

Evidence of women's oppression can be viewed on international websites devoted to democratic reform and read about in news reports and columns by editorialists that have made it their mission to convey women's stories to those of us who luxuriate in our comfortable, entitled lives. The dull blue fingers of first-time voters in Iraq and the long blue lines of burqa-enshrouded Afghan women at the polls are symbols of hope for a future of democratic participation by disenfranchised women who live their lives surrounded by danger and cultural and political oppression. However, these are Pyrrhic victories when democracy is no more than a symbol of what it is to have equal representation in the political discourse of one's country. Voting is only one manifestation of a democratic regime; if there are no women on the ballot, or only a few among a field of men, what choices do women really have in their governance?

A recent focus in the United States on politically and religiously motivated terrorism has exposed an undeniable misogyny in countries with cultures and religions that were until recently unknown to most Americans. Women are stoned for infidelity, punished for being raped, and raped as punishment for the perceived misdeeds of others. Ritual genital mutilation, forced marriages, polygamy, denial of basic health care and education, denial of participation in governance, and abject poverty, issues as old as civilization, gain a new gloss of urgency in western social consciousness. What, we ask ourselves, can we do to stop such oppression?

Although the contrast in levels of discourse seems vast between women in developing countries and the West (we sound preachy; they sound reticent, timid), we are, I believe, expressing a similar core principle: women must be proportionally equal participants in the institutions that govern us and that make the policies that determine the quality of our lives. Our mission in pursuing this principle is aided in the West by our relative comfort born of significant wealth—although we, too, have women living at subsistence levels. We can vote and work outside the home; most have access to basic health care and other benefits and resources that we take for granted. U.S. Census Bureau figures for 2004 tell us that 13.9 percent of women in the United States fall below 100 percent of the poverty level, a proportion that is reversed in most developing countries.

In contrast with our own affluence and protected rights is the heart-breaking misery of civilians, particularly women and children, in tortured countries like Afghanistan and Iraq and in many African nations. Women continue to be abused under oppressive regimes, in some circumstances abetted by U.S. policies that limit access to the knowledge, drugs, and devices needed for reproductive health. The September 2001 terrorist attacks on the United States and the subsequent "war on terrorism" opened to the public a window on this misery—misery that women's organizations in the United States and globally have known about and decried for years. One wonders if governments here and abroad would function differently—would decisions about war and peace differ substantially—if women were proportionally represented in policy-making bodies in the United States and worldwide.

In the West, feminist scholars with roots in political science, philosophy, and psychology, among others, have contributed feminist perspectives to the extensive literature on democratic theory, developing, in not a few cases, arguments that suggest the need for fundamental changes in the structure of representative government. These fundamental structural changes target how gender difference and diversity are viewed and even the way gender assignment is approached at infancy. In developing nations in Africa, the issues for feminism are much more basic: Bridging the gulf between African feminist elites and non-feminists and grassroots women in the interest of eliminating culturally based oppression as well as oppressive government policies.

In Uganda, for example, extremes between the creation of a new government with its quota of women legislators and its optimism for the future are juxtaposed with the utter desperation of women whose difficult daily existence is governed by oppressive cultural traditions that determine rigid role assignments between women and men. Reconciling these extremes seems impossible to those of us from western countries. Yet, the hope and spirited optimism voiced by Ugandan women is remarkable.[1] This optimism is attributed to laws that since 1996 specify quotas of women representatives in parliament and local councils. Although not proportionally representative, the mere acknowledgement of women as policy makers is sufficient to give heart to women advocates.

In this chapter, I discuss democracy from two perspectives: a feminist perspective on the participatory, deliberative model, and a radical feminist reconceptualization of the body politic. I argue that despite advances in women's access to government, either through quotas, in developing nations like Uganda, or through the slower evolutionary process that women have negotiated in the United States, women remain largely outsiders in the patriarchal body politic—our hold on representative power is always tenuous. The deliberative (participatory) model holds up only as long as the parties involved are equal in status to one another. Participation is compromised whenever inequalities are present.

The means to correct this tenuous hold is through a revolution in the subtle and not-so-subtle practices of sexing the body politic. An en-gendered democracy, as I see it, is a multigendered democracy that, while compatible with multiculturalism and participatory, deliberative models, resolves the structural exclusionary biases inherent in existing patriarchal systems. A polymorphous body politic is a product of a multigendered society.

"For Feminists, Democracy Has Never Existed!"

Carole Pateman's claim (1989, p. 210) seems a bold overstatement until one considers that women constitute 52 percent of the adult U.S. population and hold only a small fraction of the seats in the U.S. Congress, a slightly larger proportion in state legislatures, and an even smaller proportion of governorships. Globally, women have generally contributed to political transformations in their countries, actively and vocally through nongovernmental organizations and reformist political parties, only to be sidelined when the revolution subsides and the practical apparatuses of party politics and government begin to stabilize.

Mary Hawkesworth (2001) describes research that examines these processes in eastern European and South American countries, noting that, as the new regime stabilizes, the more participatory, social-justice-oriented goals of women activists are replaced by tactics of appeasement that are designed to appeal to conservative voters—both men and women. Nonconsensual issues like reproductive rights are neutralized or eliminated to win votes. The large-scale, participatory citizen coalitions that are necessary to overthrow old regimes give way to those of the autonomous individual who is a self-interested maximizer and desirous of advancing private interests (p. 229). The political struggle for social justice becomes a new struggle for scarce resources to meet private need.

In the United States, public policy directed at improving the quality of life for women, particularly women who are not supported by men, lags behind many European countries—not an unexpected outcome considering the few women in state and federal policy-making positions. Health care, including reproductive freedom, and poverty remain issues for women in the United States, and tragically, women in developing countries lag much further behind, struggling on multiple fronts for the most basic human resources.

Social inequalities are connected to political inequalities. Patemen calls it the two-thousand-year-old assumption that "there is no incompatibility between 'democracy' and the subjection of women or their exclusion from full and equal participation in political life" (p. 210). U.S. feminists are admonished for "whining and complaining" that, despite universal suffrage, women are not full participants in governance. The validity of women's complaints cannot be disputed, however, given the low numbers of women in elected office.

Women have been enfranchised only since 1920, seventy-two years after the Seneca Falls (New York) meeting that gave birth to the women's suffrage movement. Equal pay for equal work legislation introduced in 1948 was not passed until 1963, and gender discrimination in education was not addressed until the passage of Title IX of the 1972 Higher Education Amendments to the Civil Rights Act of 1964 (Conway, Ahern, & Steuernagel, 1999). Today, the laws that codify basic human rights for women are threatened by a lack of enforcement and potential repeal under hostile administrations.

Recognizing the tenuousness of women's aims in the political process, feminist political theorists have struggled to find models of participation in the democratic process that achieve true inclusiveness while either acknowledging a desire to do so within the existing democratic structure (in the United States) or presuming that radical change in the existing structure is not possible.

Diversity and Democracy

Feminist political theorists concur in their desire for greater participation and diversity in the political process. However, they disagree on the method for achieving this goal. One approach to diversity, multiculturalism, has been the source of lively debate among political theorists and philosophers in recent years (see Kymlicka, 2001; Kymlicka & Norman, 2000; Nagel, 1991; Rawls, 1993), centering in part on questions of the compatibility of collective rights with liberal democratic principles. For some feminist scholars, multiculturalism comes at a cost (Okin et al., 1999) when the rights of women are subverted by the rights of other entitled groups, thus rendering diversity politics no different than the majoritarian system that has proven so effective in sidelining women and minorities.

Using the notion of multiculturalism that some ascribe to Madison's writings, Brettschneider (2002, p. 12) cites within-group difference—that is, difference contained within the small group of elites that were allowed political representation at the time—as an example of what occurs when multiculturalism runs amok. Those excluded in Madison's case were numerous and far more multiculturally representative than those who were included. Majority rule is supported by the view that, through the natural give and take of citizens and their varying interests, the minority will eventually become the majority. "If we don't win this one, we will win the next one." However, this is generally not the case for marginalized and minority groups, including women, in our historically patriarchal system—indeed, it simply ensures the continuation of patriarchy. In viewing the world from the perspective of the marginalized, feminist scholars seek to preserve the character of group rights without giving preference to one group over another. This is a tough row to hoe. Further, western feminists seek to balance the rights of women who voluntarily pursue cultural and religious practices that to the western eye appear humiliating and denigrating, with truly exploitative behaviors that enslave and abuse women and deny them their humanity.

It is axiomatic that those who have the most resources control the agenda. Instead of a competition of ideas, competition is limited to contests among interest groups for a place at the table. In the United States, African Americans, other minorities, and the marginalized woman majority cannot win in this environment, unless those on the margin take responsibility for their political destinies. It is only through consistent, persistent advocacy and considerable patience that the marginalized win their moments—but mostly patience, as exemplified by the political history of women's issues in the United States. Women set the table, bake the bread, but are largely excluded from the meal, particularly in developing nations—but not exclusively so. When a woman's presence in the senior ranks at the White House and in cabinet-level positions becomes unnoticeably commonplace, we will know we're there.

In the late Dorothy Dinnerstein's (1999) view, with truly equal representation the dominant group no longer speaks for the marginalized—the marginalized can speak for themselves. The 20 percent quota for women in Uganda's parliament gives them a voice, but not a majority voice, as was exemplified in parliamentary deliberations on the right of women to own land. When a man dies intestate, established custom extends the right of ownership from the husband to the son, bypassing the wife. Women members of Uganda's parliament were successful in bringing to vote a bill that would give the wife precedence over sons; however, there were insufficient votes for passage, even though the women's caucus had been assured of majority support.

Political theorists approach women's participation in democracy variously, some taking an additive approach: encourage more women to enter politics; create a quota system. This is described by some feminists as "add women and stir" approach. Others theorize a reconceptualized participatory democracy (an ancient concept that has until recently been limited to one sex) that is open to everyone including women. Recent explorations of participatory democracy seek a model or ideal that is distinguished by the terms used to describe them: unitary (Mansbridge, 1980), strong (Barber, 1984), civic discovery (Reich, 1988), deliberative (Gutman & Thompson, 1996), and deep (Young, 2000) (see Weeks, 2000, p. 360). Each eschews the elitist participatory ideal in favor of a deliberative model that connects citizens to their communities and their government through deliberative political processes.

The Deliberative Ideal

Iris Young (2000) describes a deliberative democracy that entails five elements that, when present, contribute to what she describes as a "deep" democracy, a democracy that is inclusive and that resonates with diverse voices. Inclusion, the first element, calls for all affected parties to join in the decision-making process at the local community level. Political equality, the second element in Young's deep democracy, means that those that are affected are not only included in the process, they are included and accepted on equal terms. This kind of equality presumes that all who are included in the decision-making process are equally important, have equal status, and are able to participate in equal measure with other participants. Reasonableness, the third element, refers to a willingness to listen and be persuaded—to keep an open mind. A reasonable person may have unreasonable ideas—Young uses the term "crazy." It is not the *content* but the *intent* that counts. A reasonable person will listen, evaluate, consider, and perhaps reconsider as views are expressed and arguments made.

With these three elements of deliberative democracy as givens, the participants will, by virtue of the process, be accountable to one another and to other publics. Accountability is represented by "publicity," which is a transformational process that results in new knowledge. Participants gain this new knowledge as ideas are perfected and presented to others and as others are persuaded to abandon their own ideas in favor of new ones. This, according to Young (2000, fn. 28), is similar to the Deweyan view of democracy as collective problem solving but without the overly procedural conception prescribed by Habermas. Deep democracy is openly accepting of those who, in the current system, are marginalized or forgotten altogether.

Deep democracy, as Young describes it, poses certain challenges as a practical matter as well as fundamental and historical structural biases in social and political theory. It has the best chance of success when the community is open to diversity—and runs the greatest risk of failure in closed societies with culturally exclusive hierarchies. For example, Bugandan[2] women describe grave consequences when tribal norms are violated, most commonly social devastation from community and family ostracism. For a woman, ostracism is a ticket to prostitution, since without the shelter of her husband or family a woman has no other means of support. In the United States, exclusion is practiced as racism, homophobia, xenophobia, and sexism. For this model of democracy to work—to replace the dominant aggregative model with a deep, deliberative one—the relationship of men and women to one another and to the body politic must undergo a fundamental change.

Historical Dualism

The well-acknowledged feminist struggle with dualism is exemplified in the desire to legitimize women's autonomy on issues of reproductive choice, access to health care, and support of studies that might prolong lives by defeating breast cancer and heart disease. However, autonomy is responsible for the ubiquitous dualism that perpetuates woman as Other. Feminists have long dodged charges of essentialism while searching for a means to reconcile the seemingly contradictory pursuits of autonomy and inclusiveness. Australian philosophy professor Moira Gatens (1996) conceptualizes a theory of woman's body and the state—the body politic—that addresses the historical mind/body dualism, replacing it with a polymorphous body politic. She uses Hobbes's *Leviathan* metaphor for the body politic by way of explanation.

In *Leviathan* (1651), Hobbes uses the human body (artificial man) as metaphor for the body politic. In this, the physical attributes of the body represent the attributes of the body politic, a male body. Artificial man continues to resonate in a single voice—the male voice in the male body. Metonymically, the human body must be either a male body or a female body—there is no neutral body. In such representations, the neutral body (and the nouns, man/men when used in text) is a masculine representation. Although the body politic has been invaded by women, weakening its boundaries, those few who have entered the breach do so as actors dressed in men's clothes, speaking men's words, in a game designed and played by men. According to Gatens (1996, p. 24), women speaking in their own voices speak a foreign language.

There is no shortage of philosophical representations of the differences between men and women. The notion of women as "lack," as "deformity," or deficiency, appears in the work of philosophers from Aristotle to Lacan. That these references are no more than superficial evidence of culturally related bias has been rejected by many feminists on the view that these representations are metaphysically based in western thought and cannot be eliminated without undermining the coherence of the particular philosophical system. This deep structural bias is felt at all levels of moral, social, and political theory (Gatens, 1996, p. vii). Structural bias is so ingrained, so much a part of our western culture and heritage that men *and women* cannot help but live under and be guided by its influence. Women have been admitted into politics; however, they are playing a man's game governed by men's rules. Women are not embodied in the political, and it is this omission that feminist philosophers and political theorists seek to remedy.

For centuries, women have been denied access to the political, framed as the public sphere, and confined to the private or domestic sphere. (Public administration and political theorist, Camilla Stivers wrote of the public-private dichotomy in public administration in a 2002 forum.) Many feminist writers, following the lead of the French feminists, have begun reconceptualizing the body in non-dualistic terms.[3] The embodiment of women in the public sphere, a desired objective, is limited by market relations in which, for women, sexual labor and manual labor are historically inseparable (Gatens, 1991, p. 135). When women enter the public sphere, they do so as handmaidens by carrying their roles as mothers/wives/daughters/housekeepers from the private sphere into the public—servicing men (husbands) at home and at work (bosses), remaining forever tied to domesticity.

Feminist Views on Democratic Representation

Representation carries with it the generality that the representative will not or cannot speak for every constituent, or even for a majority of constituents on every issue. Feminist theorists seeking a theory of representation that embodies woman share a theme based on inclusion and participation—two elements that are not universally present for women (and other marginalized people) here and abroad. At issue for some feminists is defining representation from the margins without succumbing to the exclusionary tendencies of essentialism and honoring difference without lapsing into identity politics. For some this has meant quotas much as we are witnessing in newly forming democracies that set aside a portion of seats for women.

Quotas were endorsed by the Fourth World Conference on Women in 1995, in Beijing, as a fast-track method for ultimately achieving parity in women's representation in policy-making bodies. Quotas are thought to be wrongheaded by some who fear that women, when viewed as a group, are presumed to be alike when they are clearly not. However, for the women of Uganda, a 20 percent quota in parliament has given them a desperately needed voice in the affairs of their country. The complaints heard from Bugandan women with whom I spoke at an International Women's Conference in 2002 had to do with class, not gender. The quota was filled with elites—women who by virtue of their elite status were able to gain access to the political process—according to these sources.

Young (2000) theorizes three modes of representation (interests, opinions, and perspectives) that recognize that individuals are connected to one another in different and varying ways—they share affinities within and across otherwise recognizable group boundaries. Interests and opinions have self-evident meanings; however, perspective requires some explanation. Perspective presumes a differential knowledge that, in general, can only be had by walking a mile in someone else's shoes, as the saying goes. Perspective may be shared in common with one's group, yet each member of the group experiences it differently. Perspective is personal; it also transcends group boundaries—affinities of the moment are shared with people we see only in transit, literally and figuratively—riding the A-train on one's regular commute, sharing a position at a community association meeting with people with whom one has little else in common, an element of what Young (1994) has earlier described as "seriality."

It may be possible to pair perspectival representation with what I interpret as the fluid interplay of Brettschneider's *minoritizing* and *majoritizing* strategies where, practically speaking, minority coalitions are built around shared interests, dissolving when the desired results are achieved, building new coalitions around new issues. This may work well for specific, time-limited issues; however, the broader problems of on-going representation seem to remain largely unanswered in this model. Something more fundamental must occur in the interactions between men and women and in the conceptualization of our individual and collective relationships to the polity. One approach to this fundamental need is articulated by Dorothy Dinnerstein (1999) in a re-release of her 1976 work.

The Mother of Us All

Using a psychoanalytic approach with similarities to that of Melanie Klein,[4] Dinnerstein responds to the fundamental issues of representation with answers to the question of why men *and women* are reticent to elevate women to positions of power. Her work rejects the male conspiracy theories prevalent at the time of its writing—and still evident in the work of some radical feminists today. Instead, she makes the case that men and women are complicit in the symbiotic dance-like relations that have created our gendered worldview. He bows, she curtsies, he twirls her around, and she sinks gratefully into his embrace.

Dinnerstein observes that men, even men who claim to be feminists, prefer not to abdicate their "right" to rule the world and that women, even those who are ashamed to admit it, are willing to let men continue doing it. We perpetuate this imbalance because both women and men fear the will of woman. Man's dominion over the world rests on the terror of sinking back wholly into the helplessness of infancy (Dinnerstein, 1999, p. 161). The young child's perspective of the complex interactions that began at the very beginning of life and continue, lifelong, is reflected in the reality that she was strong when we were weak; she knew—and we knew she knew (p. 167).

> It is a woman who introduces us to the world before we can recognize her as a limited, mortal being like ourselves. Struggling out from under the control of this first alluring, seemingly all-powerful person is the biggest fight we ever fight. Exhausted, we fling ourselves out of the sea full of mermaids onto the dry land of minotaurs who roar and strut but who nonetheless seem much more tamable and rational in contrast to the mother still stalking in an infantile layer of our personality. (Snitow, 1999, p. x)

Our sense of strength at learning the civilizing control over body and impulse is inseparable from the dominance of mother's will. "The female will is for each of us the will of the human presence in whose sentience our own will's earliest, most intimate defeats have been reflected" (Dinnerstein, 1999, p. 168). Yet, exerting our will by resisting hers, at our considerable peril, is the child's destiny. Our subconscious fear perpetuates a social despotism that has prevailed along with a tacit agreement that women will rule childhood and men will rule the historical process, a shared self-delusion that is the basis for the historical process. "Woman is the will's first, overwhelming adversary" (Dinnerstein 1999, p. 166). Paraphrasing de Beauvoir, Dinnerstein reminds us that woman (mother) was ever-present; she knows everything about man that attacks his pride and humiliates his self-will. And, while she has witnessed his best triumphs, she was also present at his greatest defeats. Contempt for women disguises men's fear of maternal power and for women there is the distrust of the *mother* in themselves (Harris, 1999, p. 281).

The rules that socialize us are comfortable and reassuring—even as they distress us and cause us to flail against their constraining powers. Men enjoy power that women may enjoy privilege—even if the privilege is limited to allowing her to think he belongs to her. As disturbing as these powers are, giving up the familiar is hard and, for some, impossible when the alternatives are unknown. And yet, we are not unidimensional beings; we maintain ambivalences that stir us to challenge these rules. Women *and men* have loosened somewhat the constraints by publicly challenging the rules that oppress women. As a result, women now enjoy many of the privileges once reserved for men, although we remain the principal providers of child-care and home-making—unless we are privileged to afford to hire another woman to do these tasks for us.

Women, with allusions to the omnipotent mother-figure, have been demonized throughout history, from Lilith to Anita.[5] Lilith, Eve's predecessor in the Garden of Eden, was said to have evaporated following her refusal to bend to Adam's will, and was subsequently replaced by the more compliant Eve. We acknowledge the demonizing of Anita Hill in the Clarence Thomas hearings, and perhaps, have similar stories of our own to tell. In early U.S. history, the Puritans equated the soul with the feminine nature, the weak female body easily tempted by Satan. Reis refers to a 1674 statement by Harvard president Uriah Oakes that the feminine soul, in its natural propensity to sin, was a "home-bred enemy, that *mother* of all the abominations that are brought forth in the lives of men, that adversary that is ever molesting the peace, disturbing the quiet, and endangering the people of GOD" (Oakes, in Reis, 1995, p. 23). According to Ries, Oakes claimed that "the feminine soul bears within it the *mother* of all sin, the unregenerate, natural soul submitted willingly to Satan's domination" (p. 23, italics added).

This propensity to view women as possessed is demonstrated most vividly when women, particularly mothers, commit crimes. For example, Andrea Yates (with a history of clinical depression and suffering from severe postpartum depression) murdered her five children in June 2001, was demonized by the press and the public, and ultimately sentenced to life in prison. Christopher Longo murdered his three children and wife six months later, an event deplored by the press but accepted without further analysis.

Is it possible to further loosen the rules that constrain women from reaching positions of authority, to overcome the subtle—and not so subtle—demonizing? Women *and men*, radicals (in Dinnerstein's words, "those who are optimistic believers in the immediate possibility of restructuring society by political means around principles of human solidarity and equality, of cooperation and an end to exploitation" [1999, fn., p. 259]) have pressed and continue to press for justice, certainly in the most politically benign areas such as shared child-rearing and domestic responsibilities, as well as the shared public burdens of work and political action.

Shared socialization of infants is at the heart of Dinnerstein's response to the omnipresent *mother* in us all and is contingent on radical political agency. If, as she suggests, attitudes toward women in leadership positions will change when men share equally in rearing infants through whose developing eyes the feared mother is tamed and the innate fears of mother-power are overcome, then it should also hold that institutions will be altered with the embodiment of women in the body politic.

A frequently repeated admonishment during the Eighth International Women's Congress in Kampala, Uganda (2002), was the insistence that men be included in all discussions and actions related to the status of women. Furthermore, equal with education as a solution to poverty and inequality was the commonly held view that little would change in the villages without first changing the way in which children are parented.

A Polymorphous Body Politic

French feminist Luce Irigiray exposed the masculine bias in western culture by examining the relationship between philosophy and the male body. Moira Gatens makes a similar connection to the polarization of men and women in our sociopolitical history by proposing a politico-ethical stance that accommodates multiple, rather than dichotomously sexed bodies (Gatens, 1991, p. 138; 1996, p. 56). She proposes that we look to the seventeenth-century philosopher and ontologist Benedict de Spinoza for an alternative to modern constructions of the mind/body dualism. Seemingly an anachronistic, albeit enlightened choice, Spinoza's philosophy is remarkable for its lack of dependence on the dualisms that dominate traditional modern philosophy.

Spinozist work is an alternative to modern interpretations of the mind-over-matter construct that subjects the body to the will of the mind. It is by such constructions that women, whose bodies have been reputed historically to rule their minds, are eliminated from contention in the politico-theoretical space. In traditional political theory, "the particular form, structure, character and capabilities of a body confined to the domestic sphere and to the role of wife/mother may be seen as a historically specific body whose capacities are reduced by its sphere of activity and the conditions under which it recreates itself" (Gatens, 1996, p. 57). In *Ethics*, Spinoza does not view the body as separate from the mind—the object of the mind is the existing body; the body and the mind are in union with one another. This allows a conceptualization of difference that is neither dichotomized nor dualized, and that is potentially multiple (see Spinoza, 1994, p. 128). Moreover, the body in union with the mind is a *process* that is always subject to change as it interacts with its environment. This process is compatible with Young's (1994) seriality, and with notions of multigendering that are described here and elsewhere (Hutchinson, 2001).

The Multigendered Body Politic

The liberal democratic ideal and our democratic reality are conceived in the image of "man." Feminists acknowledge and reject the notion that "man" and "he" are only parts of speech used to denote both male and female. In the mind's eye, neither actually represents women but are, in fact, accurate descriptors for the image of the body politic—an inherently male image. In my view, en-gendering democracy requires a societal change far more fundamental than adopting a new participatory model. It requires a fundamentally different understanding and lived experience of gender. In this section, I wish to make the argument for the multigendered perspective.

In the rapid evolution of feminist theories over the past several decades, gender studies have amassed a prodigious literature that bespeaks the risks that feminists who are open to self-examination are willing to take. Feminists have used gender to differentiate socioeconomic, psychological, anthropological, political, and philosophical inquiry from dependence on the limiting duality of biological sex—the sexing of beings. By differentiating between masculine and feminine (social gendering) and male and female (biological sexing), feminists seek to bring into focus the social constructions that lead to the oppression of women in patriarchal societies. Sex differences are seen as immutable, gender differences as variable within and across cultures. The distinctions between sex and gender both separate them from one another and dichotomize them.

More recently, feminists, particularly those associated with poststructuralist, postmodern thinking, have been critical of this dichotomous view. Moira Gatens (1996) argues convincingly that this mind/body differential treatment of gender and sex is spurious, suggesting that the origins among feminist theorists of the mind/body (gender/sex) dichotomy were based on psychoanalyst Robert Stoller's 1968 work. Stoller used male transsexuals and transvestites as subjects, placing the genesis of sexual identity on postnatal psychological influences that could override one's biological sex. Some feminist theorists took this to mean that gender signification is learned and as such can be re-learned through a process of de-gendering and re-socialization— a body/consciousness construction that is decidedly behavioralist in its approach (Gatens, 1996, p. 6).

Gatens is clear that such notions are neither productive nor supportable. One is either sexed male or female; there is neither a neutral nor asexual body in sociocultural terms, although there are certainly biological ambiguities, as Fausto-Sterling's (2000) work reveals. Gatens and Fausto-Sterling agree that when ambiguity exists, society dictates an immediate and fundamental imperative that it be named and categorized, correctly or incorrectly, as either male or female. It is our sex, not our gender that defines us, socially and psychologically, and our perceptions of our sexed bodies cannot reasonably be separated from our understanding of our gendered selves.

The physiological differences between women and men are sufficient that they are nontransferable except in our mirror-selves (as with Lacan's mirror phase), the imaginary or phantom bodies that are the "site of historical and cultural specificity of masculine and feminine" (Gatens 1996, p. 12). It is the analysis of the imaginary body that, in Gatens's view, is the key to understanding the codes for our social construction of what is masculine and what is feminine.

Fausto-Sterling (2000) broaches the question of multigendering when describing "anomalous" persons who are born with ambiguous genitalia and struggle for a lifetime with their arbitrarily assigned sex. However, multigendering has been extended beyond the conditions described by Fausto-Sterling. It is the notion that gender attributes are not static nor should they be necessarily sex-specific. Theorists seeking to reconceptualize gender argue that recognizing gender as multiple frees women (and men) from a socially constructed, sexualized imprisonment, and the inevitable guilt and desolation that is associated with a dishonest life (Hutchinson, 2001).

Gender is a social creation; its utility is defined in the division of labor, the assignment of tasks, and the indoctrination from birth of each new member of society. The very notion of gender is the production of structured gender inequality (Lorber, 1994, pp. 292–293). In describing the components of gender, both as social institution and for the individual, Lorber points to the inevitability of gender-ascribed statuses that permeate all aspects of institutional and individual life, both limiting or creating opportunities and achievements and diminishing or enhancing them, depending on one's station in the social/cultural strata (pp. 30–31).

Characteristics and behaviors arbitrarily labeled masculine or feminine can and do cross gender lines. Those who are closely associated with young people witness the blurring of dress, speech, and demeanor, particularly among young women, although young men seem to be enjoying a newfound freedom, too. These outward manifestations of "gender-bending" perhaps foreshadow an evolution toward a multigendered society in which the stifling limits and artificial boundaries that restrict both sexes, women and men will erode the statuses that Lorber claims have thus far been impervious to resistance and rebellion. If we are to enjoy Young's deep democracy, the statuses that are the core of our discontent must become a part of an anomalous past.

En-gendering Democracy

As we struggle with the structure imposed by language and seek to alter the substance of this image, we encounter those who admit a preference for democratic institutions and the notion that, left in the capable hands of women, the world would be a better place than it is today (add women and stir). Apropos of the "add women and stir" approach are newly democratizing nations where women's struggle is of the most basic nature—about daily survival in the midst of desperate poverty. The addition of women to positions of authority in legislative and administrative bodies is a boon. However, Aina (1998) warns that the chasm between elite women, those with power, and the grassroots women eking out a daily living in the towns, cities, and the countryside must be closed before African feminism will take root.[6] Moreover, their positions are sufficiently tenuous that a regime change could threaten, perhaps eliminate, their participation altogether.

Others convincingly argue that democratic institutions must be reconceptualized to admit all who are systematically marginalized, that is, racial minorities, ethnic minorities, and women of all hues. Along these lines, Marla Brettschneider (2002) and Iris Young (2000) propose modes of representation that are inclusive and fluid. Brettschneider seeks a diversity-based politics in which fluid coalitions constitute and reconstitute in a pattern of "joining." In this way, marginalized groups influence issues that affect them without forcing the issue of identity quotas. (Quotas guarantee identity groups' political representation but may have the undesirable side effects of freezing group identity and increasing complacency among those for whom the quota is established.)

Deep democracy has at its core a notion of representativeness that not only respects difference but insists on diversity, as well as the differences of the heart that transcend identities. Young's view of democracy draws upon her earlier proposition that women can be viewed as a social collective without the necessity for signifying a particular political philosophy (e.g., radical, liberal, psychoanalytic, cultural feminism). Seeking inclusiveness without the destructiveness that categories create, Young (1994) used Sartre's term "seriality" to describe the many-layered, multidimensional, loosely coupled experiences and affiliations reflected in our interactions with one another and our environment.

Representatives, acknowledged as a necessity in a large country, approach their duty, for it must be a duty, with an obligation to understand and empathize with their constituents—all of them. To do so requires an honor-bound sense of obligation; it also demands constant multiple-way communication with constituents that constitutes a differentiated relationship over space and time (Young, 2000, p. 123). It is this relationship that ensures that the issues of all groups are understood and represented. Accomplishing this form of representation requires localizing the political process as well as the active and willing participation in the process by the citizenry. One need not be a woman to represent women.

However, some form of proportional representation would give women and other marginalized groups a voice along the lines of the supermajority proposals made by Lani Guinier (1992). This is accomplished by ensuring that representativeness occurs in all of the elements of policy making and that it not be confined to official government bodies (but it is central to institutional decision-making). Deep democracy requires the "free associative life of civil society" where the formation and expression of ideas, interests, and opinions can flourish (Young, 2000, p. 153). Like Brettschneider, Young seeks a multicultural, community-based politics of justice; however, Brettschneider's approach lacks the subtleties of Young's model.

Deliberative and radical diversity democracies still must struggle with externally imposed and self-described definitional categories and groups, and the problems associated with identity politics. While Brettschneider speaks of fluid relations between and among groups, Young views the group as a mix of diverse individuals with some common and some disparate views on issues. The fluidity of which she speaks is not of coalitions but of the perspectives and interests of individuals that are sometimes compatible, sometimes divergent and contradictory within the same ethnic, racial, or gendered group. Representation is not valid unless it is attentive to these individual perspectives and interests. For these models to succeed, however, a more fundamental change must take place, one that does not simply recognize diversity, but one that absorbs diversity into the political structure and culture—into gender.

Dinnerstein and Gatens approach representation of women with proposals that address core issues of sexism in democracy: the patriarchal body politic. Thirty years after Dinnerstein's proposal to alter the basic arrangements of infancy by tempering the omnipresent mother with an equally attentive father, there is some evidence of changes in the parenting roles. Fathers appear to be more interested in participating in the parenting role than a generation ago. However, Silverstein and Auerbach (1999) remain skeptical about real change occurring on any grand scale, suggesting that workplace norms must change if men are to have equivalent responsibility for childcare.

It remains to be seen whether Dinnerstein's proposal will result in greater political representation for women when the children of these enlightened parents become voting adults. An appeal for encouraging men through edu-

cation to become involved with their infant children was echoed repeat-
edly at the Kampala conference by Bugandan women *and men* and their
colleagues from neighboring countries as the only means by which long-
standing, rigid, culturally imposed roles for both women and men can be
eliminated.

Dinnerstein's pragmatism is in contrast to Gatens's approach to theory-
building, which proposes a polymorphic body politic using Spinozist work,
discussed above, as the ontological basis for overcoming the ubiquitous mind/
body dualism.[7] Spinoza describes the human body as made up of a number
of other bodies that can never be a finished product since it is constantly
interchanging with its environment. It is apparent that this is a key element in
common to each of the authors discussed in this chapter.

Conclusion

In this chapter, I have presented two feminist perspectives on democracy: the
participatory, deliberative, "deep" democracy developed by Young (2000)
and a radical feminist reconceptualization of the body politic proposed by
Gatens (1996). I have also discussed Dinnerstein's (1999) explanation of
mother-fear in justification for our reticence to elevate women to positions of
power and as a partial explanation for existing political inequalities. I take
the position that deep democracy and other new participatory democratic
models will fail, if true participation is really the goal, as long as there are
basic inequalities between men and women that prevent women from full
and proportionally equal participation. I also suggest that an en-gendered
democracy is a multigendered democracy. Multigendering is based on the
notion that gender is not static, but is relational, fluid, and changing in refer-
ence to the environment, elements that are shared in common in the work of
the authors discussed in this chapter. The relational aspects of gendering,
once understood and accepted, may be an answer to the dilemma of the representation of women and our equal participation in the institutions that govern our lives.

In the meantime, our voices should not be lulled into silence by the safety
and comfort of middle-class privilege and security. We must accept the responsibility to remain attentive to the misery and suffering of women in this
and other countries, and to do what is within our power to eliminate it. That
includes questioning the morality of the institutions and political systems to
which we entrust our lives and the lives of those we love.

We are making our voices heard. May the world stop to listen.

Nahid Toubia (1988). *Women of the Arab World*

Notes

1. Women's World 2002, Eighth International Interdisciplinary Congress on Women, Kampala, Uganda.

2. The name used by Uganda's people for themselves.

3. Examples of dualisms include public/private, mind/body, reason/passion, masculine/feminine.

4. Klein (1882–1960), born in Austria, was a psychoanalyst influenced by Freud's work.

5. Anita Hill, a law professor, came forward during the Supreme Court confirmation hearings for Clarence Thomas in 1991, claiming that Thomas, her former boss, had sexually harassed her while both worked for the U.S. Department of Education.

6. Academic arguments over naming a women's movement in Africa suggests a cleavage that I did not witness at the Kampala conference. Nevertheless, Clenora Hudson-Weems claims coinage of the term, Africana-Womanism, in 1987.

7. Ontology is the science of being. Spinoza was a seventeenth-century ontological philosopher (or ontologist) whose explanation of the "single substance" responded to the "god/nature," "mind/body" arguments by proposing a case for a single substance (life essence) that suggests that these dichotomies are one—not two.

References

Aina, O. (1998). African women at the grassroots: The silent partners of the women's movement. In O. Nnaemeka (Ed.), *Sisterhood, feminisms, & power: From Africa to the diaspora* (pp. 65–88). Trenton, NJ: Africa World Press.

Barber, B. (1984). *Strong democracy: Participatory politics for a new age.* Berkeley, CA: University of California Press.

Brettschneider, M. (2002). *Democratic theorizing from the margins.* Philadelphia: Temple University Press.

Conway, M. M., Ahern, D. W., & Steuernagel, G. A. (1999). *Women and public policy* (2nd ed.). Washington, DC: CQ Press.

Dinnerstein, D. (Ed.). (1999). *The mermaid and the minotaur* (2nd ed.). New York: Other Press.

Fausto-Sterling, A. (2000). *Sexing the body: Gender politics and the construction of sexuality.* New York: Basic Books.

Gatens, M. (1991). *Feminisms and philosophy: Perspectives on difference and equality.* Bloomington, IN: Indiana University Press.

Gatens, M. (1996). *Imaginary bodies: Ethics, power and corporeality.* London: Routledge.

Guinier, L. (1992). Second proms and second primaries: The limits of majority rule. *Boston Review.* Retrieved January 5, 2006, from http://bostonreview.net/BR17.5/guinier.html.

Gutmann, A., & Thompson, D. (1996). *Democracy and disagreement.* Cambridge, MA: Harvard University Press.

Harris, A. (1999). Afterward. In D. Dinnerstein (Ed.), *The mermaid and the minotaur* (pp. 279–284). New York: Other Press.

Hawkesworth, M. E. (2001). Democratization: Reflections on gendered dislocations in the public sphere. In R. M. Kelly, J. H. Bayes, M. E. Hawkesworth, & B. Young

(Eds.), *Gender, globalization, and democratization* (pp. 223–236). Lanham, MD: Rowman & Littlefield.

Hutchinson, J. R. (2001). Multigendering PA: Anti-administration, anti-blues. *Administrative Theory & Praxis, 23*, 589–604.

Kymlicka, W. (2001). *Politics in the vernacular: Nationalism, multiculturalism, and citizenship.* Oxford: Oxford University Press.

Kymlicka, W., & Norman, W. (2000). *Citizenship in diverse societies.* Oxford: Oxford University Press.

Lichter, D. T., & Crowley, M. L. (2002). Poverty in America: Beyond welfare reform. *Population Bulletin, 57*(2), 1–34.

Lorber, J. L. (1994). *Paradoxes of gender.* New Haven, CT: Yale University Press.

Mansbridge, J. J. (1980). *Beyond adversary democracy.* NY: Basic Books.

Nagel, T. (1991). *Equality and partiality.* Oxford: Oxford University Press.

National Foundation for Women Legislators. Facts about women legislators (n.d.) Retrieved January 5, 2006, from www.womenlegislators.org/facts/.

Okin, S. M., Cohen, J., Howard, M., & Nussbaum, M. (1999). *Is multiculturalism bad for women?* Princeton, NJ: Princeton University Press.

Pateman, C. (1989). *The disorder of women: Democracy, feminism and political theory.* Stanford, CA: Stanford University Press.

Rawls, J. (1993). *Political liberalism.* New York: Columbia University Press.

Reich, R. B. (1988). *The power of public ideas.* Cambridge, MA: Harvard University Press.

Reis, E. (1995). The devil, the body and the feminine soul in Puritan New England. *Journal of American History, 82*, 15–36.

Silverstein, L. B., & Auerbach, C. F. (1999). Deconstructing the essential father. *American Psychologist, 54*, 397–407.

Snitow, A. (1999). Forward. In D. Dinnerstein (Ed.), *The mermaid and the minotaur* (pp. ix–xxiii). New York: Other Press.

Spinoza, B. de. (1994). *A Spinoza reader: The ethics and other works* (E. Curley, Ed. & Trans.). Princeton, NJ: Princeton University Press.

Stivers, C. (2002). Toward administrative space: Hannah Arendt meets the municipal housekeepers. *Administration & Society, 34*, 98–101.

Stivers, C. (2005). Dreaming the world: Feminisms in public administration. *Administrative Theory & Praxis, 27,* 364–369.

Toubia, N. (1988). *Women of the Arab World.* London: Zed Press.

U.S. Bureau of Labor Statistics, & U.S. Bureau of the Census. (2005). Annual demographic survey, March supplement. Retrieved November 25, 2005, from http://pubdb3.census.gov/macro/032005/pov/new01_100_01.htm.

Weeks, E. C. (2000). The practice of deliberative democracy: Results from four large-scale trials. *Public Administration Review, 60*, 360–372.

Women's Health Research at Yale. (2002). Retrieved June 13, 2002, from http://info.med.yale.edu/womenshealth/index.html.

Young, I. M. (1994). Gender as seriality: Thinking about women as a social collective. *Signs, 19*, 713–738.

Young, I. M. (2000). *Inclusion and democracy.* Oxford: Oxford University Press.

Democratic Administration in a Multicultural Environment

Mohamad G. Alkadry

In the twenty-first century, public administrators are expected to be responsive to citizens. Most western nations, however, are multicultural and diverse in terms of race, ethnicity, gender, identity, situation, and standpoint. Multiculturalism impacts public administration in two major domains: within public organizations and in the greater society. Public administrators work in diverse organizations and deal with a diverse citizenry. Internally, managing a multicultural workforce is a major challenge facing public organizations. Externally, public organizations are impacted by the challenge of serving, and being responsive to, a multicultural society.

Since the late 1960s, public administration has been attempting to deal with the challenges of multiculturalism. In the Minnowbrook conference in 1968, young public administration scholars wanting to ensure that public organizations were representative of the diversity in society argued that public administrators should act as advocates for the underrepresented and just interests. Passive and active forms of representation are essential to ensure equity, justice, and equality among all citizens. However, this chapter argues that such forms of representation are group-based and therefore do not by themselves meet the needs of multiculturalism in a democratic society. The chapter suggests that new social science and public administration theories—such as feminism and postmodernism—offer hope that true multiculturalism can be practiced.

There are four sections in this chapter. First, I define what is meant by multiculturalism. In doing so, I distinguish between culture and identity and between cultural pluralism and pluralistic integration. I also make the case that while group politics is essential to a democracy, we need to be very cognizant of the dangers of such politics—primarily the risk of "homogenizing hegemony." Second, I examine the past approaches to multiculturalism in the field of public administration. I specifically present the historical evolution of the notion of representative bureaucracy and the difference between active and passive representation and a critique of these two concepts. Third, I present the two challenges to representation as we have seen them in public administration. The two challenges include the inability of current manifestations of multiculturalism to reach beyond the narrow scope of group politics, and the inability of bureaucracy to fully embrace multiculturalism because of the nature of bureaucratic organizations. The final section in this chapter looks forward to the future, especially in light of contemporary public administration theories that provide hope that multiculturalism, within and outside public organizations, is within the reach of public administrators. In the conclusion of the chapter, I make the case that principles of multiculturalism can be used to provide public administrators with a toolbox for interacting among themselves and with citizens. Multiculturalism provides an opportunity for public administration to be more responsive than ever before.

What Is Multiculturalism?

No nation-state can hide from its diversity in the twenty-first century, even those with homogenous racial and ethnic populations. Historically, multiculturalism and diversity were used interchangeably to refer to ethnic and racial heterogeneity within society. However, multiculturalism extends beyond racial, ethnic, and gender diversity.

What do we mean we say that a nation is multicultural? Are there nations that are unicultural and ones that are multicultural? There are three defining moments in the discourse on multiculturalism. First, there is a distinction between culture and identity, which makes culture individual and drives multiculturalism into the accommodation of individuals and not groups. Second, there is a distinction between cultural pluralism and pluralistic integration, with multiculturalism resting on the former. Third, a critique of group politics cautions that multiculturalism that is based on accommodating group "cultures" could yield a form of cultural hegemony within groups.

The three defining moments collectively invite an inclusive definition of multiculturalism that assumes that no two people share the same culture. While it appears that this definition complicates our ability to be inclusive, this chapter merely invites a different paradigm of approaching multicultural administration. Past and current approaches to diversity and representative bureaucracy might help our organizations appear more diverse, but they do little to help us achieve multiculturalism. Multiculturalism is a good everyday strategy not only to yield equity and justice for employees and citizens, but also to enhance the responsiveness and democratic principles of public administration.

Culture and Identity

The term *culture* is often loosely used to refer to ethnic or racial traditions and identity. However, culture is essentially distinct from both traditions and identity. While group identity may exist, group culture is something that cannot possibly exist. Edward Said (1993) views culture as a collective of various meanings and experiences. To Said (1993, pp. xii–xiii), culture is "all those practices, like the arts of description, communication, and representation, that have relative autonomy from the economic, social, and political realms and that often exist in aesthetic forms, one of whose principle aims is pleasure." Goodenough (1964, p. 37) argues that culture is "what people have to learn as distinct from their biological heritage." Culture is distinct from ethnic background although ethnic background could play a major role in shaping one's experiences—a shared experience of being subjected to racism by blacks in the United States, Moroccans in France, Turks in Germany, or Kurds in Turkey, for instance. Such shared experiences, however, cannot be used to argue that there is a black culture, Moroccan culture, or Kurdish culture that is internally homogeneous. On the other hand, it is customary for us to talk about a black identity, a Moroccan identity, or a Kurdish identity.

While group identity could be defined as the unifying commonality among different individuals, a group culture is much more troublesome. While individuals within a group could share a common identity (e.g., Cuban American women), they would have different experiences and therefore different cultures. Despite the fact that my own brother and I attended the same grade school, the same high school, the same undergraduate universities, and lived in the same neighborhoods for most of our lives, we do not share the same culture. But we both identify as "Arab American men," despite the difference in our personal experiences, values, and therefore cultures. It is important to realize that citizens, even those who share the same identity, have different experiences, different realities, different needs, different standpoints, and therefore different cultures. This makes it difficult for us to associate multiculturalism with group politics, but rather drives multiculturalism essentially into the domain of individual politics. Defining people as part of a cultural group creates a homogenizing hegemony that oppresses intra-group differences.

Homogenizing Hegemony and Multiculturalism

While multiculturalism is essentially driven by a desire to create a more fair and inclusive society, group-based multiculturalism has its risks. The most significant of these risks is the tendency to associate multiculturalism with the representation of cultural groups—essentially groups of people who share an ethnic, gender, or racial identity. K. Anthony Appiah (1994) argues that our understanding of multiculturalism is based on conceptions of "collective identity that are remarkably unsubtle in their understandings of the processes by which identities, both individual and collective, develop" (p. 156). Appiah argues that the process of group recognition (identifying as a group) ties individuals to scripts over which they have little control. In the way that gender identity, grounded in the sexual body, proposes norms of behavior and character, ethnocultural identities propose norms of behavior and a "habitual life in culture" (Appiah, 1994; Spivak & Gunew, 1993). This is precisely the problem with interjecting culture into group politics. We would not be representing group cultures, which I argue are a figment of our imagination, but rather forcing individuals to adhere to certain scripts (shared/common identity attributes) as a prerequisite for inclusion. With group-centered multiculturalism, we are not unconditionally accepting differences and embracing them. We are rather accepting differences on our terms and as long as these differences are consistent with a common attribute of a group.

In a discussion of multiculturalism in Australia and the United States, Spivak and Gunew (1993) criticize multiculturalism's emphasis on groups for its tendency to emphasize group identity over individual identity. Spivak and Gunew, for instance, argue that:

> The question of "speaking as" involves a distancing from oneself. The moment I have to think of the ways in which I will speak as an Indian, or as a feminist, the ways in which I will speak as a woman, what I am doing is trying to generalize myself, make myself a representative, trying to distance myself from some kind of inchoate speaking as such. There are many subject positions one must inhabit; one is not just one thing. . . . But when the cardcarrying listeners, the hegemonic people, the dominant people, talk about listening to someone "speaking as" something or the other, I think there one encounters a problem. When they want to hear an Indian speaking as an Indian, a Third World woman speaking as a Third World woman, they cover over the fact of the ignorance that they are allowed to possess, into a kind of homogenization. (p. 195)

In other words, with multiculturalism, we run the risk of protecting exactly what we are supposed to be guarding individuals against—cultural hegemony.

Central to this discussion is the role of the state and the way it tackles the issue of multiculturalism. A multicultural strategy that emphasizes "group cultures" would be counterproductive because group culture masks differences within groups. In doing so, states would also be encouraging a form of cultural and heritage preservation—preserving the attributes that are essential to the group's identity. In some western countries, like Canada and Australia, the government effectively funds groups that act to preserve culture and heritage. Jürgen Habermas (1994) makes a rather convincing argument that the state should respect but not preserve cultural identities. Any attempt by the state to recognize cultural groups helps preserve the cultural identity of these groups. Preserving cultural identities goes against individuals' right to revise or reject their inherited identities. The guarantee of cultural preservation, according to Habermas, goes against the individual rights of free association and nondiscrimination (Gutmann, 1993, p. 171). In a sense, the state restricts the vitality and growth of cultures by associating them with traditions and encouraging the survival of these traditions. If the state were to ensure that traditions are preserved in the United States or Canada for instance, it would be preserving nineteenth-century values on representation, gender equality, and civil rights.

Group-based multiculturalism forces ethnocultural groups to retain their heritage and traditions—oftentimes the only commonality among members of these groups. The loss of these common traditions could result in the loss of status as a group. No group commonality translates into no group identity, which in turn translates into no recognition, inclusion, or representation. These conditions of inclusion apply to peripheral groups seeking recognition and inclusion and rarely apply to dominant groups. In reality, this ethnic center still has the legitimizing power to admit or not to admit different cultures (West, 1993). According to Iris Young (1989, p. 259),

> In a society where some groups are privileged while others are oppressed, insisting that citizens should not leave behind their particular affiliations and experiences to adopt a general point of view serves only to reinforce the privilege, for the perspective and interests of the privileged, marginalizing or silencing those of other groups.

If multiculturalism stresses the interaction of cultural groups and not individuals, then at its basis is the idea of cultural conformity. The mere act of belonging to a group does not safeguard members of that group against hegemony.

To date, government accommodation of cultural diversity has been limited to a recognition of cultural groups and accommodation of these group cultures. The gap between what the government has to offer and what ethnic groups expect is best explained in the following quote from Daniel Salée (1995, p. 279):

> The actual recognition of difference—the realization of inclusion—is more often than not an unsatisfactory and disappointing experience for many of the groups or communities striving for that recognition. The gap between the recognition sought and the recognition effectively granted is character-

istically wide, if not unbridgeable. The integration of divergent or hardly reconcilable identity claims within the same political, administrative and institutional framework is a practical impossibility, mostly when it involves ethnocultural divergence. The reality of pluriethnicity or multiculturalism in liberal societies poses a public policy challenge that most of them are hard pressed to meet.

Salée's words are a case in point. The dominant, also often dubbed as the cultural, center is often willing to give up whatever does not reduce its power, while groups seek empowering actions and not merely symbolic gestures.

In western democracies, multiculturalism has often been manifested in representation and inclusion policies that are essentially group-based representations. The above critique of group-based politics should not be misread as a criticism of group-based politics. It is rather an attempt to caution against the negative aspects of group-based cultural politics. All attempts to represent traditionally underrepresented individuals or groups are worthy of praise. However, public administrators need to be cognizant of the troubles with group-based cultural politics. There are strategies, such as cultural pluralism or cultural relativism, that emphasize unconditional acceptance of difference and at the same time act to de-center cultural domination.

Cultural Pluralism and Pluralistic Integration

Cultural pluralism and pluralistic integration are two important concepts adapted from Jeff Spinner's (1994) *The Boundaries of Citizenship*. Spinner argues that "by emphasizing specific practices and not cultures, pluralistic integration rejects the idea that cultures are somehow sacrosanct and need to be protected at all costs" (p. 76). Pluralistic integration emphasizes mainstream society, or the ethnic center, for that will be the one to define what is "liberal and what is illiberal" or what is "good" and what is "bad." Cultural pluralism, on the other hand, is the acceptance of all cultures and cultural values for what they are.

Pluralistic integration's main distinction from cultural pluralism, or what Amy Gutmann (1993) refers to as cultural relativism, is a form of polycentric multiculturalism based on unconditionally recognizing and accepting "differences" and "otherness." Cultural pluralism, or cultural relativism, suggests that the views on social justice held by different societies, communities, or even cultures be interpreted in the perspective and in the context of the culture within which they exists—truth is in the eye of the beholder.

Gutmann (1993) argues that by definition individuals are multicultural, and the only way to achieve multiculturalism in organizations and in society is through cultural relativism. Cultural relativism involves accepting differences and otherness. This poses the question of the ability of representative democracy to not only accept but to accommodate these differences. The only way to do this seems to be through a bureaucracy of all society. Even then, hierarchy will impose internal inequalities. There is an array of scholars who argue that multiculturalism risks enslavement to Eurocentric, ethnocentric, or colonial images and symbols of ethnicities (Bullivant, 1990; Said, 1993; Shohat & Stam, 1994; Wilson, 1993).

If we were to apply Spinner's distinction on pluralistic integration and cultural pluralism, one could easily argue that governments generally advocate pluralistic integration. There are two reasons for this tendency. First, pluralistic integration is easier to implement than cultural pluralism. Once the center is defined, peripheries could relate to that center. This is very true in the case of organizations and how they handle new ideas and new members. On the other hand, implementing a form of cultural pluralism is much more complicated. Second, pluralistic integration is more consistent with the interest in the protection and celebration of cultural practices that are compatible with liberalism (Spinner, 1994, pp. 7–8). Pluralistic integration is much more equipped to discourage, or even forbid, illiberal practices.

Pluralistic integration is very close to the main ethos of many public organizations—both internally and externally. Internally, public administrators will follow habitual scripts and would have little power to write their own scripts in the bureaucracy. An example would be the admitting of a very diverse workforce into a dominating organizational culture that will absorb diversity not on diversity's own terms, but rather on the terms of the bureaucracy. Externally, citizens receive services also prescribed from within realities of the organization and not their own realities. Cultural relativism (Gutmann, 1993) or cultural pluralism (Spinner, 1994) is consistent with "multiculturalism" as advocated in this chapter.

Diversity, Multiculturalism, and Representation in Public Administration

Multiculturalism impacts public administration in two very profound ways: the creation and management of multicultural organizations, and the ability of organizations to be responsive to a multicultural citizenry. The most prominent public administration response to these two realities was in the 1968 Minnowbrook conference—what became known as the New Public Administration. Conference attendees and subsequent writings provided the foundations of representative bureaucracy. This section discussed the Minnowbrook conference and then draws a distinction between passive and active representation.

New Public Administration and Minnowbrook

In 1968, a group of young public administration scholars met in Minnowbrook, New York, and called essentially for a representative public administration relevant to social problems. The Minnowbrook conference came after decades of theorizing a neutral public administration that is technically driven and separated from politics and policy making. At the conference, invited young public administration scholars were responding to new social and political realities arising from the civil rights movement. Regardless of the success of the Minnowbrook scholars in translating their declarations into actions, the movement provided the foundation for a representative and a relative public administration. The Minnowbrook conference declarations became known as the New Public Administration.

Frank Marini (1971) describes the main issues of the conference: "We were reminded of relevance, social problems, personal morality, innovation, clients, the evils of hierarchy and bureaucracy" (p. 5). The conference was a recognition that bureaucracy has powers and was expected to use them and to be more responsive to, and representative of, the public (Frederickson, 1997). New Public Administration argues that the main value driving governance is the "equalization of economic and political power" (Thompson, 1975, p. 66). This value-oriented approach defines the success or failure of a certain organization according to how well it serves its values. It undermines judging organizations by their responsiveness "to an unconcerned majority or [their] efficiency in achieving [their] assigned goals" (Thompson, 1975, p. 66).

The complexity of the New Public Administration approach lies in the diversity of the citizenry. The New Public Administration finds itself ahead of a complex issue of representing a citizenry whose diversity is beyond comprehension. The issue of who and how to represent by itself poses a great challenge to the popular sovereignty approach of the New Public Administration and representative bureaucracy.

Active and Passive Representation

Representative bureaucracy is based on the notion that "the social composition of the bureaucracy should reflect that of the population as a whole; and that larger numbers from certain underrepresented groups should be brought [into] the public service" (Kernaghan & Siegel, 1991, p. 470). As the principles of equality and participatory democracy started unfolding in the 1960s and 1970s, the inequalities of representation became clearer. Riggs (1970, pp. 570–573) suggests that there is:

> a need for diverse elements in a population to be adequately represented [in the government apparatus] in order for a government to command their loyalty as a legitimate expression of common welfare. . . . The effectiveness of any government depends not only on how well its machinery for implementing decisions operates, but also on its ability to command the continuing support and loyalty of its population.

This notion has clearly given the supposedly neutral public service the political role of representation. Riggs goes further to relate representation in "all organizations of government" to the stability of that government. He uses examples from various countries to show how the failure to have an equitable representation in the political dimensions of government and its administration could result in public rebellion. He also argues that there is a "need for diverse elements in a population to be adequately represented in order for a government to command their loyalty as a legitimate expression of common welfare" (p. 570). He argues that

> if we concentrate on the effort to improve capacity by administrative reform without simultaneously making sure that the need for more political equality is met, then revolutionary turbulence will undermine and destroy whatever gains might have been made in the struggle for greater efficiency. . . . Sometimes the best way to improve administration may be to work for a more representative political system and, conversely, of course, . . . the most promising road to political reform will sometimes be to strive for greater administrative capabilities. (pp. 573–574)

The main premise of representative bureaucracy has been that an organization that mirrors the ethnic and gender diversity of society would be representative of, but also by default responsive to, that society. This makes achieving representative or diverse organizations an end in itself—a form of representation often referred to as passive representation. Representative bureaucracy is not seen as a mean to enhance social justice or equality, but the premise of representative bureaucracy is that this will occur automatically once diversity exists at all levels of organizations.

This discussion is usually presented in terms of passive versus active representation. Active representation results in representation in the decision-making and implementation stages, and impacts the groups represented in the policy-making forum. Passive representation is achieved when the bureaucracy mirrors society in terms of group representation (Hindera & Young, 1998; Thompson, 1975). Both active and passive forms of representation emphasize the representation of groups—both internally as employees and externally as customers/consumers/clients/citizens.

The main flaw of passive representation rests in its inability to provide meaningful results-oriented representation. The most that such a form of representation could hope for is a bureaucracy that reflects the visible diversity in society. Such a form of representative bureaucracy would not necessarily serve the functions of participatory democracy. Distributive justice, a product of liberal political theory, and the birthplace of passive representative bureaucracy, is a concept that Young (1989, 1990) criticizes, primarily because of its failure to yield meaningful levels of participatory democracy. Young clearly advocates a progressive emancipatory conception of justice. She argues that people should be able to make decisions about their jobs and communities and to "have their experiences and perspectives recognized in significant cultural contexts" (Young, 1989, p. 259). The essentially liberal notion of passive representation fails to consider group perspectives, experiences, and interests. She argues that social groups' interests, and not only numbers, should be represented—essentially an argument for a form of active representation. To a great extent, the notion of representative bureaucracy risks falling into the trap of passive representation where the appearance of representation becomes a goal rather than a means of including various segments in the decision-making process.

Active and passive forms of representation are not necessarily exclusive of one another. Meier (1993) argues that passive representation will yield active representation only after members of target groups constitute a significant proportion of the decision-making forum's personnel. Hindera and Young (1998, p. 656) suggest that "the relationship between passive and active representations changes at three critical points: when the critical mass is reached; when the group constitutes a plurality (i.e., social prominence) of agency personnel; and when the group constitutes a majority (i.e., social dominance)."

Multiculturalism and Representation: Two Challenges

There are two challenges to multiculturalism in public administration. The first involves doubts about the ability of bureaucracy, an organization dominated by norms and habits, to allow multicultural pluralism within its borders. The second challenge relates to the fact that representative bureaucracy has been essentially a form of group-based multiculturalism, and could be problematic.

The Challenge of Intra-Group Difference

Group-based politics and policies, including representative bureaucracy, fail to address the existence of differences within various social groups. Young advocates an emancipatory conception of justice that is more progressive than redistributive justice. She wants people to make decisions about their jobs and communities and to "have their experiences and perspectives recognized in significant cultural contexts" (Young, 1989, p. 257). This compares to pacifying (overlooking?) individual differences under the notion of redistributive justice. The essentially liberal notion of group or proportional representation of groups fails to consider "group perspectives, experiences and interests," Young (1989, p. 259) argues.

It is essential to understand the notions of proportional representation and identity politics or the politics of difference as advanced by Riggs (1970) and Young (1989). Two essential issues arise here. First, what defines representativeness? Second, what prevents representation from turning into some form of tokenism and even elitism? Representative bureaucracy is assumed to exist when people from various segments of society are employed by the organization. The question of how much the conservative Supreme Court justice Clarence Thomas can be representative of black Americans' interests in the highest court comes to mind. In this case, would a progressive non-black judge be more representative of black interests than Clarence Thomas? And, what would the contribution of the appointment of Thomas be to the whole notion of representation? This is really the difference between Young and Riggs. Riggs (1970) would argue that since Thomas is black, his appointment counts as a move toward increasing representation of blacks on the Supreme Court. Young, on the other hand, argues that social groups' interests, and not only numbers, should be represented.

However, Young's suggestion of increasing the representativeness of the different social groups' interests does very little to acknowledge the diversity of different social groups and the diversity of ideas within each social group. For instance, an Arab American group is essentially considered an ethnic group and could be only one of hundreds to be represented in the ethnic category in the decision-making process. Within the Arab American social group, there are various ideas and identities. Within that group, there exist gays, lesbians, women, elderly, the back-to-traditions camp, the progressive camp, Lebanese, Syrians, Palestinians, Moroccans, etc. Besides, within each of these Arab American sub-groups, there is a diversity of conflicting values. How Arab American interests would be represented in the bureaucracy is a question that is often left unanswered by Young. Young criticizes communitarians for their attempts to marginalize differences within groups. However, to represent each social group with its distinct individual identities, as Young suggests, could be somewhat utopian. Her idea of reform raises the question of where to draw the line and could entail problems similar to those of "representative bureaucracy."

So, the criticism of passive representation is not a blind invitation to active representation. Active representation still has its problems. The challenge to active and passive representation is that both are group-based. In other words, the only available mechanisms for representation in bureaucracy, even active representation, are group-based. Groups targeted for representation are defined according to age, gender, race, ability, and other factors that place assign group identities to individuals. Such forms of representation cross-reference representation in an organization to representation of these identified groups. This occurs for a political but also tactical reason. The political reasons for group-based representation derive from demands that are usually placed on the political system by groups (Pal, 1993; Spinner, 1994). The tactical reasons involve the absence of any alternate mechanism that would provide better results. This reason notwithstanding, the result of group-based representation is ethnic and gender diversity, but not necessarily cultural pluralism.

While there are many differences within a group, a certain group has one single identity (Spinner, 1994). A group can have a compound identity, e.g., lesbian Hispanic. Groups that have been identified for inclusion in the bureaucracy are still diverse from within, and the mere inclusion of one member of that group fails by far to represent the whole group. Take, for instance, the identification of minorities as target groups for affirmative action by human resources managers. Minority is a term that is often used to refer to all persons of color. There is no homogenous group of people called a minority group. Minorities are not only blacks. Blacks are not only African in origin. African blacks are not all men. African black men are not all heterosexuals. African black heterosexual men are not always able-bodied. Able-bodied African black heterosexual men are not always highly educated. Highly educated able-bodied African black heterosexual men do not always come from the same socioeconomic class. Rich, highly educated, able-bodied African black heterosexual men do not always have the same political affiliations. And the list can go on. The main question that this example raises is: Who should represent societal minorities in the bureaucracy? The biggest problem with this approach is that we will continually have to accept new identities, which emerge from these mega-identities that are based on group definitions that are manageable (e.g., visible minorities, women, homosexuals, etc.). Defining groups in a narrow way would yield a management problem and a program impossible to run.

Defining group membership and belonging based on ethnic identity or gender simply obscures the differences of gender, religion, class, and race. Hooks (1981) criticizes the way early feminists of the contemporary feminist movement have excluded the experience of women of color. While feminists, in a sense, assumed the center of that movement, the writings of early feminists came to reflect everything but the experience of women of color. Friedan's (1963) book, *The Feminine Mystique,* which is largely considered the classic of contemporary feminism, has no mention of the experience of women of color (Yeatman, 1994, p. 4). Hooks points to legitimate concerns that group representation unfortunately fails to address. We have to also look at some neo-Marxists who argue that class hegemony has always existed in American society. If one were to accept the definition of the hegemony of a political class as the situation where a "class had succeeded in persuading the other classes of society to accept its moral, political and cultural values," then the dangers of a class practicing internal hegemony within a social group are very real (Bullivant, 1990).

Over the years, representative bureaucracy has manifested itself through several different names. One of these manifestation was the concept of organizational multiculturalisms (Bak, 1993; Harris, 1995; Jun, 1996; Laudicina, 1995). This is an even more obscure way of defining group "oneness" and "sameness" based on culture. The trend is to look at cultures through ethnic, gender, and sexually oriented glasses.

The Bureaucratic Challenge: Reconciling the Irreconcilable

When discussing multiculturalism, one cannot ignore the wealth of literature that alleges that bureaucracy is by definition unicultural—characterized by the dominance of the organizational culture (often defined by white, heterosexual, middle-aged men in power). Some theorists pose an irreconcilable challenge to organizations and to the notion of representative bureaucracy. Some scholars have led this fight to isolate domination in bureaucratic culture and intra-organizational behavior (Bologh, 1982; Denhardt & Perkins, 1976). Organizations' "superior domination through hierarchical patterns of authority is not essential to the achievement of important goals but in fact is restrictive of the growth of the group and its individual members" (Denhardt & Perkins, 1976, p. 379). Participation in this organization leaves people with the choice of "selling out" or remaining on its margins forever.

Ferguson (1984) suggests that bureaucratic organizations cannot but produce conformity. Ferguson seems to reiterate Lenin's (1949) notion that a good bureaucracy is no bureaucracy. Entering into the bureaucracy is, however, "necessary to some extent, if for no other reason than to be able to speak against it; in order to articulate the virtues of female experiences, women have to transcend its constraints" (Ferguson, 1984, p. 29). To Ferguson, the price of success for women in the bureaucracy is conformity and the abandonment of critical consciousness. Rich (1979, p. 43) has already warned us that for women to fit too well in the bureaucracy is to lose the "outsider's view and the outsider's consciousness." Individuals are encountering bureaucracy on its own terms, and not the other way around (Golembiewski, 1995; Griggs & Louw, 1995; Henderson, 1994; Hopson & Hopson, 1992). This is troubling for attempts to exercise any form of cultural pluralism or cultural relativism within public organizations.

There are two key questions posed by the above discussion. Will the bureaucracy co-opt people into "the one way of doing things" or will bureaucracy be co-opted into a multicultural discourse? If the latter, what are the consequences for bureaucracy as we know it? If admission to the bureaucracy is conditioned upon integration into its culture and values—essentially the definition of cultural integration—then how can we assume that a multicultural discourse or any form of cultural pluralism is feasible? These questions cannot be properly addressed without establishing the prevalence of bureaucratic characteristics in today's public organizations—an issue that is beyond the scope of this chapter.

Is Multiculturalism the Future? Standpoint and Multi-Realities

Representative bureaucracy is public administration's response to the civil rights movement. While it was certainly a move forward, it has not produced the form of cultural pluralism or relativism that would be associated with multiculturalism. The trouble with the field of public administration is that it has not properly engaged the issue of multiculturalism from perspectives other than passive or active representation of groups or group interests. There are some new and emerging theories that can help us move from representative bureaucracy to better forms of cultural pluralism or multiculturalism. Such theories have indirectly articulated the case that multiculturalism, cultural pluralism, is not an option but an essential tool to govern a citizenry with as many realities as the citizens themselves. In this chapter I would like to particularly refer the reader to critical standpoint epistemology and postmodernism as strategies of cultural pluralism.

Emphasizing the Standpoint

Government in the twentieth century, especially after the Progressive-era reforms, became more involved in issues that deal with the welfare of citizens. This makes information about consumers important for crafting public policy (Schachter, 1995). At the heart of this information-gathering process is the assumption that policy makers can gather information about a "collective public," which in itself has become a suspect concept (Hummel, 1997;

Yeatman, 1994). There is doubt about the ability of administrators to form knowledge claims about the consumers of public services when these consumers do not participate directly in the administrative process (Miller, Alkadry, & Donohue, 2001). This doubt is particularly about the ability of public administrators to remove themselves from observed phenomena and make so-called objective claims about a "reality" and a policy situation that is being judged, observed, or resolved. Standpoint epistemology indirectly proposes that the participation of individual citizens, and not information about a collective public, provides the better source of intelligence about consumer preferences and needs. Knowledge of consumer preference is essential to the ability of administrators to be responsive.

Harding (1986, 1987, 1993), a proponent of "standpoint epistemology," argues that science's objectivity is essentially compromised by the failure of scientific methods to examine the context of science. She rejects the objectivity assumption that science is value free and independent or external to social context. The subject is male and the context is patriarchal and male dominated. Thus, according to Harding, a feminist epistemology's largest contribution is to initiate scientific observation from the experiences and "lives" of the marginalized people (Bar-On, 1993, p. 83). This will make scientific questions more critical and will reveal more comprehensive results.

With standpoint epistemology, feminist scholars question the ability of policy makers and scientists to obtain objective knowledge. They suggest that the more subjective and standpoint-based the observation is, the closer we might get to observing realities. These become realities from where people/citizens stand.

There are two major implications for the above discussion of standpoint knowledge. First, objective claims about reality become suspect because the objectivity of the observer, the observation, and the observed reality are also suspect. Second, the acclamation of the subjective nature of knowledge invites the representation of various perspectives other than, but not excluding, the dominant one. Citizens are privy to information that the administrator, the policy analyst, and the politician do not have. For example, a welfare recipient is privy to information about being on welfare that salaried politicians and administrators do not have. This is by itself a source of power to participants in the administrative process. The lack of objective knowledge and the ability of administrators to make universal knowledge claims bring new focus to the need to empower both the consumer and the front-line administrator. This will ensure that gathered intelligence from the public and about the public is dealt with on an individual basis and not on the basis of a collective public.

Postmodernism and the End of Meta-Narratives

Feminists have not been the only ones to question the ability of administrators to make judgments about the realities of citizens. Postmodernists also question such ability. Postmodernists question the existence of a single reality (Hassard & Parker, 1993; Lyotard, 1979/1984). There is no one truth, no one reality, but rather many realities and many truths (Yeatman, 1994). The lack of a single reality translates into a lack of a single reality about policy problems and a single public for which the policy fits. In its effort to legitimize grand narratives of policy, postmodernism legitimizes local narratives and mini-realities. The implications of postmodernism to public administration and public policy include the inability of traditional policy-analysis tools to capture information about the public. The goal of policy analysis to make statements about a reality that exists "out there" is shattered by postmodern, and phenomenological, arguments that reality is inside each of us and not "out there." There is no readily available reality that we can define through existing policies or procedures. There are rather many realities that are ready to be made by citizens. Such realities are better stated by the citizens themselves and not by an observer who may be tainted by claims to objective knowledge that is not so objective.

Although imported into the field of public administration through the works of some feminist and postmodernist scholars, the postmodern critique of meta-narratives and the feminist emphasis on standpoint have thus far steered away from cultural politics discussed in earlier sections of this chapter. However, both sets of theories provide the foundation for an organizational multiculturalism that emphasizes the individuality of public administrators and the individuality of the citizens they serve.

Conclusion

Ella Shohat and Robert Stam (1994) argue that multiculturalism "means seeing world history and contemporary social life from the perspective of the radical equality of peoples in status, potential and rights." To Shohat and Stam, "multiculturalism decolonizes representation not only in terms of cultural artifacts—literary canons, museum exhibits, film series—but also in terms of power relations between communities" (p. 5). Multiculturalism in the field of public administration has been a mere response to a system of ethnic and social hegemony in distress. The distress was highlighted by the civil rights movements, which gave rise to voices of inclusion and recognition of differences in society (Pal, 1993). Passive representation might serve to provide this façade of multiculturalism—essentially a diverse workforce— without the bother of a more complex remedy to representation.

This chapter has made three key arguments. First, multiculturalism is not the same as diversity. Only a form of cultural relativism or cultural pluralism that steers away from group-culture politics qualifies as multiculturalism. Second, representative bureaucracy—the official response of public administration to the need to accommodate difference—falls short of achieving multicultural administration. At best, it achieves a façade of diversity that may or may not represent the interests of ethnic, gender, and racial groups. Even when it does so, it acts to obscure differences within groups, and in some cases oppresses difference within groups. Third, a new approach to public administration could emphasize the importance of individual realities and standpoints. Such an approach would not only yield better responsiveness, but would also act to meet the fundamental principles of cultural pluralism.

If public administration aims to achieve a diverse workforce in terms of gender, race, and ethnicity, then representative bureaucracy is certainly the route to achieve that diversity. However, if public administration's goal is to be responsive to a multicultural society, then we need to supplement strategies of representative bureaucracy with strategies that are sensitive to cultural relativism as discussed in this chapter. That does not mean that representative bureaucracy strategies are not important. Representative bureaucracy is a very basic, and fundamental, response to years of disadvantage and exclusion of women and minorities from the public sector. Representative bureaucracy is the floor, and not the ceiling, of what should be expected from a democratic public administration in a multicultural society.

References

Appiah, K. A. (1994). Identity, authenticity, survival: Multicultural societies and social reproduction. In A. Gutmann (Ed.), *Multiculturalism: Examining the politics of recognition* (pp. 149–164). Princeton, NJ: Princeton University Press.

Bak, H. (1993). *Multiculturalism and the canon of American culture*. Amsterdam: VU University Press.

Bar-On, B-A. (1993). Marginality and epistemic privilege. In L. Alcoff & E. Potter (Eds.), *Feminist epistemologies* (pp. 83–100). New York: Routledge.

Bologh, R. W. (1982). Beyond Weber's analysis and critique of bureaucracy. Paper presented at the First International Conference on the Comparative, Historical, and Critical Analysis of Bureaucracy, Gottlieb Duttweiler Institute, Zurich, October 1982.

Bullivant, B. M. (1990). Multiculturalism: Pluralist orthodoxy or ethnic hegemony? *Canadian Ethnic Studies, 13*(2), 1–22.

Denhardt, R. B., & Perkins, J. (1976). The coming death of administrative man. *Women in Public Administration, 36,* 379–384.

Ferguson, K. E. (1984). *The feminist case against bureaucracy.* Philadelphia: Temple University Press.

Fredrickson, H. G. (1997). *The spirit of public administration.* San Francisco: Jossey-Bass.

Friedan, B. (1963). *The feminine mystique.* New York: Dell.

Golembiewski, R. T. (1995). *Managing diversity in organizations.* Tuscaloosa: University of Alabama Press.

Goodenough, W. (1964). Cultural anthropology and linguistics. In D. Hymes (Ed.), *Language in culture and society: A reader in linguistics and anthropology* (pp. 36–39). New York: Harper & Row.

Griggs, L. B., & Louw, L. L. (1995). *Valuing diversity: New tools for a new reality.* New York: McGraw-Hill.

Gutmann, A. (1993). The challenge of multiculturalism in political ethics. *Philosophy & Public Affairs, 22,* 171–206.

Habermas, J. (1994). Struggles for recognition in the democratic constitutional state. In A. Gutmann (Ed.), *Multiculturalism: Examining the politics of recognition* (pp. 107–148). Princeton, NJ: Princeton University Press.

Harding, S. (1986). The instability of the analytical categories of feminist theory. *Signs, 11,* 645–664.

Harding, S. (1987). The instability of the analytical categories of feminist theory. In S. Harding & J. F. O'Barr (Eds.), *Sex and scientific inquiry* (pp. 283–308). Chicago: University of Chicago Press.

Harding, S. (1993). Rethinking standpoint epistemology: What is strong objectivity? In L. Alcoff & E. Potter (Eds.), *Feminist epistemologies* (pp. 49–82). New York: Routledge.

Harris, D. A. (Ed.). (1995). *Multiculturalism from the margins: Non-dominant voices on difference and diversity.* Westport, CT: Greenwood.

Hassard, J., & Parker, M. (1993). *Postmodernism and organizations.* Thousand Oaks, CA: Sage.

Henderson, G. (1994). *Cultural diversity in the workplace: Issues and strategies.* Westport, CT: Quorum Books.

Hindera, J. J., & Young, C. D. (1998). Representative bureaucracy: The theoretical implications of statistical interaction. *Political Research Quarterly, 51,* 655–671.

Hooks, b. (1981). *Ain't I a woman: Black women and feminism.* Boston: Southend.

Hopson, D. P., & Hopson, D. S. (1992). *Different and wonderful: Raising black children in a race-conscious society.* New York: Simon & Schuster.

Hummel, R. (1997). Ideocracy: The cultural uses of modern post-ism in a late capital economy. In H. T. Miller & C. Fox (Eds.), *Postmodernism, "reality" and public administration: A discourse* (pp. 19–40). Burke, VA: Chatelaine.

Jun, J. S. (1996). Changing perspectives on organizational culture: Embracing multiculturalism. *International Journal of Public Administration 19,* 345–375.

Kernaghan, K., & Siegel, D. (1991). *Public administration in Canada* (2nd ed.). Scarborough, Canada: Nelson.

Laudicina, E. V. (1995). Managing workforce diversity in government: An initial assessment. *Public Administration Quarterly, 19,* 170–192.

Lenin, V. (1969). *Selected works.* London: Lawrence & Wishart.

Lyotard, J.-F. (1979/1984). *The postmodern condition: A report on knowledge.* Minneapolis: University of Minnesota Press.

Marini, F. (1971). *Toward a new public administration.* Scranton, PA: Chandler.

Meier, K. J. (1993). Representative bureaucracy: A theoretical and empirical exposition. In J. Perry (Ed.), *Research in public administration* (pp. 1–35). Greenwich, CT: JAI.

Miller, H. T., Alkadry, M. G., & Donohue, J. (2001). Rumbling doubt about managerial effectiveness and a turn toward discourse. In T. Liou (Ed.), *Handbook of public management and reform* (pp. 607–618). New York: Marcel Dekker.

Pal, L. A. (1993). *Interest of state: The politics of language, multiculturalism, and feminism in Canada.* Montreal: McGill-Queen's University Press.

Rich, A. (1979). Privilege, power, and tokenism. *MS, 8,* 42–44.

Riggs, F. (1970). *Administrative reform and political responsiveness: A theory of dynamic balancing.* Thousand Oaks, CA: Sage.

Said, E. W. (1993). *Culture and imperialism.* New York: Vintage Books.

Salée, D. (1995). Identities in conflict: The aboriginal question and the politics of recognition. *Ethnic and Racial Studies, 18,* 277–314.

Schachter, H. L. (1995). *Reinventing government or reinventing ourselves: The role of citizen owners in making a better government.* Albany: State University of New York Press.

Shohat, E., & Stam, R. (1994). *Unthinking Eurocentrism: Multiculturalism and the media.* London: Routledge.

Spinner, J. (1994). *The boundaries of citizenship.* Baltimore: Johns Hopkins University Press.

Spivak, G. C., & Gunew, S. (1993). Questions of multiculturalism. In S. During (Ed.), *The cultural studies reader* (pp. 193–202). London: Routledge.

Thompson, V. A. (1975). *Without sympathy or enthusiasm: The problem of administrative compassion.* Birmingham: University of Alabama Press.

West, C. (1993). The new cultural politics of difference. In S. During (Ed.), *The cultural studies reader* (pp. 203–220). London: Routledge.

Wilson, V. S. (1993). The tapestry vision of Canadian multiculturalism. *Canadian Journal of Political Science, 26,* 645–669.

Yeatman, A. (1994). *Postmodern revisionings of the political.* New York: Routledge.

Young, I. M. (1989). Polity and group difference: A critique of the ideal of universal citizenship. *Ethics, 99,* 250–274.

Young, I. M. (1990). *Justice and the politics of difference.* Princeton, NJ: Princeton University Press.

Nonprofit Organizations, Philanthropy, and Democracy in the United States

Angela M. Eikenberry

Nonprofit organizations are becoming increasingly important as social service providers. Beyond questions of accountability for efficiency and effectiveness, very little discussion has taken place regarding the democratic impacts—procedural and substantive—of relying on nonprofit organizations and philanthropy to provide these services, especially basic social services to the poor. In this broader context, nonprofit and other philanthropic institutions can both enhance and detract from democracy. This chapter suggests that public administrators might look beyond principal-agent models to guide their relationships with nonprofit organizations and consider the broader democratic implications of relying on these organizations to provide social services to the poor. To discuss these issues, the chapter is divided into three sections. The first section briefly summarizes the current trend to rely on nonprofit organizations to provide social services in the United States and the narrow and inadequate principal-agent focus public administration seems to have regarding the role of nonprofits. The second section provides an overview of the ways in which nonprofit and other philanthropic institutions both create and negate democracy. Finally, based on findings from a study of giving circles, the third section provides a discussion of ways in which we might create a more democratic nonprofit and philanthropic sector and the limitations involved in this pursuit.

Before proceeding to the first section, a note on key terms is in order. Within the chapter the terms "nonprofit organization," "voluntary association," and "philanthropy" will be used. Nonprofit organizations are those organizations designated by a state as a nonprofit corporation and typically by the federal Internal Revenue Service as tax-exempt. Though there are many types of nonprofit organizations, for this study it is human service organizations that are primarily considered. Voluntary associations both pre-date and continue to exist alongside nonprofit organizations. They are groups of individuals who voluntarily come together to accomplish a purpose. This group may or may not be a tax-exempt nonprofit organization. Philanthropy is understood as encompassing the act of giving money and other resources, including time (volunteering), to aid individuals, causes, and organizations. In this chapter, philanthropy will be used to also encompass institutions—such as voluntary associations, nonprofit and tax-exempt organizations, and other funding mechanisms—that enable individuals to give their resources.

A Growing Reliance on Nonprofit Organizations: Creating the "Hollow" State

In recent decades there has been an increased call for and reliance on non-profit organizations and their philanthropic supporters to provide social ser-vices in the United States. These include services that provide for life's necessities, needs that at a minimum must be met for personal survival (i.e., direct income and other material support) and for individuals to develop their potential richly and fully (Addams, 1902). Proponents of the relatively re-cent welfare reform changes have argued that if social services are needed, local philanthropic organizations can provide them as they did during the nineteenth century "golden age of charity" (Beito, Gordon, & Tabarrok, 2002; Olasky, 1992). They see the welfare state as displacing or "crowding out" other institutions and sapping democracy's strength and argue that philan-thropic organizations can draw on local social and financial capital to fill the void in government welfare spending.

Government rhetoric and reality in the past two decades have followed this line of reasoning, initiating policies that rely to a greater degree on the nonprofit and philanthropic sector. Beginning in the 1980s, Ronald Reagan and George Bush, Sr., called for Americans to increase philanthropic support and voluntary action, linking them directly to their campaign to reduce the size of "big" government (Hall, 2003, pp. 377–378; Poppendieck, 1998, p. 139). Influenced by the Reinventing Government movement, the Clinton administration oversaw sweeping changes in the government's relationship with nonprofit organizations (Grønbjerg & Salamon, 2002, p. 447). Welfare reform legislation included a "charitable choice" amendment that encour-aged state and local officials to use charitable and faith-based organizations to provide welfare-related services (Rom, 1999). George W. Bush has con-tinued in this direction with his call for greater reliance on local faith-based organizations and community groups to help the poor (Executive Order Nos. 13198 & 13199, 2001). Part of the appeal of Bush's proposal to privilege faith-based charities is the potential replacement of formal, professionalized nonprofit organizations with informal church groups staffed by volunteers. Yet, as Salamon (2002, p. 20) writes, "this reinforces a quaint nineteenth-century image of how charitable organizations are supposed to operate, an image that competitive pressures, accountability demands, and technological change have made increasingly untenable."

Ensuring Democratic Accountability: Shortcomings of a Principal-Agent Focus

Thus, in recent decades there has been a transfer of responsibility for social service delivery from governmental agencies to private firms and charities, including faith-based organizations, creating what some have termed the "hollow state" (Milward, Provan, & Else, 1993). Democratic accountability has become a growing concern within this environment because nonprofit service providers "are only tangentially accountable to the elected officials who enact and oversee the programs" (Salamon, 1981, p. 261). Workers in these organizations essentially become "street level bureaucrats" with a more diluted line of authority (Milward, 1994). In this context, it becomes the job of government agencies to ensure that nonprofit providers use public funds efficiently and effectively, and the most popular means for this is through the use of legal and bureaucratic control mechanisms (Dicke, 2002). These efforts are informed by notions of principal-agent theory that posit that there is typically

> a fundamental tension between the interests of a principal [in this case government] and an agent [in this case the nonprofit service provider] in a contracting relationship. Agents are assumed to be self-interested utility maximizers who will pursue their own self-interests over and above the wishes of the principal in the absence of threats, sanctions, or inducements. (Dicke, 2002, p. 456)

This an extremely narrow view of the role nonprofit organizations play in society (see below), and moreover these external control-based measures are often inadequate or fail to influence desired outcomes. Scholars have noted the many problems associated with external, control-based measures, both for public administrators and nonprofit providers. For public administrators, problems include contract failure, inadequate resources for oversight, and a general lack of capacity among providers (Dwivedi & Jabbra, 1988; Frederickson & London, 2000; Kettl, 1993). In addition, Dicke (2002) found in a study of external control methods limitations such as: questionable validity of the information obtained from monitoring due to infrequent visits and evaluations based on snapshot depictions of on-site conditions susceptible to manipulation by the provider; time constraints; falsified and inaccurate documentation, sometimes due to inadequate training and lack of understanding of what is required or disorganization; environmental conditions such as staff turnover and inadequate resources that render the control ineffective for assessing quality of services; and an unwillingness by government agencies to sanction poorly performing nonprofit providers.

Likewise, nonprofit providers experience problems associated with these external, control-based oversight measures by public agencies. For example, conveying the views of several nonprofit managers in New York City, Bernstein (1991) shows the many difficulties managers have with the "chaos" of government budget cycles, rules, and contract compliance procedures. The implications are that community-based nonprofits relying heavily upon public funding "might be forced to shift focus from meeting community needs to meeting contract compliance requirements" (Smith & Lipsky, 1993, in Frederickson & London, 2000, p. 231). Furthermore, Wolch (1990) predicts the voluntary sector will "lose its soul" as it relies increasingly on government funding because it will not be able to maintain advocacy efforts for the poor and others. Faith-based advocates also worry that public agency oversight of faith-based service providers will serve to "turn religion against religion" and "make religion a servant of the state" (Cnaan & Boddie, 2002; Matsui & Chuman, 2001, p. 31). Ultimately, control mechanisms and measurements are inadequate for tracking what could be considered the core of nonprofit service provision: concern for mission over profit and an ethic of care (Dicke, 2002, p. 466). They also fail to consider the broader democratic implications of nonprofit service provision.

A More Expansive View of Democracy and Philanthropy

Though there are several models of democracy (Held, 1996), in the United States the notion has been influenced most by two major philosophical streams. Classical liberalism with its emphasis on individualism has influenced the dominant view of democracy in the United States, making it our "first language" of moral discourse (Bellah et al., 1985, p. 334). Classical liberalism assumes that individuals pursue their private self-interests while government exists to balance these interests. In this context, the state does not aim to develop citizens, only to act as a neutral mediator of competing interests and rights and guarantor of some of these rights. Classical liberal theory supports the notion that popular sovereignty rests solely within representational mechanisms, where citizen participation is limited primarily to voting for governmental representatives (Sandel, 1996, chap. 1). Principal-agent theories are derived from this philosophical context.

Though liberalism has been dominant throughout most of American history, a classical republican undercurrent has also existed and has reemerged in importance at various times in the United States (Bellah et al., 1985, pp. 28–31; Box, 1998, pp. 12–13; McSwite, 1997, chaps. 3, 4). Self-government and community are at the heart of this philosophy. Classical republicans believe in a high level of interaction among citizens and between citizens and government. This approach is based on a tradition of face-to-face problem solving, with an implicit belief that people can "rise above their particular interests to pursue a common good" (Kemmis, 1990, p. 11). To do this, citizens must be able to deliberate on the issues of the day and come to some consensus on what is best for the community, as well as feel a sense of mutual responsibility for one another (Follett, 1998). The ability to do this depends not only on a virtuous citizenry equally capable of participation, but also on the ability of citizens to understand each other and come to some notion of the common good. It is a reemphasis on this "second language" of moral discourse (Bellah et al., 1985, pp. 28–31) that provides the foundation for a notion of democracy useful for viewing nonprofit organizations from a broader perspective. Thus, a definition of democracy for this broader view considers participatory and substantive notions of democracy emphasized to a greater degree by republicanism. This is the "full democracy" described by Adams et al. (1990, pp. 228–229):

> Full democratic rule (a) ensures that all adults have a genuine opportunity to participate in public discussions of issues that affect the conditions of their lives and to exercise decisive judgment about public actions that may affect those conditions, and (b) achieves outcomes that are consistent with choices the people collectively make about the public conditions of their lives.

Philanthropy's Benefits to Democracy

Ideas of philanthropy have long played an important role in Western political and social theory. Communitarian, liberal, and left thinkers have promoted philanthropic activity as an important basis for good democratic governance and for limiting, supporting, or extending the state (Passey & Tonkiss, 2000, p. 33). To advocates, philanthropic institutions' "special strength is in providing a democratic political opportunity structure, encouraging indigenous leadership capabilities, shifting to an asset rather than a deficit-based understanding of communities, and providing a forum for citizenship" (Clarke, 2001, p. 141). This is largely what Tocqueville (1835/2000) wrote about in his mid-nineteenth-century publication, *Democracy in America.* Tocqueville observed that "Americans of all ages, all conditions, and all dispositions" (p. 630) continually joined together in informal voluntary associations for mutual benefit. Based on Tocqueville's observations, voluntary associations were seen as means for citizens to achieve the virtues necessary for democratic citizenship. As "laboratories for democracy," they helped citizens learn the civic virtues of trust, moderation, compromise, and reciprocity, and the skills of democratic discussion and organization (Newton, 1997, p. 579), and linked individuals' private interests to broader community interests. Thus, philanthropy and voluntarism are often seen as a key to enhancing political participation in the wider community (Almond & Verba, 1963; Barber, 1998; Evans & Boyte, 1986; Skocpol, 2003; Verba, Schlozman, & Brady, 1995).

In contemporary discourse, associational life has moved to the center of many democratic theories (Warren, 2001, p. 4). Following Tocqueville, some see the vitality of association as an indication of the health of democracy in particular and society in general (Berger & Neuhaus, 1996, p. 163; Van Til, 2000). Civic republicans such as Sandel and Bellah have emphasized the positive impact of association on civic virtues (Warren, 2001, p. 9). This is important in the context of modernity where associations can mediate between the private sphere of the individual and the public sphere of the state (Berger & Neuhaus, 1996), counteracting the processes of fragmentation and individualization within modern society (Durkheim, 1984). According to Warren (2001), critical theorists such as Habermas, Cohen and Arato, Offe, Preuss, and Beck, who favor radical democracy, believe "associations can provide the social infrastructure of robust democracy by enabling direct self-governance, providing venues for participating in public conversations and opinions, and securing influence over states and markets" (p. 10). There is also an emerging group of associative democrats such as Hirst (1994) and Cohen and Rogers (1995), "who see associations as means of unburdening the state and revitalizing smaller-scale, functionally delineated arenas of democratic decision making" (Warren, 2001, p. 10). They can do this by providing information, equalizing representation, educating citizens, and providing alternative forms of governance (Cohen & Rogers, 1995).

Similarly, Putnam (1993, 2000) suggests that voluntary associations are significant contributors to the effectiveness and stability of democratic governance. This is due to the internal effects on members who develop habits of cooperation, solidarity, and public spiritedness and the external effects, which include effective social collaboration and self-government. Putnam believes voluntary associations have the potential to strengthen citizenship. He claims members of associations display more political sophistication, social trust, and political participation than others and argues that since voluntary associations represent horizontal relations of reciprocity and cooperation, rather than vertical relations of authority and dependency, they are essential to the production and reproduction of social capital. Putnam (1993, p. 167) defines social capital as the "features of social organization, such as trust, norms, and networks that can improve the efficiency of society by facilitating coordinated actions." Nonprofit organizations, emerging as modern versions of voluntary associations in the welfare state, allow for a broad array of activities and services to be available to Americans that may not be provided otherwise. They also permit a range of values and points of view to be expressed within society (Salamon, 1995). Such a pluralist environment preserves choices and enables individuals to act on their own ideas and values in relation to the common good. It also ensures that the government remains accountable to these individuals and others by both augmenting and restricting the political system (Berger & Neuhaus, 1996, chap. 6).

Philanthropy's Detriments to Democracy

Though philanthropy and its institutions contribute to democracy in several ways as noted above, they also have several negative aspects that are problematic for democracy. These include reduced volunteerism and citizen participation due to a modernization of the philanthropic sector as well as several inherent anti-democratic elements.

The Modernization of the Philanthropic Sector

Since the early days of the American republic, the rise of modernity and its component parts—rational bureaucratic organization, liberal individualism, and the capitalist economic system—have played a dominant role in shaping the United States' culture, economy, and politics. Though modernity has brought many benefits, it has also led to several social and economic challenges such as an excessive focus on individualism, the separation of public and private spheres, alienation and anxiety, deterioration of the public sphere, and economic inequality. These have all had detrimental effects on civic engagement and democracy. Because philanthropy is embedded in the social, political, and economic environment, it has mirrored changes in the larger society. As early as the mid-nineteenth century (Gross, 2003), and continuing through the scientific charity and philanthropy movements (Lubove, 1965) and to today (Eikenberry, 2005; Putnam, 1995, 2000; Skocpol, 2002), nonprofit organizations and philanthropy have become more modernized—rationalized, professionalized, and marketized—which has meant less opportunity for democratic, face-to-face, local citizen participation in the sense praised by Tocqueville and others.

The most recent manifestation of the modernization of the sector is the replacement of traditional voluntary associations—such as Kiwanis, Lions, Rotary, and League of Women Voters—by a new wave of national associational launchings. These new organizations are a different breed: professionally led advocacy groups. According to Skocpol (2003), "social movements of the 1960s and 1970s helped to trigger a reorganization of national civic life, in which professionally managed associations and institutions proliferated while cross-class membership associations lost ground" (p. 13). These groups (such as the AARP or Sierra Club) have narrower missions, and either few or no members (Brody, 2002, p. 832; Putnam, 2000, p. 49; Van Til, 2000, p. 194) or thin memberships based on computer-directed mailings to individuals (skewed toward the upper end of the U.S. income distribution) who send checks (Skocpol, 1999; 2002, p. 132) and perhaps occasionally read a newsletter (Putnam, 1995, p. 71). Individualized contact and narrow, instrumental foci are the norm (Skocpol, 2003, pp. 156–158). Within these groups, there is no longer face-to-face contact with membership or a concern for fellow citizenship; thus, ordinary citizens are less likely to be mobilized at the local level. Member ties are through common symbols, common leaders, and perhaps common ideals, but not with one another (Putnam, 1995, p. 71). Putnam (2000, pp. 49–53) argues that these so-called tertiary organizations, which are very different from the face-to-face associations described by Tocqueville, may not play an adequate role in preparing citizens for their role in a democracy.

The Anti-Democratic Side of the Philanthropic Sector

Added to the problems created by the modernization of the field is the negative or anti-democratic side of philanthropy that few neo-Tocquevillians and other philanthropic supporters consider in their praise of philanthropy and nonprofit organizations. Philanthropy and its institutions may not only serve as mechanisms for civic participation, as Tocqueville observed, but also as threats to political and social institutions by maintaining social and economic divisions and inequality. This is so because philanthropy generally does not redistribute resources to where they may be most needed, is fragmented and focuses on the short-term, maintains elite hegemonic control, and creates an "us versus them" asymmetric relationship among citizens, all of which are detrimental to democracy.

Inadequate Distribution of Resources

One of the reasons Americans continue to be philanthropic is their belief that nonprofit organizations and other philanthropic institutions largely benefit the poor and the most disadvantaged (Diaz, 2002, p. 517). But who does the philanthropic sector actually serve? Although philanthropy performs many necessary functions, it cannot guarantee equity of support for a variety of institutions, causes, and citizens because both private giving and volunteering are inherently limited by choice and geography. Philanthropic particularism (the way nonprofits, their donors, and volunteers choose to focus on particular causes) and philanthropic disparity (the charitable differences among communities) invariably affect the role that individual giving and volunteering play in financing the philanthropic sector (Hodgkinson, 2002, pp. 390–391). According to Hodgkinson (2002, p. 391), "such particularism can cause fundraising to exacerbate the mismatch between society's needs and available resources." For example, "the American Cancer Society and the American Heart Association, both dealing with major threats to our health, are the giant fundraisers. Yet, the nation's fourth biggest killer, kidney disease, ranks at the bottom in health fundraising efforts" (p. 391). In addition, because the philanthropic sector is so decentralized and locally focused, it does not or cannot reallocate resources from affluent to distressed communities. This is a significant problem when one considers that about 90 percent of charitable contributions are raised and spent locally (Wolpert, 1997, p. 106), affluent communities are more generous than distressed communities where there are wider variations in income and racial/ethnic populations (Wolpert, 1993), and since the 1970s there has been an increasing residential segregation of Americans by income (Wolpert, 1999, p. 238).

Research shows that philanthropic giving does not go to those most in need. Private charitable donations go primarily to religious organizations and private higher education rather than to areas like human services (AAFRC, 2004). In fact, since the 1970s, giving to higher education, the arts, and private foundations has increased as a percentage of total individual giving, while giving to human services, health, and international aid has declined (Hodgkinson, 2002, p. 396). Wolpert (1997, p. 101) estimates that only about 10 percent of charitable contributions are targeted to the poor. These giving patterns reflect the fact that people give to whom and what they know, and to causes with which they can identify and are physically or emotionally attached (Ostrander & Schervish, 1990, p. 74; Schervish, 1995; Schervish & Herman, 1988). According to Schervish and Havens (2001, p. 91), "the more closely donors are associated with charitable causes, and the more intensely donors feel the beneficiaries of their giving share a fate with them, the greater is the amount of charitable giving." Thus, wealthy philanthropists—who provide the bulk of philanthropic dollars—tend to give the majority of their donations to organizations from which they or their family directly benefit, such as the symphony, church, or their alma mater (Odendahl, 1990, p. 67;

Ostrower, 1995) as well as to amenity services such as education, culture, and health (Wolpert, 1993, p. 7).

This is true as well for non-wealthy individuals. Overall, most donations go to support community churches and synagogues, YMCAs, museums, and parochial schools—"services that donors themselves use—and are not freely available to target the neediest and to sustain safety nets" (Wolpert, 1997, p. 101). Philanthropy has appeared to become even more amenities-focused in the past twenty or more years (Diaz, 2002, p. 519). Even when individuals give beyond their immediate family, it is usually to relatives and friends more so than to nonprofit organizations or charitable causes. A recent national survey found that 56 percent of respondents indicated their household gave an average of $1,527 (3.3 percent of average household income) to assist relatives and friends who did not live with them. This is compared to an average household charitable contribution of $902 (2 percent of household income) for the same respondents (Steuerle & Hodgkinson, 1999, p. 76).

Additionally, organizations that rely heavily on philanthropic donations are less likely to serve poor populations. Salamon (1992) found in a study of human service organizations that the majority of organizations studied did not provide services or advocacy for the poor. Of 1,474 agencies reporting on whether they served poor clients (family income below the official poverty line), only 27 percent indicated that most of their clients were poor. Another 20 percent indicated that they serviced some poor clients (between 21 percent and 50 percent of the total client base), suggesting that the remaining 53 percent had few poor clients (below 20 percent). Among those that did serve the poor, the bulk of their funding was from government sources rather than private giving. Diaz (2002, p. 518) surmises that by and large the types of organizations that benefit from private philanthropy are elite institutions that serve non-poor, non-Hispanic whites.

Beyond these issues of redistribution, it is clear from available data that the philanthropic sector does not have the capacity to provide needed services. Certainly, the philanthropic sector is a significant force in the United States. According to the Independent Sector, it consists of more than 1.2 million nonprofit organizations, receives over $665 billion in revenue annually, and employs 7 percent of the nation's work force (Independent Sector, 2001, p. 3). In 2003, private contributions amounted to $241 billion (AAFRC, 2004). The Independent Sector estimates that over 70 percent of American households give money to charities, while over 50 percent give their time (Independent Sector, 2001, p. 3). Yet, if one analyzes the past thirty years, charitable giving in the United States continues to represent less than 2 percent of personal income and 2 percent of the U.S. gross domestic product (Burke, 2001, p. 187). In fact, Burke (2001) notes: "As measured by individual contributions as a percentage of after-tax (disposable) income, Americans became *less* generous despite great increases in standards of living, education, and the reach of liberally oriented mass media since the 1960s" (p. 185, italics added). This is despite a significant growth in personal wealth in recent decades where the number of households with a net worth of $1 million or more has grown from 3.5 million in 1994 to an estimated 8.3 million in 2000 (Hodgkinson, 2002, p. 395).

Part of the reason for this decline may be attributed to recent changes in tax policy. According to Hodgkinson (2002), "beginning with the Reagan tax cuts of 1981, Congress has generally acted over the past two decades to lower income tax rates, capital gains tax rates, and estate tax rates" (p. 402). These changes may reduce the incentive to give at death by increasing the cost of such giving (Abramson, Salamon, & Steuerle, 1999, p. 114). The U.S. Department of Treasury reports that only 19 percent of those paying federal estate taxes (estates valued at $600,000 or more) reported charitable bequests in 1992. This totaled $8 million, or only about 8 percent of the total net worth of those surveyed (Joulfaian, 1998, p. 20). Another reason for a decline in giving may be due to growing economic inequality in the past few decades (Krugman, 2002). A growing gap between the rich and poor has significant implications for household giving. National surveys of giving and volunteering in the United States conducted by the Independent Sector show that financial worry is the most prevalent reason individuals cite for not giving (Hodgkinson, 2002).

One result of this decline is that private giving to charitable organizations, as a share of their total income, has declined substantially in recent years. According to Wolpert (1997), "as recently as the mid-1950s, charitable organizations raised 70% of their income from donations" (p. 100). However, more recently, Hodgkinson and Weitzman (2000, p. 11) show that private contributions as a percent of charitable organizations' total annual funds declined from 26 percent in 1977 to 18 percent in 1992. More specifically, the share of all private contributions going to human service organizations declined from 10 percent to 8 percent between the 1970s and mid-1990s (Burke, 2000, p. 46), while United Way funding—which typically goes to human service organizations—hardly grew during this time (Smith, 2002, p. 169). Private giving for all tax-exempt organizations remains at around 20 percent of total revenue today (Independent Sector, 2001, p. 5).

Private giving for social welfare services is not only substantially less than government funding, nonprofit organizations rely on government for much of their support. Boris and Steuerle (1999) note that private donations to charitable organizations represent less than 10 percent of the federal government's spending on welfare. Additionally, in 1997, funding from the government accounted for over 30 percent of charitable organizations' funding (Independent Sector, 2001, p. 5). There is strong evidence that the philanthropic sector has historically been reliant on government support (Burke, 2000; Salamon, 1995; Skocpol, 2003, p. 12) and private giving is significantly linked to government funding levels. Wolpert (1993) shows that "places that are generous in their state and local government programs tend to be generous in their charitable contributions as well" (p. 2).

Fragmented and Short-term Focus

Even where certain charitable causes or nonprofit organizations serving the poor enjoy popularity among donors, and where there are many organizations that provide services, there are difficulties associated with meeting the needs of the poor and addressing deep-seated societal problems. The emergency food relief system is a good example. The current emergency food system, begun in the 1980s, consists of tens of thousands of emergency food programs serving nearly one-tenth of the American population (Poppendieck, 1998, p. 3). Volunteers and donors from all walks of life and economic levels show their support for food banks and soup kitchens—from Boy Scout canned food drives to multi-million-dollar corporate food donation programs. Yet, even with such widespread support, there are many problems with the system. For example, according to Poppendieck (1998, pp. 213–222):

- The food available is often insufficient in quantity and quality. Donated items are often given in too small or too large amounts and/or are given because they are not good enough for others to purchase. Additionally, it is impossible to choose and serve the kinds of food people will like.
- The nutritional value of donated items is often inadequate. A 1986 study of soup kitchen meals in the state of New York found that over half the soup kitchens studied did not provide at least one-third of the Recommended Dietary Allowances for an adult.
- Many programs are inaccessible. There is lack of convergence between need and supply, and thus there are gaps in coverage. Additionally, many of those who need help the most do not have reliable transportation to access food.

Though each individual emergency food organization may be extremely efficient, the system as a whole is inefficient and inadequate because of these problems, which are indicative of those found in many organizations and causes that depend on private giving and volunteering. This is because the inherent character of philanthropy is fragmented, inconstant, and has a tendency toward short-term problem solving rather than addressing long-term, underlying social problems. Philanthropy and its institutions are often parochial, episodic, and "too dependent upon the moral imagination of its affluent members" (May, 2000, p. xx) and have the vice of "inconstancy" because philanthropists usually give out of surplus and a doctrine of "love without ties"—they want to give without getting entangled in the on-going toils of the receiver (p. xxii). Giving and volunteering are often viewed as an individual (heroic) effort based on individual choice; there is typically little incentive or even ability for individuals to look at more comprehensive efforts for fundamental, long-term change (Ostrander, 1989, p. 228).

Because of these inherent difficulties, philanthropy largely serves as a Band-Aid or even mask for deep structural problems. Poppendieck (1998, chap. 9) shows in the case of emergency food relief that many in this industry are so busy building bigger, stronger, and better food programs, they lose sight of the reasons people need such services in the first place. This sentiment is not new among scholars and philosophers. Henry David Thoreau attacked the hypocrisy of philanthropists "who relieve misery just enough to perpetuate the system producing that misery" (Fischer, 1995, p. 281), and John Stuart Mill argued that "it is the great error of reformers and philanthropists in our time to nibble at the consequences of unjust power, instead of redressing the injustice itself" (Fischer, 1995, p. 282). In the early days of the American republic, James Madison was well aware of the "mischief of faction," or problem of fragmentation caused by a heavy reliance on voluntarism. He knew that associations could not maintain equality of condition, only equality of opportunity, and that there was a need for a high level of civic consciousness among citizens if democracy was to succeed in this environment (Cohen & Rogers, 1995, p. 7). Rousseau outlawed secondary associations all together in *On the Social Contract* because he thought they were incompatible with the common good (Warren, 2001, p. 11).

Poppendieck (1998, pp. 26–27) suggests the general popularity of giving and volunteering can perhaps best be explained by its function as a moral safety valve to relieve the discomfort people feel when they are confronted with privation and suffering amid general comfort and abundance. In this context, charity serves to mitigate guilt while economic and political systems maintain poverty and inequality. Poppendieck believes emergency food programs serve as an illusion of effective community action, lulling the public into complacency. For example, canned food drives give people a warm, fuzzy feeling but do not cause them to think about why people continue to be in need (p. 38). Philanthropy, as in the case with emergency food, convinces politicians and the public at large that the immediate problem is under control and that it is the appropriate response to poverty and economic inequality (p. 302). With the outward appearance that no one will starve, emergency food makes it easier for society to shed its responsibility for the poor. Poppendieck (1998) writes: "By harnessing a wealth of volunteer effort and donations, it makes private programs appear cheaper and more cost effective than their public counterparts, thus reinforcing an ideology of voluntarism that obscures the fundamental destruction of rights" (p. 6). This represents a larger trend in American public policy, prevalent since the 1980s, to retreat from rights to gifts.

Maintains Elite Control

Philanthropy often allows wealthy elites to cover up their hegemonic control over society, which perpetuates their wealth and powerful positions. Tocqueville himself warned that private associations could form something like a separate nation within a nation (Whittington, 1998, p. 24). He and others saw that such intermediary bodies often formed around special interests that not only diminished the sovereignty of the state, but also favored propertied minorities with the resources to devote to their establishment and perpetuation (Hall, 1999, pp. 9–10).

Elite philanthropic foundations especially have long been criticized in the United States for their undemocratic nature and use of assets to bring about change in their own interest. In 1915, at the federal level, the Walsh Commission attacked foundations as bastions of corporate capitalism and as subversive to American democracy (Nielsen, 1972, pp. 5–6). Foundations became the objects of criticism again during the hysteria of the McCarthy period after World War II when they "were criticized for what were viewed as 'suspect' liberal ideologies" (Brilliant, 2000, p. 11). The Select Committee to Investigate Foundations and Comparable Organizations, established in April 1952 and led by Congressman E. Eugene Cox, accused foundations of giving money to support anti-American, pro-communist causes (Nielsen, 1972, p. 6). More recently, Gramscian scholars have criticized wealthy philanthropists, especially foundations, for using their resources to create a "hegemonic class" of intellectuals who support their commitment to industrial capitalism (Arnove, 1980; Fisher, 1983; Roelofs, 1995). Arnove (1980) argues that foundations have a corrosive influence on a democratic society because "they represent relatively unregulated and unaccountable concentrations of power and wealth which buy talent, promote causes, and, in effect, establish an agenda of what merits society's attention. They serve as 'cooling out' agencies, delaying and preventing more radical, structural change" (Arnove, 1980, p. 1). Foundations and other philanthropic organizations are typically governed by private, self-perpetuating boards, which can "divert decision mak-

ing in the arts, culture, education, health, and welfare from public representatives to a private power elite" (Odendahl, 1990, p. 3), providing the philanthropic elite with a vehicle to make public decisions with little accountability
to, or scrutiny by, the general public and elected officials. This means that
many major policy decisions are unseen and un-debated in the larger public
arena (Wagner, 2000, p. 94).

Creates an "Us Versus Them" Ethic

There is typically an "us versus them" ethic, or asymmetric relationship,
promoted by philanthropy that further threatens democracy. Embedded in
the philanthropic system is the perception that people who need help are
inferior and the help they receive is a gift in response to a deficit rather than
an entitlement or earning. For example, images of emergency food clients
used to attract donors are often of patient sufferers, humbly waiting for help
(Poppendieck, 1998, p. 303). The homeless present a similar case, where
they are forced to remain supplicants and objects of charity if they want to
receive help. If the homeless organize and make demands, they lose appeal
as a charitable cause. This "inhibits direct, aggressive action by poor people
on their own behalf, which is essential to the initiation of political reform"
(Katz, 1989, p. 194).

When the social world becomes divided into givers and receivers, "haves"
and "have-nots," a conceit or moral superiority is encouraged among bene-
factors and a feeling of demeaning inferiority among beneficiaries. A society
relying too exclusively on philanthropy can easily fall into moral traps because it creates the fiction of a self-sufficient giver. In this context, donors
become too overbearing and too demeaning, are given to covert control, become too insensitive to long-range negative side effects of interventions, are
too given to monumentalism, are too oriented to their own glory, and are
sometimes too narrow or inflexible (May, 2000, p. xxi). Psychologically,
beneficiaries are put in a position that is demeaning and destructive to the
human spirit because asking for help can be perceived as an admission of
inadequacy (Menninger, 2000, p. 211). This "us versus them" dichotomy
can eventually lead to extreme and dangerous behavior. Wagner (2000, p. 5)
notes: "The rhetoric of virtue has always coexisted with a deep-seated streak
of violent repression in America: the physical and cultural genocide against
American Indians, the enslavement of Africans, and the conquering of foreign lands." Ultimately, philanthropy may serve to erode "the cultural pre-
requisites for a vigorous democracy [because] we become a society of givers
and receivers, rather than a commonwealth of fellow citizens" (Poppendieck,
1998, p. 255).

The Need to Build a More Democratic Philanthropy

Given trends of a growing modernization of philanthropy and its subsequent effects on civic engagement and democracy, as well as the negative aspects of philanthropy that have persisted since at least the American founding, a strong argument could be made to eliminate the philanthropic sector altogether. Yet, the nature of the social and political environment in the United States necessitates reliance on nongovernmental entities. Americans have always had a certain fear or dislike of excessive state power, and it is clear from the past that the market cannot always be depended upon to adequately address citizens' needs (e.g., the Great Depression of the 1930s). This explains to some degree the sustained existence of large foundations, charitable organizations, and a reliance on philanthropy in general (Nagai, Lerner, & Rothman, 1994, p. 4). If there is little choice but to rely on nonprofit and philanthropic institutions, then it becomes increasingly important, in the current political and socioeconomic environment, to understand how to add to nonprofit organizations' and philanthropy's ability to enhance democracy.

What would a democratic nonprofit and philanthropic sector look like? According to Eikenberry (2005), it might:

1. Provide more individuals of diverse backgrounds with opportunities for increased participation in philanthropy as well as opportunities for face-to-face discourse among citizens and equal opportunities to participate in decision-making, agenda-setting, and capacity-building. This builds on classical republican notions of participatory democracy that put great store on citizens' participation and role in decision-making within their communities.
2. Broaden individual participants' identification with the needs of others. This builds upon theories of bridging social capital as described by Putnam (2000) as well as the social ethics of Jane Addams (1902), linking them to Schervish and his colleagues' understandings of philanthropic motivation (Schervish, 1995; Schervish & Herman, 1988). In this context, democratization can be defined in relation to philanthropy's role in linking citizens to one another across social and economic boundaries.
3. Expand who benefits from philanthropy. Building on substantive notions of democracy, this considers philanthropy's potential role for redistributing resources by expanding the types of groups and organizations that receive funding, as well as expanding members' giving to issues and areas that are beyond their or their families' direct benefit.

These three areas might serve as keys to expanding the breadth and depth of philanthropic participation to not only counter the effects of modernization, but also to combat elite control, the creation of asymmetric relationships among citizens, and unequal philanthropic outcomes; broadening the identification individuals have with the needs of others to counter asymmetric relationships and bring about more equitable outcomes; and expanding philanthropic outcomes to increase the redistribution of resources and nullify the fragmentation and short-term focus of traditional philanthropy.

The New Philanthropy and Giving Circles

Aspects of what has become called the "new philanthropy" may serve to create a more democratic philanthropy. There has been revived attention to community in recent years (Staeheli, 1997), especially at the local level in the United States (see for example: Box, 1998; Kemmis, 1995; Putnam, 2000; Sandel, 1996). Embedded within these larger societal trends, several scholars, practitioners, and journalists claim a new era has begun in American philanthropy (Bianchi, 2000; Byrne, 2002; Cobb, 2002; McCully, 2000; Streisand, 2002). Cobb (2002, p. 126) writes that the emergence of a new philanthropy has largely been in response to several socioeconomic factors, including technological innovation, the creation of large new fortunes, the dominance of market ideology, new demographics—particularly the growing disparity between rich and poor—and government retrenchment. Unlike the modern or "mainstream" philanthropy, which has been led by large philanthropic institutions such as foundations and federated giving programs and has been characterized by rationalization, professionalization, and marketization as well as dominance by large charitable institutions, the new philanthropy is guided by individual donors and emphasizes collaboration across groups and sectors, hands-on, unconventional modes of giving and volunteering, and a focus on small organizations and grassroots problem-solving (Ellis L. Phillips Foundation, 2000, pp. 60–62).

Leading this shift in philanthropy are what some call "new and emerging donors" (Philanthropic Initiative, 2000, chap. 4). Dissatisfied with the mainstream approach to philanthropy, these donors have sought out a more engaged philanthropy (Grace & Wendroff, 2001, chap. 7). As noted by a donor, "the traditional approach of writing a check to a charitable organization or serving on a board did not seem very fulfilling. There was a desire to be more engaged in the process of giving back" (Brainerd, 1999, p. 502). New and emerging donors are described primarily as the high-tech wealthy, executives of major corporations, investment executives, consultants, and other beneficiaries of the new economy; though new and emerging donors may also come from other walks of life—especially significant within this group are women (Philanthropic Initiative, 2000, chap. 4). New and emerging donors: are typically new to wealth and giving; are younger than traditional philanthropists; recognize the value of strategic partnerships; want to control where and how theirs gifts are spent; focus on issues rather than institutions; are entrepreneurial in their giving; emphasize impact and accountability with funding recipients; and mistrust large, bureaucratic philanthropic institutions (Grace & Wendroff, 2001, chap. 7; Philanthropic Initiative, 2000, chap. 4). The hands-on, engaged philanthropy and collaboration of these new donors indicates a shift from modern philanthropy. This shift has manifested itself in several ways, including the introduction of new funding mechanisms and philosophies to enable donors to reach their philanthropic goals. One such funding mechanism is the "giving circle."

Giving circles are described as a cross between a book club and an investment group (Jones, 2000) and entail individuals "pooling their resources in support of organizations of mutual interest" (Schweitzer, 2000, p. 32). Though founded in an old idea, giving circles are new forms of collaborative giving that have been said to represent the "democratization of philanthropy" (Paulson, 2001, p. 18). Building on this assertion, and based on the notion of a democratic nonprofit and philanthropic sector outlined above, Eikenberry (2005) conducted a study of giving circles in the United States (and Canada). She identified three major types of giving circles: small groups, loose networks, and formal organizations that serve to democratize philanthropy to varying degrees depending on their size, structure, and activities.

According to Eikenberry (2005), small groups seem to be the most democratic internally—they provide the most opportunities for all members to participate in decision-making, agenda-setting, deliberation, and capacity-building within the group. However, creating these opportunities depends largely on having a small, informal structure, which also serves to limit activities that take place beyond the group. Especially for those without staff support, small groups are unable to have a comprehensive view of the needs of the community and thus fill in the gaps appropriately. Loose networks are even less comprehensive in their approach to finding funding opportunities, but they have the redeeming qualities of trying to empower members while maintaining as nonbureaucratic a structure as possible. They also seem to do the most to enable members to identify with others on a more personal, one-on-one level because loose networks tend to give money directly to individuals in need or doing good work. Formal organizations are unique in that they are much more structured and organized than the other types of giving circles, and more bureaucratic. On the one hand then, members lose the equal participation and intimacy of a small group and the informal, nonbureaucratic feel of the loose network. On the other hand, formal organizations are the most systematic about identifying needs in the community, educating members about these needs, finding appropriate funding opportunities, and enabling members to engage directly with funding recipients. They also seem to be the most dedicated to attracting diverse populations to participate.

Thus, though each type of giving circle democratizes philanthropy in different ways and to different degrees, none do it to the extent necessary to counter all of the problems of philanthropy. Even in a best-case scenario, where a majority of the membership is highly engaged in the giving circle, comprehensively educated in an issue area, and receptive to minority participants—as in the case with formal organizations—giving circles still appear to be largely upper-class, homogenous groups with a relatively small amount of resources to give away. This leads to the conclusion that, though philanthropy contributes much to society, it cannot and should not be relied upon to provide for basic needs in society.

Conclusion and Implications for Public Administration

Understanding a broader role for nonprofit organizations and philanthropy in society is important for public administrators. In this era of contracting out public services to private, nonprofit providers, public administrators might look beyond principal-agent models to guide their relationships with nonprofit organizations and consider the broader democratic implications of relying on these organizations to provide social services to the poor. The new philanthropy and giving circles highlight the importance of this. Understanding and connecting with citizens in these groups could enable public administrators to gather citizen input and engage citizens to solve problems. Donors' desire for more engagement through their philanthropy, or desire to make a difference in the community through nonbureaucratic means, may serve as a sign to public administrators that citizens want a more direct understanding and say—a closer relationship—with solving community problems.

This is relevant for public administration scholars who are interested in ways to engage citizens in governance. Several public administration scholars believe that a collaborative relationship between citizens and public administrators is desirable—even necessary—for a legitimate and effective public administration (Box, 1998; Denhardt & Denhardt, 2000; King & Stivers, 1998; McSwite, 1997; Stivers, 1994). These scholars emphasize "giving citizens the knowledge and techniques they need to deal with public policy issues and providing an open and non-threatening forum for deliberation and decision making" (Box, Marshall, Reed, & Reed, 2001, p. 616). Giving circles could serve as a forum for public administrators to engage and educate citizens in this way, as well as to empower citizens—especially women—to be involved in governance. There is a word of caution, however. Public administrators should keep in mind that giving circle members are most likely not representative of the community at large and their resources are limited. It is also not clear, as indicated earlier, how well "outside" influence would be accepted within these independent groups.

On an instrumental level, the new philanthropy and giving circles may also serve as an avenue for bringing resources to bear on certain community problems. Giving circles focusing on specific community issues may be able to help meliorate problems, though this will necessarily be done on giving circle members' terms rather than through a mandate from government officials. This means that giving circle funding might prove helpful but cannot be counted upon as a reliable source for solving community problems. Nonetheless, giving circles might be considered partners in battling some community problems, much in the way that local governments have relied on private philanthropy in the past for one-time projects such as libraries or parks (Irvin & Carr, 2004).

Ultimately, given the findings from this study, citizens and policy makers need to discuss the proper role for philanthropy in our society. Should it be relied upon to provide for basic human needs? Philanthropy does well at addressing small short-term problems and enhancing quality of life. It does not do so well at reducing, preventing, or eliminating need. In fact, philanthropy's most important role in society may be nothing more or less than enabling people to be philanthropic: to liberate the "human aspiration to give" and "enable human beings to develop their full human potential" (Gunderman, 2003, pp. 9–10). This is an important role in society, and much needed. Thus, is it appropriate to require philanthropy to do something different, that it cannot do? These are issues to consider as citizens, public administrators, and politicians decide how to create a better society for all.

References

AAFRC Trust for Philanthropy (2004). *Giving USA charts.* Retrieved February 9, 2004, from www.aafrc.org/gusa/.

Abramson, A. J., Salamon, L. M., & Steuerle, C. E. (1999). The nonprofit sector and the federal budget: Recent history and future directions. In E. T. Boris & C. E. Steuerle (Eds.), *Nonprofits and government* (pp. 99–139). Washington, DC: Urban Institute.

Adams, G. B., Bowerman, P. V., Dolbeare, K. M., & Stivers, C. (1990). Joining purpose to practice: A democratic identity for the public service. In H. D. Kass & B. L. Catron (Eds.), *Images and identities in public administration* (pp. 219–240). Newbury Park, CA: Sage.

Addams, J. (1902). *Democracy and social ethics.* New York: Macmillan.

Almond, G. A., & Verba, S. (1963). *The civic culture: Political attitudes and democracy in five nations.* Princeton, NJ: Princeton University Press.

Arnove, R. F. (1980). Introduction. In R. F. Arnove (Ed.), *Philanthropy and cultural imperialism: The foundations at home and abroad* (pp. 1–24). Bloomington: Indiana University Press.

Barber, B. R. (1998). *A place for us: How to make society civil and democracy strong.* New York: Hill & Wang.

Beito, D. T., Gordon, P., & Tabarrok, A. (2002). *The voluntary city: Choice, community, and civil society.* Ann Arbor: University of Michigan Press.

Bellah, R. N., Madsen, R., Sullivan, W. M., Swidler, A., & Tipton, S. M. (1985). *Habits of the heart: Individualism and commitment in American life.* New York: Harper & Row.

Berger, P. L., & Neuhaus, R. J. (1996). *To empower people: From state to civil society* (2nd ed.). Washington, DC: AEI Press.

Bernstein, S. R. (1991). *Managing contracted services in the nonprofit agency: Administrative, ethical, and political issues.* Philadelphia: Temple University Press.

Bianchi, A. (2000, October). Serving nonprofits: The new philanthropy. *Inc.*, 23–25.

Boris, E., & Steuerle, E. (1999, October 1). What charities cannot do. *Christian Science Monitor*, p. 11.

Box, R. C. (1998). *Citizen governance: Leading American communities into the 21st century.* Thousand Oaks, CA: Sage.

Box, R. C., Marshall, G. S., Reed, B. J., & Reed, C. M. (2001). New public management and substantive democracy. *Public Administration Review, 61*, 608–619.

Brainerd, P. (1999). Social Venture Partners: Engaging a new generation of givers. *Nonprofit & Voluntary Sector Quarterly, 28*, 502–507.

Brilliant, E. L. (2000). *Private charity and public inquiry: A history of the Filer and Peterson Commissions.* Bloomington: Indiana University Press.

Brody, E. (2002). Entrance, voice, and exit: The constitutional bounds of the right of association. *U.C. Davis Law Review, 35*, 821–832.

Burke, C. C. (2000, November). *Establishing a context: The elusive history of America's nonprofit domain—numbers count—if someone counted* (Working Paper 261). New Haven, CT: Yale University Program on Non-Profit Organizations.

Burke, C. C. (2001). Nonprofit history's new numbers (and the need for more). *Nonprofit & Voluntary Sector Quarterly, 30*, 174–203.

Byrne, J. A. (2002, December 2). The new face of philanthropy. *Business Week*, pp. 82–94.

Clarke, S. E. (2001). The prospects for local democratic governance: The governance roles of nonprofit organizations. *Policy Studies Review, 18*, 129–145.

Cnaan, R. A., & Boddie, S. C. (2002). Charitable choice and faith-based welfare: A call for social work. *Social Work, 47*, 224–235.

Cobb, N. K. (2002). The new philanthropy: Its impact on funding arts and culture. *Journal of Arts Management, Law, and Society, 32*, 125–143.

Cohen, J., & Rogers, J. (1995). *Associations and democracy.* London: Verso.

Denhardt, R. B., & Denhardt, J. V. (2000). The new public service: Serving rather than steering. *Public Administration Review, 60*, 549–559.

Diaz, W. (2002). For whom and for what? The contributions of the nonprofit sector. In L. M. Salamon (Ed.), *The state of nonprofit America* (pp. 517–536). Washington, DC: Brookings Institution.

Dicke, L. A. (2002). Ensuring accountability in human services contracting: Can stewardship theory fill the bill? *American Review of Public Administration, 32*, 455–470.

Durkheim, E. (1984). *The division of labor in society.* New York: Free Press.

Dwivedi, O. P., & Jabbra, J. G. (1988). Public service responsibility and accountability. In J. G. Jabbra & O. P. Dwivedi (Eds.), *Public service accountability* (pp. 1–16). West Hartford, CT: Kumarian.

Eikenberry, A. M. (2005). *Giving circles and the democratization of philanthropy.* Unpublished manuscript.

Ellis L. Phillips Foundation. (2000). The paradigm-shift in philanthropy. *The Catalogue for Philanthropy* (p. 61). Boston: Author.

Evans, S. M., & Boyte, H. C. (1986). *Free spaces: The sources of democratic change in America.* New York: Harper & Row.

Executive Order Nos. 13198 & 13199, 66 C.F.R. 8497–8500 (2001).

Fischer, M. (1995). Philanthropy and injustice in Mill and Addams. *Nonprofit and Voluntary Sector Quarterly, 24*, 281–292.

Fisher, D. (1983). The role of philanthropic foundations in the reproduction and production of hegemony. *Sociology, 17*, 206–233.

Follett, M. P. (1998). *The new state: Group organization, the solution of popular government.* University Park: Pennsylvania State University Press. (Original work published 1918)

Frederickson, P., & London, R. (2000). Disconnect in the hollow state: The pivotal role of organizational capacity in community-based development organizations. *Public Administration Review, 60*, 230–239.

Grace, K. S., & Wendroff, A. L. (2001). *High impact philanthropy: How donors, boards, and nonprofit organizations can transform communities.* New York: John Wiley & Sons.

Grønbjerg, K. A., & Salamon, L. M. (2002). Devolution, marketization, and the changing shape of government-nonprofit relations. In L. M. Salamon (Ed.), *The state of nonprofit America* (pp. 447–470). Washington, DC: Brookings Institution.

Gross, R. (2003). Giving in America: From charity to philanthropy. In L. J. Friedman & M. D. McGarvie (Eds.), *Charity, philanthropy, and civility in American history* (pp. 29–48). Cambridge, UK: Cambridge University Press.

Gunderman, R. B. (2003, December). Giving and human excellence: The paradigm of liberal philanthropy. Retrieved August 20, 2004, from www. thephilanthropicenterprise.org/main/library.php/87/p.

Hall, P. D. (1999). Resolving the dilemmas of democratic governance: The historical development of trusteeship in America, 1636–1996. In E. C. Lagemann (Ed.), *Philanthropic foundations: New scholarship, new possibilities* (pp. 3–42). Bloomington: Indiana University Press.

Hall, P. D. (2003). The welfare state and the careers of public and private institutions since 1945. In L. J. Friedman & M. D. McGarvie (Eds.), *Charity, philanthropy, and civility in American history* (pp. 363–383). Cambridge, UK: Cambridge University Press.

Held, D. (1996). *Models of democracy.* Stanford, CA: Stanford University Press.

Hirst, P. (1994). *Associative democracy: New forms of economic and social governance.* Amherst: University of Massachusetts Press.

Hodgkinson, V. A. (with Nelson, K. E., & Sivak, E. D., Jr.) (2002). Individual giving and volunteering. In L. M. Salamon (Ed.), *The state of nonprofit America* (pp. 387–420). Washington, DC: Brookings Institution.

Hodgkinson, V. A., & Weitzman, M. S. (2000). Overview: The state of the independent sector. In J. S. Ott (Ed.), *The nature of the nonprofit sector* (pp. 9–22). Boulder, CO: Westview.

Independent Sector (2001). *The nonprofit almanac in brief: Facts and figures on the*

Independent Sector 2001. Washington, DC: Author. Retrieved November 2001, from www.IndependentSector.org.

Irvin, R. A., & Carr, P. (2004, November). *The emerging role of private philanthropy in local government finance*. Paper presented at the 33rd Annual ARNOVA Conference, Los Angeles.

Jones, M. M. (2000, August 1). Circular reasoning can prove most charitable indeed: "Giving circles" help focus, fuel philanthropy. *Concord Monitor.* Retrieved December 12, 2002, from www.givingnewengland.org/press_top_00_08.html.

Joulfaian, D. (1998, December). *The federal estate and gift tax: Description, profile of taxpayers, and economic consequences* (Office of Tax Analysis Paper 80). Washington, DC: U.S. Department of Treasury. Retrieved July 21, 2002, from www.ustreas.gov/ota/otapapers.html.

Katz, M. B. (1989). *The undeserving poor: From the war on poverty to the war on welfare*. New York: Pantheon.

Kemmis, D. (1990). *Community and the politics of place*. Norman: University of Oklahoma Press.

Kettl, D. (1993). *Sharing power.* Washington, DC: Brookings Institution.

King, C. S., & Stivers, C. (1998). Introduction: The anti-government era. In C. S. King & C. Stivers (Eds.), *Government is us: Public administration in an anti-government era* (pp. 3–18). Thousand Oaks, CA: Sage.

Krugman, P. (2002, October 20). For richer. *New York Times Magazine*, p. 62.

Lubove, R. (1965). *The professional altruist: The emergence of social work as a career, 1880–1930*. Cambridge, MA: Harvard University Press.

Matsui, E., & Chuman, J. (2001, January/February). The case against charitable choice. *Humanist*, pp. 31–33.

May, W. F. (2000). Introduction. In W. F. May & A. L. Soens, Jr. (Eds.), *The ethics of giving and receiving: Am I my foolish brother's keeper?* (pp. xvii–xl). Dallas: Cary M. Maguire Center for Ethics and Public Responsibility and Southern Methodist University Press.

McCully, G. (2000, March/April). Is this a paradigm shift? *Foundation News & Commentary*, pp. 20–22.

McSwite, O. C. (1997). *Legitimacy in public administration: A discourse analysis*. Newbury Park, CA: Sage.

Menninger, R. W. (2000). Observations on the psychology of giving and receiving money. In W. F. May & A. L. Soens, Jr. (Eds.), *The ethics of giving and receiving: Am I my foolish brother's keeper?* (pp. 202–215). Dallas: Cary M. Maguire Center for Ethics and Public Responsibility and Southern Methodist University Press.

Milward, H. B. (1994). Nonprofit contracting and the hollow state. *Public Administration Review, 54*, 73–77.

Milward, H. B., Provan, K., & Smith, L. J. (1994). Human service contracting and coordination: The market for mental health services. In J. Perry (Ed.), *Research in public administration* (Vol. 3, pp. 231–279). Greenwich, CT: JAI.

Milward, H. B., Provan, K., & Else, B. (1993). What does the hollow state look like? In B. Bozeman (Ed.), *Public management theory: The state of the art* (pp. 309-323). San Francisco: Jossey Bass.

Nagai, A., Lerner, R., & Rothman, S. (1994). *Giving for social change: Foundations, public policy, and the American political agenda*. Westport, CT: Praeger.

Newton, K. (1997, March/April). Social capital and democracy. *American Behavioral Scientist, 40*, 575–586.

Nielsen, W. A. (1972). *The big foundations*. New York: Columbia University Press.

Odendahl, T. (1990). *Charity begins at home: Generosity and self-interest among the philanthropic elite.* New York: Basic Books.

Olasky, M. (1992). *The tragedy of American compassion.* Washington, DC: Regnery Gateway.

Ostrander, S. A. (1989). The problem of poverty and why philanthropy neglects it. In V. A. Hodgkinson & R. W. Lyman & Associates (Eds.), *The future of the nonprofit sector: Challenges, changes, and policy considerations* (pp. 219–236). San Francisco: Jossey-Bass.

Ostrander, S. A., & Schervish, P. G. (1990). Giving and getting: Philanthropy as a social relation. In J. Van Til (Ed.), *Critical issues in American philanthropy: Strengthening theory and practice* (pp. 67–98). San Francisco: Jossey-Bass.

Ostrower, F. (1995). *Why the wealthy give: The culture of elite philanthropy.* Princeton, NJ: Princeton University Press.

Passey, A., & Tonkiss, F. (2000). Trust, voluntary association and civil society. In F. Tonkiss, A. Passey, N. Fenton, & L. C. Hems (Eds.), *Trust and civil society* (pp. 31–51). New York: St. Martins.

Paulson, A. (2001, October 1). A pooling of funds to boost donors' impact. *Christian Science Monitor, 93*, p. 18.

Philanthropic Initiative (2000). *What's a donor to do? The state of donor resources in America today.* Retrieved June 23, 2002, from www.tpi.org/_tpi/ promoting/ research.htm.

Poppendieck, J. (1998). *Sweet charity? Emergency food and the end of entitlement.* New York: Penguin.

Putnam, R. D. (1993). *Making democracy work: Civic traditions in modern Italy.* Princeton, NJ: Princeton University Press.

Putnam, R. D. (1995). Bowling alone: America's declining social capital. *Journal of Democracy, 6,* 65–78.

Putnam, R. D. (2000). *Bowling alone: The collapse and revival of American community.* New York: Simon & Schuster.

Roelofs, J. (1995). The third sector as a protective layer for capitalism. *Monthly Review, 47,* pp. 16–25.

Rom, M. C. (1999). From welfare state to opportunity inc. *American Behavioral Scientist, 43,* 155–176.

Salamon, L. M. (1981). Rethinking public management: Third-party government and the changing forms of government action. *Public Policy, 29,* 255–275.

Salamon, L. M. (1992). Social services. In C. T. Clotfelter (Ed.), *Who benefits from the nonprofit sector?* (pp. 134–173). Chicago: University of Chicago Press.

Salamon, L. M. (1995). *Partners in public service: Government-nonprofit relations in the modern welfare state.* Baltimore: Johns Hopkins University Press.

Salamon, L. M. (2002). The resilient sector: The state of nonprofit America. In L. M. Salamon (Ed.), *The state of nonprofit America* (pp. 3–61). Washington, DC: Brookings Institution.

Sandel, M. J. (1996). *Democracy's discontent: America in search of a public philosophy.* Cambridge, MA: Belknap Press of Harvard University Press.

Schervish, P. G. (1995). Gentle as doves and wise as serpents: The philosophy of care and sociology of transmission. In P. G. Schervish, V. A. Hodgkinson, & M. Gates (Eds.), *Care and community in modern society: Passing on the tradition of service to future generations* (pp. 1–20). San Francisco: Jossey-Bass.

Schervish, P. G., & Havens, J. J. (2001). The mind of the millionaire: Findings from a national survey on wealth and responsibility. In E. R. Tempel (Ed.), *New directions for philanthropic fundraising: Understanding donor dynamics* (pp. 75–107). San Francisco: Jossey-Bass.

Schervish, P. G., & Herman, A. (1988, July). *Empowerment and beneficence: Strategies of living and giving among the wealthy.* Final Report: The Study on Wealth and Philanthropy. Boston: Boston College Social Welfare Research Institute.

Schweitzer, C. (2000, October). Building on new foundations. *Association Management, 28–39.*

Skocpol, T. (1999). Associations without members. *American Prospect, 45*, 66–73.

Skocpol, T. (2002). The United States: From membership to advocacy. In R. D. Putnam (Ed.), *Democracies in flux: The evolution of social capital in contemporary society* (pp. 103–136). Oxford: Oxford University Press.

Skocpol, T. (2003). *Diminished democracy: From membership to management in American civic life.* Norman: University of Oklahoma Press.

Smith, S. R. (2002). Social services. In L. M. Salamon (Ed.), *The state of nonprofit America* (pp. 149–186). Washington, DC: Brookings Institution.

Staeheli, L. A. (1997). Citizenship and the search for community. In L. A. Staeheli, J. E. Kodras, & C. Flint (Eds.), *State devolution in America: Implications for a diverse society* (pp. 60–75). Thousand Oaks, CA: Sage.

Steuerle, C. E., & Hodgkinson, V. A. (1999). Meeting social needs: Comparing the resources of the independent sector and government. In E. T. Boris & C. E. Steuerle (Eds.), *Nonprofits and government: Collaboration and conflict* (pp. 71–98). Washington, DC: Urban Institute Press.

Stivers, C. (1994). The listening bureaucrat: Responsiveness in public administration. *Public Administration Review, 54*, 364–369.

Streisand, B. (2002, June 11). The new philanthropy. *U.S. News & World Report, 130*, 40–42.

Tocqueville, A. de. (2000). *Democracy in America.* New York: Bantam Books. (Original work published 1835)

Van Til, J. (2000). *Growing civil society: From nonprofit sector to third space.* Bloomington: Indiana University Press.

Verba, S., Schlozman, K. L., & Brady, H. E. (1995). *Voice and equality: Civic voluntarism in American politics.* Cambridge, MA: Harvard University Press.

Wagner, D. (2000). *What's love got to do with it? A critical look at American charity.* New York: New York Press.

Warren, M. E. (2001). *Democracy and association.* Princeton, NJ: Princeton University Press.

Whittington, K. E. (1998). Revisiting Tocqueville's America: Society, politics, and association in the nineteenth century. *American Behavioral Scientist, 42*, 21–32.

Wolch, J. R. (1990). *The shadow state: Government and voluntary sector in transition.* New York: Foundation Center.

Wolpert, J. (1993). Decentralization and equity in public and nonprofit sectors. *Nonprofit and Voluntary Sector Quarterly, 22*, 281–296.

Wolpert, J. (1997). How federal cutbacks affect the charitable sector. In L. Staeheli, J. Kodras, & C. Flint (Eds.), *State devolution in America: Implications for a diverse society* (pp. 97–117). Thousand Oaks, CA: Sage.

Wolpert, J. (1999). Communities, networks, and the future of philanthropy. In C. T. Clotfelter (Ed.), *Philanthropy and the nonprofit sector in a changing America* (pp. 231–247). Indianapolis: Indiana University Press.

The Public Service Practitioner as Agent of Social Change

Richard C. Box

The current emphasis in public administration on economic efficiency, quantification, policy analysis, and control of bureaucracy slights matters that in the past have been considered especially important. Among these are constitutionalism and law, citizen self-governance, the role of the individual public service practitioner in a democratic society, the public good, and social equity. One may hope this emphasis is part of a temporary swing toward the private end of what historian Arthur Schlesinger (1986) calls "cycles of American history," periodic shifts in "national involvement between public purpose and private interest" (p. 27). However naïve that hope may be, we might occasionally recall key issues in public administration that today are given less attention than they have received in other times.

This chapter is about the role of the public service practitioner in facilitating social change. The term "public service practitioner" is used to distinguish between public and private or nonprofit sector workers, and between career employees and political appointees. Thus, the subject here is the career public employee, a person filling a role position that includes characteristics expected in a bureaucracy based on merit, including a defined professional area of knowledge and practice and some degree of autonomy from political influence. The public service practitioner is the unit of analysis rather than the organization, policies, or "reforms" that emphasize maximization of economic value, though these are contextual elements of the practitioner's role.

There are any number of normative values a public service practitioner interested in facilitating social change might choose to pursue. The value of interest in this chapter is social equity, the idea that public professionals might use the administrative discretion and legal and organizational resources available to them to shift "downward" the distribution of goods such as education, infrastructure, public safety, access to public decision-making, and so on, with the intent of narrowing the widening gap between the wealthy and everyone else, especially the poor. A central premise of the chapter is that social equity or any normative value in public administration is made more meaningful if pursued with knowledge of the historical, political, and economic context. A practitioner who is aware of debates about, and the current status of, perspectives on matters such as representative versus direct democracy, the role of the public service practitioner in a democratic society, structural forms of government, social equity, and so on may be better prepared to handle the challenges presented by the daily work environment.

The position of social equity in American society is equivocal at best. There were "civic republican" themes in Colonial Era and Founding Era thought that emphasized community over the individual and included disapproval of public displays of wealth, class, and social superiority (Wood, 1969). However, this line of thought was, if not overshadowed, then diluted by classical liberalism, the Enlightenment emphasis on individual liberty and reason (Sinopoli, 1992). Communitarian writers in the past few decades have worked to strengthen a sense of shared rights and responsibilities. In public administration, a number of authors have urged greater emphasis on direct democracy and public discourse about key issues, on the assumptions that people involved in such processes acquire new information, their initial positions may be transformed through encounters with others, and greater citizen involvement produces more democratic outcomes. However, despite the success of such efforts in some places at certain times, changes in decision-making processes do not guarantee a shift toward more equitable distribution of resources controlled by government or of private sector resources influenced by governmental regulation.

Today, in a context of globalized neoliberalism and the increasing penetration of the public sector by language, techniques, and attitudes toward citizens drawn from the private market, the challenge for public administration practitioners and scholars interested in social equity is substantial—it is difficult for them to deviate from the emphasis on economic efficiency. Both practitioners and academicians might ask themselves three questions related to social change: who benefits from my work, what constraints restrict action in favor of social change, and what alternative courses of action are available to improve social equity?

This chapter examines the potential for the practitioner to function as an agent of social change, advancing social equity through choices made about the operation of public services. A critical theoretic framework is offered as a way to conceptualize societal conditions and the need for action. Six categories of action are suggested that practitioners can take to shift the balance of wealth and power in society. Below, the societal context of the public sector is described in preparation for discussion of the role of the public service practitioner and models of the practitioner as agent of social change.

Societal Conditions and the Public Sector

It would take considerable space to thoroughly describe the theoretical bases implied here for interpreting global and societal conditions and their effects on public sector theory and practice. However, comments can be offered about this in summary form, leaving the reader free to agree, disagree, or extend the analysis.

The question of inequality in society is complex. One measure of inequality is the distribution of financial resources. Empirically, it is a contested question whether globally, nationally, or in specific states and localities differences in income and wealth are increasing. On the broadest level, it seems apparent that income inequality in the United States has grown significantly in the past three decades, such that "by 2000, the top one percent of the population was getting a bigger share of after-tax income than the bottom 40 percent. In other words, 2.8 million Americans were out-earning 100 million" (Inequality.org, 2005, p. 2). In 2001 the top 1 percent of the people owned 33 percent of the wealth and the income inequality in the United States was considerably greater than that in other developed countries (Inequality.org, 2005, pp. 4–5).

People who study income and wealth inequality in the United States often contrast the period from 1980 to the present, during which inequality has been growing, with the period 1950–1970, during which inequality was stable or in decline. Economist Paul Krugman (2002) takes a longer view, characterizing the last few decades as a return to conditions that existed in the Gilded Age of the late nineteenth century and through the 1920s. For Krugman, events during the Great Depression and World War II led to postwar growth of the middle class, which is now being reversed by rising inequality. It appears from a cursory review of available material in this area that while concentration of resources at the top levels has occurred during the past decades, it is open to question whether it has been accompanied by decreases among people at other socioeconomic levels, or whether the question at hand is one of fairness in distribution of a larger economic "pie."

Technical and ideological debates in the study of income and wealth inequality cannot be sorted out here, and there is much more to social inequality than money. The time period of interest to people documenting apparent increases in financial inequality is also a period during which advances in social welfare, urban regeneration, civil rights, civil liberties, and environmental protection made in the postwar period have been under attack. In addition, at the heart of the matter of inequality for practitioners and academicians in public administration is the question of citizen access to, and influence over, the public policy process at all levels of government; put another way, this is the matter of the status of democracy. As members of the Task Force on Inequality and American Democracy of the American Political Science Association (2004, p. 1) put it,

> Equal political voice and democratically responsive government are widely cherished American ideals. Indeed, the United States is vigorously promoting democracy abroad. Yet, what is happening to democracy at home? Our country's ideals of equal citizenship and responsive government may be under growing threat in an era of persistent and rising inequalities. Disparities of income, wealth, and access to opportunity are growing more sharply in the United States than in many other nations, and gaps between races and ethnic groups persist. Progress toward realizing American ideals of democracy may have stalled, and in some arenas reversed.

Broadly, the theoretic framework used here is critical. It assumes that liberal-democratic societies with capitalist economic systems will be characterized by: economic success for many at the expense of many others; a constant tension between the private sector and the governmental role in restraining the worst abuses of the market; periodic crises such as economic downturns and wars that are "built in" to such economies; environmental waste and destruction; consumerism that distracts people from the problems in society; and strong influence over the media and public opinion by governmental and corporate leaders expressing corporate interests. Because of constitutional protections for individual liberties, there is significant freedom for dissent and society is intensely pluralistic, though social conformity, suppression of dissent, and curtailment of civil liberties can be significant. (Examples include passage of the Alien and Sedition Acts during the Adams administration in the 1790s, incarceration of American citizens of Japanese ancestry during World War II, the McCarthy era of the 1950s, the Vietnam era of the 1960s and 1970s, and the period immediately following September 11, 2001.)

This theoretical framework is also pragmatic in accepting the broad outlines of the societal system as it is, recognizing there are currently no known acceptable alternatives. It is assumed that societal conditions in the United States are today oriented toward market dominance and shifting of resources from the bottom to the top of the socioeconomic scale nationally and internationally through mechanisms such as taxation policy, military interventions, erosion of the social safety net, blurring of the boundaries between the public and private/nonprofit sectors, and so on. Symbolic issues such as patriotism, supposed democratization of other countries, abortion, and gay marriage distract the public from the underlying economic agenda. Some people are well informed and "connected" with public affairs, though forms of involvement are moving from direct participation in groups to individual electronic information gathering and joining and contributing online to lobbying and political action organizations. This is part of the fragmented, hyperplural "postmodern" condition. Overall, some may feel a sense of narrowing of opportunities for progressive, constructive change.

Generalization about the effects of these circumstances on the public sector is difficult. It can safely be said that the emphasis on efficiency has intensified, leading to use of language, techniques, and attitudes toward management that are modeled on the private sector. Economic efficiency/productivity appears today to be the primary objective of much scholarship and practice in public administration. It has always been important in public administration, an applied field that values getting the most result from expenditure of tax dollars, but today the language of the market is found in textbooks, classrooms, and workplaces in a way that seems unprecedented. Contracts, productivity, metrics, performance measurement, grants, incentives, money to be made from "homeland security," quantified policy analysis, and so on are especially prominent in PA. This is not to suggest that efficiency is inappropriate as one of several concerns, especially at the micro, operational level—an applied field needs to pay attention to economic efficiency in its daily affairs. However, as others have noted, today the necessity of efficiency at the micro, operational level has become confused with the macro-level reasons for existence of the public sector, displacing other important matters of concern as noted at the beginning of the chapter.

The effects of the political and economic environment are felt differently by people depending on their work setting. Vulnerable occupations are likely to include those created for purposes that run counter to the present emphasis on economics and shrinking government's role in moderating the effects of the market. Social service caseworkers may experience the effects of cutbacks in a time when human services are not a priority. Land use planners may be affected by negative public attitudes about the role of government in shaping and protecting the physical and cultural environment.

Despite current societal conditions, it is apparent that some practitioners and academicians remain interested in alternative values, including social equity. It is not uncommon to encounter students in public administration classrooms who are upset about today's situation and want to facilitate meaningful social change. Given the challenges present in the environment of public administration, when and why will some practitioners and academicians choose to exercise discretion in the direction of social equity? What might be the long-term effects on governmental structures and public attitudes? What can be accomplished through isolated acts of conscience? Thorough answers to these broad questions are beyond this brief discussion of the role of the practitioner in facilitating social change, but the questions help define the issues at hand. We can move toward addressing the practitioner's role in social change by outlining how that role has developed over time, or at least how scholarly understanding of it has developed.

Models of the Role of the Public Service Practitioner

The public administration literature is rich with models of the role of the public service practitioner. This review of a few models is not exhaustive, but it is useful for outlining themes and perspectives. Such models are in part descriptive because they are informed by knowledge of extant conditions and they are in part normative because they express preferences for the future.

Since Woodrow Wilson's 1887 essay arguing for a distinct professional role, many authors have written about the relationship between policy making and implementation. Though the literature of public administration may appear to say that the politics-administration "dichotomy" was central to the field until World War II, after which it was discarded, the reality is that practitioners early and late have recognized the fuzziness of the boundary between the two areas and at the same time its importance in their daily work. Both the difference between, and the interaction of, deciding and acting are central to the nature of public affairs. Many practitioners are involved in sensing public needs and formulating and presenting policy proposals and many elected officials and political appointees are involved in the details of administrative work. The variety of political settings, governmental structures, and localized practices on a national and international basis make it difficult to generalize about the politics-administration relationship, but that a relationship exists that is important to the study and practice of public governance is unarguable. Given the circumstance of elected leaders who are for the most part not experts in governmental administration and unelected professionals who manage the work of government, a role tension is present that offers fertile ground for scholarly study and discussion.

Two broad bodies of work may be identified that have sought to re-theorize the role of the public service practitioner in the post–World War II period. The "New Public Administration" of the 1960s and 1970s advocated social equity as an important companion, or supplement, to the dominant value of efficiency (Frederickson, 1980). It arose in response to perceived social imbalances such as racial discrimination and widespread poverty. It was a time when government appeared to be mobilizing to address these problems; a hopeful, constructive, and progressive view of the role of public administrators seemed realistic and achievable.

However, with the shift in national politics in the 1980s, this hopeful view of public administration waned. In an era of declining resources and "bureaucrat bashing," the Blacksburg Manifesto (Wamsley et al., 1987)—and related articles and books—argued in the 1980s and 1990s for an enhanced status for public administration in the constitutional order. This "legitimacy" perspective encountered difficulties due to the historical and cultural resistance in American society to a more formal, authoritative state, and its constitutional orientation is less relevant to the larger body of public employees in state and particularly local government than it is for national-level practitioners. Nevertheless, it illustrates the concern for greater administrative latitude to function as a policy actor as well as implementer.

These two perspectives recognize that characteristics of society produce inequity. New PA sought public sector action to alleviate suffering and inequity, but it did not reject or propose fundamental change to the underlying systems and institutions of society. The legitimacy perspective explicitly names the capitalist economic system, with its gratification of market desires, as a cause of social imbalance. Authors of the Blacksburg Manifesto suggest that public administration may "serve as a cooling, containing, and directing foil" (Wamsley et al., 1987, p. 309) to this system. Both perspectives intend to correct imbalances but do not suggest that the economic-political system is fundamentally flawed and in need of change.

Another way to approach the issue of the administrative role is to begin with the individual as the unit of analysis, building upward from descriptions of individual behavior to construct typologies. Barry Hammond and Bayard Catron (1990) offered a summary of thought on the role of the public service practitioner, in the form of seven "images." Hammond and Catron (p. 242) are careful to note that these images are not mutually exclusive and an individual practitioner may make use of parts of one or more of them at various times. The seven images are: functionary (the traditional neutrality role); opportunist/pragmatist (administrator as utility maximizer); interest broker/market manager (the public choice administrator); professional expert/technician (the autonomous technicist); agent/trustee (guardian or steward of the public interest); communitarian facilitator (enabling face-to-face discourse); and transformational social critic (protecting citizens from conditions in society).

This sort of role typology is not uncommon in the public administration literature. Another example is the typology of city manager roles described by William Fannin in 1983, based on interviews and a survey instrument used to sample managers and city council members in Texas. Fannin's five manager types are the "administrative craftsman," the "administrative technician," the "expert advisor," the "political activist," and the "policy nonactor." He found that city managers and council members both preferred the "expert advisor" role, though Fannin's expert is not Hammond and Catron's autonomous technician, but instead a person who engages with the local community and formulates policy for consideration by elected officials (Fannin, 1983). Some other researchers have found disagreement between elected officials and administrators on the appropriate role for the public professional, but the point here is that the relationship of unelected, professional public practitioners to citizens and elected officials has for some time been a central issue in public administration.

This relationship can be visualized as a continuum of administrative discretion, with on one polar end the practitioner as neutral implementer of policy direction from above (an embodiment of the politics-administration dichotomy), and on the other end the practitioner as an agent of change, using independent judgment to act in ways that may alter societal conditions. The "change agent" end of the continuum often draws heated criticism from those who believe in clear subordination of public administration in a constitutional or representative democracy. These critics may be classical liberals, "conservatives," or people skeptical about the role of government in society.

Today, as the globalized market with its value of efficiency becomes increasingly dominant and its ideology penetrates even the best-hidden corners of the public sector, it becomes more difficult for those advocating social equity to be heard and to craft meaningful action. To make progress, it may be helpful to adopt a theory of action that includes critique of the given system as a conceptual backdrop for the value of social equity. People who favor greater social equity are likely to believe that something fundamental is wrong in a societal order with a large and growing disparity of wealth and power between classes. Their ability to act with purpose and coherent direction may be enhanced by theoretical critique of existing society and how it can be changed.

The description above of societal conditions and their effects on the role of the public service practitioner is a beginning toward theorizing the context that shapes and constrains the actions of public professionals. This conceptual framework is an adapted version of critical theory, and it offers a conceptual framework for action that favors democracy and social equity. It is not necessary to believe that the political-economic order must be overthrown to think that it has serious flaws deserving of constructive change. Also, it is not necessary to wait for large-scale change to initiate limited, focused actions to promote social equity.

The Practitioner as Agent of Social Change

This chapter began with three questions for practitioners and academicians: "who benefits from my work, what constraints restrict action in favor of social change, and what alternative courses of action are available to improve social equity?" The question of benefit rests within the context of the critical description of society offered above. It is appealing to think of public professionals as street-level functionaries close to the general public, and this characterization is accurate for many. However, for some practitioners being close to the public is not the same thing as sharing their interests; police officers in areas of racial unrest and resistance to authority are an example. For others who work in offices and manage services, the public may be largely an abstraction, a rather distant one as they perform complex administrative tasks, go to meetings with other professionals, and in midday have lunch with other professionals or community leaders. For the most part it is the wealthy, the powerful, and those with specialized training who determine the public policy agenda, the outcomes of the decision-making process, and ways in which public services are delivered. This reality suggests that practitioners and academicians who care about social change and equity need to exercise imagination in service to their sense of mission.

Societal constraints on change can be formidable. In contemporary American liberal-capitalist society, the idea that public service practitioners might promote social change is problematic. Career public professionals are not elected, and it is assumed by many that they should serve as agents of elected officials, not pursue their own policy preferences. However, if public professionals do not act as agents of change, change in institutions and systems as well as in the way government addresses social equity, then who will do so?

It is probably unrealistic to expect some portion of the public to rise up to demand social change; in these "postmodern," or late-modern times, it becomes difficult to identify a cohesive public that is interested in public affairs and willing to take part in informed self-governance (Box, 2005, chap. 7). It has even become difficult to get people to vote, that minimal act of citizenship in which they take a few minutes to express their often uninformed opinion about candidates who may or may not have the capacity to effect meaningful change. In today's world of consumerism and multiplying and diverse interests and communities of association, for public practitioners to gather, inform, and carry on dialogue with something resembling a representative public may seem a fantasy of the past (though in a number of places nationwide active citizen self-governance and neighborhood initiatives are doing well; see, for example, Musso, Weare, Oztas, & Loges, 2006).

A critical analysis of public involvement in change finds the public at large misinformed by the media about the nature of the political-economic system and preoccupied by consumerist distractions. Though much attention has focused on the Internet as a source of information and group membership, it is unclear whether technology is affecting knowledge and participation in public affairs for a large percentage of the population, or whether the effects are experienced mostly by the small portion that were already inclined to participate. Further, it is uncertain whether technology makes governance more effective and timely or causes further fragmentation and lack of coherence. In short, it might not be reasonable to expect the public to initiate change.

In *Organizational America* (1979), William G. Scott and David K. Hart observe that the "significant" people and the "insignificant" people in society are not likely to challenge the "organizational imperative" of hierarchical corporate domination. The significant people have too much to lose and the insignificant people are dependent on the significant people for employment and consumer goods. Scott and Hart argue there is public support for change and that if any group of organization-bound citizens could prevent the nation from "drifting into totalitarianism" (p. 215), it would be the "professional people" who "have the technical and organizational expertise to galvanize this support into a reform movement" (p. 220).

Beyond the problem of societal acceptance of public service practitioners as agents of social change, the proportion of practitioners who are in circumstances to act in this role is probably relatively small and, of those, only some are inclined to do so. In addressing the question of alternative courses of action available to improve social equity, the logic of our inquiry leads to certain public sector positions and people who might take action. These positions include "boundary-spanning" jobs whose occupants work directly with the public, management-level jobs in which there is direct access to decision-makers, and technical positions that offer the opportunity to shape decisions by providing information. It is especially among public employees who believe social change is necessary, that we will find those best positioned to take action.

We may highlight two current approaches to the role of the public service practitioner in the American PA literature that are built on critical analysis of the nature of society. They are found in two recent books, *Transformational Public Service: Portraits of Theory in Practice* (2005) by Cheryl Simrell King and Lisa A. Zanetti, and *Critical Social Theory in Public Administration* (2005), by Richard C. Box. These authors do not advocate immediate utopian change, but they use critical analysis of existing political and economic systems to present descriptions of, and prescriptions for, the public professional's role in constructive social change. King and Zanetti interweave stories of the work of practitioners who are committed to social and organizational change with critical theories of transformation. Box uses critical theory to construct a model of practice that involves professional use of reason and imagination in the service of citizen self-determination.

The point here is not to detail two approaches to the practitioner's role, but to use them as examples of theory-based, analytic ways of conceptualizing that role in relation to social change, and in particular, social equity. There may be any number of actions practitioners have taken and can take to effect social change. The listing of six categories of actions below is a beginning toward identifying categories of action; there is nothing new or surprising about these concepts, which may be found throughout the public administration literature. However, the intent here is to focus these ideas for greater effect by organizing them around theoretic analysis of societal conditions and bringing them together in a "toolkit" that could serve the goal of social equity. Practitioners who share the critical view of society and who want to effect change may be taking some or all of these actions and perhaps some that are not discussed. These categories of action are arranged on a continuum from those taken within an organization to those that cross organizational boundaries to affect the broader public.

Sense and Describe Needs

This first category of action is basic to the professional role. It involves gathering and analyzing information about current conditions immediately related to organizational mission, in addition to broader knowledge of best practices, alternative futures, and trends in social and environmental change. This professional function is a mixture of normative choice and relatively value-free fact gathering. Ideally, conscious and explicit choices are made about what information to gather and for what purposes, then the acquisition and analysis of information is carried out as precisely and objectively as possible.

Though the collection and display of information may seem apolitical and uncontroversial, the sorts of knowledge gathered may call into question ways an organization operates in relation to issues such as social equity, efficiency, rational versus political decision-making, and use of public power and resources by elites to benefit themselves and their associates. In addition, the process of gathering information may include interacting with individual citizens and groups, potentially bringing the practitioner in conflict with elected officials or political appointees who fear the practitioner is developing an independent constituency. Citizens, elected officials, or the practitioner may find it difficult to distinguish professional from political activity in interaction with citizens; is this a matter of gathering information, or of helping people recognize needs and preferences?

The role of the nonelected public professional in American society can be ambiguous and difficult to navigate. The politics-administration relationship is inherent in the role, and it is not a dichotomy but a continuum, ranging from the practitioner as passive instrument of established policy to the practitioner as agent of change. The appropriate or preferred location on the continuum is something each practitioner chooses in a particular time and set of circumstances.

Modify Operating Procedures

Within the organization, practitioners may modify operating procedures in ways that serve the goal of social equity. Svara and Brunet (2005, p. 257) write that "services and benefits should be distributed equally or in such a way that those who are less advantaged receive greater benefits." Rosenbloom (2005) is concerned that pursuit of social equity could lead practitioners to take actions that are not legitimate in the Constitutional order. Citing Victor Thompson's (1975) warning against "stealing" popular sovereignty, Rosenbloom (2005, pp. 250–251), notes that "public administrators need a mandate from the constitutional branches of government to legitimate their pursuit of redistribution and social change." Thus, "advocacy, not imposition of personal and professional values, should be the rule" (p. 251).

Of course, public service practitioners function within a legal and institutional order that constrains their actions and they have a duty to the public to remain faithful to these constraints. (I use the terms "legal" and "institutional" here to be inclusive of local government, for which the constitutional order is less immediately relevant.) However, there is no way to screen out "personal and professional values," becoming a value-free automaton carrying out orders. This is an old debate, perhaps becoming evident with the Friedrich-Finer exchange six decades ago and running through the "legitimacy" dialogue of the 1990s (see, for example, the symposium on "public administration and the Constitution" in the May/June 1993 issue of *Public Administration Review*).

Though it is possible to suppress creativity, imagination, and empathy in public employees by assigning mind-numbing work or threatening negative consequences for deviation from the official line, every professional sees the world through her or his particular set of personal and professional values. Within the constraints of the legal and institutional order, there is considerable room for independent judgment and action. Contrary to Lowi's (1969) "juridical democracy," it is not feasible to specify with precision what most public employees do, nor, in principal-agent terms, is it efficient to monitor them to the point that deviation from predetermined standards can be prevented. The daily work of a police chief or state human services manager, for example, proceeds within the role expectations of the given position. However, these people apply personal and professional experience, beliefs, and standards of performance as they intentionally or unintentionally shape both policy and the environment in which it is created and changed over time. They establish and modify operating procedures, shift staff and material resources among areas, and communicate their values and concerns to agency staff; the potential for impact on social equity is considerable. It may not be appropriate to say that social equity "should" be a primary value or guide to practice—there is no apparent foundational rationale for such a claim—but practitioners may decide on their own that social change and social equity are sufficiently important to be incorporated into their daily work.

Propose Programs and Policies

This category of practitioner action is consistent with Rosenbloom's "advocacy." It follows the "sense and describe needs" category above, using gathered information to bridge the gap between professional knowledge and the relevant governing body or bodies. It is part of the action loop that includes: aggregation of interests that rise to the level of the public policy agenda; a period of public discourse; a decision that adopts a policy; implementation; and feedback on progress potentially leading to policy modification.

The practitioner formulates a recommendation for change to be presented, possibly with intermediate steps in the hierarchy, to the ultimate decision-maker. This could be a cabinet secretary at the national or state levels, Congress or a state legislature, or at the local level the city manager, mayor, or council. Making any recommendation can carry risk. Making a recommendation that includes, explicitly or implicitly, a shift from the status quo toward social equity may be especially risky because it involves movement of resources, power, or both and may be resisted by those who benefit from the current situation. The person who would make the recommendation will consider the risk and potential benefits, deciding whether the goal of social equity outweighs potential consequences.

Provide Information to the Public

This is the first of the action categories focused on spanning the boundary of the organization and linking with citizens. As noted above, acquisition of knowledge can present risks, and making it available to the public at large magnifies that potential. However, providing citizens with as much information as possible about current conditions, best practices, and alternative futures is essential to practice informed by the critical perspective. To the extent citizens choose to become informed about, and involved in, the policy process, they need a full range of information and interpretation. The practitioner guided by a critical theoretic view will see this action option as a way to "enlighten" citizens, potentially giving them the knowledge needed to initiate social change.

Provide Meaningful Access to Policy Processes

It becomes increasingly difficult for many people to take part in the traditional public policy process, for a variety of reasons including lack of knowledge about government, the cost of time needed to acquire information and participate, and changes in lifestyle and personal interests (Bennett, 1998). The national government was not created to promote participation by individual citizens, and those who participate often do so through membership in large advocacy organizations. Individual participation at the state level is not much easier. At the local level there can be greater potential for involvement due to proximity and access, though access may be limited by governance practices that emphasize decision-making by elites (Box, 1998). In any event, in most times and places only a small percentage of citizens participate in governance.

It is not necessarily widely accepted among practitioners that involving citizens is either important or efficient. Some consider it neither, but instead an intrusion on administrative discretion, a misuse of time (Irvin & Stansbury, 2004), or a violation of the authority of elected officials. Elected officials may also regard citizen involvement as a misuse of time or threat to their authority, and they may also consider it a potential threat to their financial or other interests, or the interests of those whom they feel they represent.

This is not to deny there are times and places in which public professionals or elected officials welcome and encourage citizen involvement in governance—of course there are. As an ideal, public service practitioners ensure that participatory processes and settings (electronic as well as traditional meetings and face-to-face dialogue) are as understandable, open, transparent, and welcoming as possible. Providing such settings may require advocacy and persuasion within the organization and may entail some risk of opposition and failure. However, the potential benefits in relation to democracy and social equity are considerable.

Protect Private Lives

Aside from the question of whether most people have the time and knowledge to participate in governance, there is the normative question of whether they *should* do so. To answer affirmatively is to adopt the Athenian/ communitarian/classical republican model of citizenship as a primary human goal. This model often underlies discussion in the public administration literature of citizen involvement in governance. As noted directly above, in contemporary urban society we cannot assume that most people either will or would want to participate in public decision-making, but in addition it seems somewhat presumptuous to assume normatively that they should. Why, exactly, ought this concept be considered universal, invariant over time and place?

An opposing argument can be made from the classical liberal perspective that government should function only to protect the individual from harm by others, but this perspective suffers from a poor fit with contemporary society. It was conceived before the rise of urban society and corporations, so its emphasis on "negative liberty" (protecting the individual from the state and from other individuals) is not especially helpful when the individual faces global corporate society, people need public services to deal with collective problems, and government itself is often influenced or controlled by the interests from whom individuals need protection.

Part of giving attention to social equity may involve recognizing that not everyone has open and easy access to the policy process and, even with the time, knowledge, and resources to participate, not everyone would choose to do so. This does not mean that people with little access because of circumstances or people who choose not to participate should be written off, ignored, while those in power and their friends decide what to do with public money. It does mean that public administrators might use imagination (Box, 2001; 2005) and social conscience to keep in mind the effects of their actions and policy proposals on private lives, striving for both equity and protection of personal liberties. In a society structured to benefit those with greater financial resources, this sort of imagination can be an important part of the practitioner's social equity tool kit.

Conclusion: "Micro Outbreaks of Reason and Imagination"

The critical theoretic framework outlined in this chapter is not intended to provide a universal and unitary interpretation of the motivations or interests of citizens, elected representatives, or public service practitioners. None of these groups are uniform or homogeneous in their activities or preferences.

Though the critical framework assumes motivations of power and wealth by governing elites, citizen interests that counter those of elites, and public service practitioners who would like to assist the public in governance, there are any number of examples amongst elected officials of benevolence, public-spirited thought, and selfless service; citizens exhibit the full human range of motivations, some self-interested and some showing concern for the broader community; and the beliefs and motivations of public practitioners are as varied as those of the public at large. Nevertheless, this analytic framework offers a useful way to understand contemporary society and the obstacles it places in the path of the practitioner who values social equity.

Efficiency is an enduring and dominant value in public administration, but many values are important to people in public service. Among those that have been neglected in recent years is social equity. It may not be foundational or essential in the field, but a number of practitioners and academicians find it to be of particular importance. This chapter has sought to address the questions: who benefits from the work of public service practitioners, what constraints restrict action in favor of social change, and what alternative courses of action are available to improve social equity? It will be useful here to address two other questions asked earlier about practitioner action in favor of social change, and to explore what academicians might do to facilitate the use of social equity as one among several values guiding practice.

The two questions are: what might be the long-term effects on governmental structures and public attitudes, and what can be accomplished through isolated acts of conscience? The answers to these questions rest within the critical framework, which assumes the economic-political system is hostile to social equity and that it will remain so for the foreseeable future. In this situation, only some practitioners have been or are interested in serving as agents of social change, and when they do, they may take isolated actions based on a personal/professional commitment to constructive change. The long-term effects on governmental structures and public attitudes are difficult to foresee, but for people who believe change is needed, it may be that the important thing is to try, to make small changes that are meaningful to those affected. We might call these efforts "micro outbreaks of reason and imagination," using reason to identify relationships of power and wealth that impede social change, and imagination to suggest possible alternative futures. Whether or not some find this inappropriate within the legal and institutional order, if change is needed and there are few groups willing or able to initiate it, there have been and will be public service practitioners who take on the challenge.

Something might be said about the role of public affairs academicians in relation to social equity. Academicians with this interest can research and write about social conditions and efforts by public professionals to create change. They can also teach critical analysis of the economic and political institutions of society, framing it within national historical narratives. For example, an element of such teaching can be the dialogue between the Anti-Federalists and Federalists over perspectives on the structure and function of government, citizenship, and inequalities of power and wealth. It can be uncomfortable and risky to challenge preconceptions held by students whose views are shaped by decades of exposure to corporate-owned media and superficial, one-dimensional teaching of history, but it can also be especially rewarding.

The purpose of this chapter is not to prescribe a universal perspective that "should" be adopted by all in the public sector. Instead, the purpose is to suggest a theoretic framework that might in some way enrich and facilitate the work of those who care about democracy and social equity.

References

American Political Science Association. (2004). *American democracy in an age of rising inequality* (Report of the Task Force on Inequality and American Democracy). Retrieved September 25, 2005, from www.apsanet.org/section_256.cfm.

Bennett, L. W. (1998). The uncivic culture: Communication, identity, and the rise of lifestyle politics. *Political Science & Politics, 31*, 741–761.

Box, R. C. (1998). *Citizen governance: Leading American communities into the 21st century.* Thousand Oaks, CA: Sage.

Box, R. C. (2001). Private lives and anti-administration. *Administrative Theory & Praxis, 23*, 541–558.

Box, R. C. (2005). *Critical social theory in public administration.* Armonk, NY: M.E. Sharpe.

Fannin, W. R. (1983). City manager policy roles as a source of city council/city manager conflict. *International Journal of Public Administration, 5*, 381–399.

Frederickson, H. G. (1980). *New public administration.* University: University of Alabama Press.

Hammond, B. R., & Catron, B. L. (1990). Epilogue: Reflections on practical wisdom—enacting images and developing identity. In H. D. Kass & B. L. Catron (Eds.), *Images and identities in public administration* (pp. 241–251). Newbury Park, CA: Sage.

Inequality.org. (2005). *How unequal are we, anyway?* Retrieved September 21, 2005, from www.inequality.org.

Irvin, R. A., & Stansbury, J. (2004). Citizen participation in decision making: Is it worth it? *Public Administration Review, 64*, 55–65.

King, C. S., & Zanetti, L. A. (2005). *Transformational public service: Portraits of theory in practice.* Armonk, NY: M.E. Sharpe.

Krugman, P. (2002, October 20). For richer. *New York Times Magazine*, section 6, p. 62.

Lowi, T. J. (1969). *The end of liberalism: Ideology, policy, and the crisis of public authority.* New York: W. W. Norton.

Musso, J. A., Weare, C., Oztas, N., & Loges, W. E. (2006). Neighborhood governance reform and networks of community power in Los Angeles. *American Review of Public Administration, 36,* 79–97.

Rosenbloom, D. (2005). Taking social equity seriously in MPA education. *Journal of Public Affairs Education, 3,* 247–252.

Schlesinger, A. M. (1986). *The cycles of American history.* Boston: Houghton Mifflin.

Scott, W. G., & Hart, D. K. (1979). *Organizational America.* Boston: Houghton Mifflin.

Sinopoli, R. C. (1992). *The foundations of American citizenship: Liberalism, the Constitution, and civic virtue.* Oxford: Oxford University Press.

Svara, J. H., & Brunet, J. R. (2005). Social equity is a pillar of public administration. *Journal of Public Affairs Education, 3,* 253–258.

Thompson, V. A. (1975). *Without sympathy or enthusiasm: The problem of administrative compassion.* University: University of Alabama Press.

Wamsley, G. L., Goodsell, C. T., Rohr, J. A., Stivers, C. M., White, O. F., & Wolf, J. F. (1987). The public administration and the governance process: Refocusing the American dialogue. In R. C. Chandler (Ed.), *A centennial history of the American administrative state* (pp. 291–317). New York: Free Press.

Wood, G. S. (1969). *The creation of the American republic 1776–1787.* Chapel Hill: University of North Carolina Press.

About the Editor and Contributors

Richard C. Box is a professor in the School of Public Administration, University of Nebraska at Omaha. He served for thirteen years in local governments in Oregon and California before completing a D.P.A. at the University of Southern California in 1990. His research focuses on democracy, citizen self-governance, and the application of critical theory in public administration. Dr. Box is the author of *Citizen Governance: Leading American Communities into the 21st Century* (Sage Publications, 1998), *Public Administration and Society: Critical Issues in American Governance* (M.E. Sharpe, 2004), and *Critical Social Theory in Public Administration* (M.E. Sharpe, 2005).

Mohamad G. Alkadry is a member of the graduate faculty, associate professor of public administration, and director of the MPA program at West Virginia University (WVU). He received his Ph.D. from Florida Atlantic University. Prior to joining WVU, he worked as a senior associate at the Center for Urban Redevelopment and Empowerment and as a performance auditor at the Office of the Auditor General of Canada. Dr. Alkadry has written over twenty peer-reviewed publications and has authored more than forty community and professional studies in areas of economic and community development. His current research focuses on organizational behavior, community development, multiculturalism, and democracy.

Carol Ebdon, Ph.D., is the finance director for the City of Omaha, Nebraska. She was previously an associate professor in the School of Public Administration at the University of Nebraska at Omaha. Her research interests are in the areas of public budgeting and finance.

Angela M. Eikenberry is an assistant professor in the School of Public and International Affairs, Center for Public Administration and Policy, at Virginia Tech. She completed her Ph.D. in public administration at the University of Nebraska at Omaha. Before returning to school, she was a development and grant-writing consultant. Her main research interests include civil society, nonprofit organizations, and philanthropy, and their role in democratic society.

Aimee L. Franklin, Ph.D., is an associate professor and the graduate program director in the Political Science Department at the University of Oklahoma. She teaches in the areas of strategic planning, budgeting and financial management, regulatory policy, and managing public programs. Her research interests and publications are currently in topics such as citizen participation, Indian and commercial gaming expansion, and library funding policies. She is the coauthor of *An Introduction to Public Administration: Theories, Challenges and Choices* and publishes in a variety of public administration and public policy journals.

Mary R. Hamilton is senior executive in residence in the School of Public Administration at the University of Nebraska at Omaha. Previously she was the executive director of the American Society for Public Administration (ASPA), and a senior executive with the U.S. General Accounting Office (GAO). Dr. Hamilton received her Ph.D. in sociology from the University of Maryland College Park, her M.A. in sociology and political science from the University of North Carolina at Chapel Hill, and her B.A. in sociology and psychology from Bethel College, St. Paul, Minnesota.

Alfred T. Ho is an associate professor at the School of Public and Environmental Affairs, Indiana University–Purdue University Indianapolis. His research focuses on state and local public finance, performance management, and e-government development. In 2001–4, he and Paul Coates at Iowa State University co-led the Iowa Citizen-Initiated Performance Assessment (CIPA) project, which was funded by the Alfred P. Sloan Foundation. Ho has published in *American Review of Public Administration*, *Public Administration Review*, *Public Performance & Management Review*, and *State and Local Government Review*, among others.

Janet R. Hutchinson is an associate professor of public administration with a faculty affiliation in women's studies at the L. Douglas Wilder School of Government and Public Affairs, Virginia Commonwealth University. She earned her Ph.D. from the Graduate School of Public and International Affairs, University of Pittsburgh. Her recent scholarship has focused on the theoretical analyses of issues related to gender in public administration. She has written one book based on her professional experiences in child welfare and published a number of articles on gender and multigendering in public administration.

Cheryl Simrell King, Ph.D., is a member of the faculty of the Evergreen State College, teaching primarily in the Graduate Program in Public Administration (MPA). Coauthor of *Transformative Public Service: Portraits of Theory in Practice* (M.E. Sharpe, 2005) and *Government Is Us: Public Administration in an Anti-Government Era* (Sage Publications, 1998) as well as author of articles in trade press and academic journals, she writes and practices in the areas of democratizing and transforming public administration, accountability, and the relationships amongst and between citizens and their governments.

Dale Krane, Ph.D., University of Minnesota, is a professor at the School of Public Administration, University of Nebraska at Omaha. His research interests include policy implementation and evaluation, federalism and intergovernmental relations, and state and local government administration. Since 2001 he has served as the editor of the annual *Publius* issue on the state of American federalism. Professor Krane has served as a consultant to the Council of State Governments, the National Commission for Employment Policy, the U.S. Department of Education, and the U.S. Geological Survey, and he has provided technical assistance to governments in Afghanistan, Brazil, Canada, Moldova, Romania, Tajikistan, and Venezuela.

Gary S. Marshall, Ph.D., is an associate professor in the School of Public Administration at the University of Nebraska at Omaha. His research emphasizes the centrality of human identity as it relates to work in public agencies. This research focus is being conducted at two levels. At the level of social theory, the emphasis is on the study of public administration from a Lacanian orientation. At the level of management theory, the emphasis is on the study of public managers using a reflexive identity model that encompasses role theory, discourse theory, and psychoanalytic theory. Professor Marshall has published in *Administration & Society*, *Administrative Theory & Praxis*, *Public Administration Review*, and *American Behavioral Scientist.*

Christine M. Reed is a professor in the School of Public Administration at the University of Nebraska at Omaha, where she has taught administrative law in the MPA program for almost twenty years. Her research interests in recent years have included community-based environmental mediation and participation by small local governments in EPA rulemaking procedures. Dr. Reed is the past chair of both the Section on Public Law and Administration and the Section on Environmental and Natural Resource Administration of the American Society for Public Administration. She is an Associate Member of the American Bar Association and a member of the Section of Administrative Law & Regulatory Practice.

Index

A

Abramson, A.J., 179
Accountability, public
citizen participation and, 87
of nonprofit organizations, 171–172,
182–183
performance measurement and, 75, 109,
110
Action research model of organizational
analysis, 49
Activation, in network model, 57
Active representation, 158, 159, 161
Adams, B., 96
Adams, G.B., 173
Addams, J., 170
Adjudication, democratic practice in,
124–127
Administrative Behavior (Simon), 50
Administrative law
civic republican ideas about, 120–121,
122, 129
constitutional limits and, 119–120
democratic practice and, 122–128
provisions of, 120, 126
Administrative man, 51
Administrative Procedures Act, 34, 121,
124–125, 126, 127
Administrative science, 50, 51
Agenda setting, 28–30
Agranoff, R., 57
Ahern, D.W., 134
Aina, O., 145

Alkadry, Mohamad G., xii, 150–168, 164,
213
Almond, G.A., 174
Alter, Catherine, 56
American Cancer Society, 177
American Heart Association, 177
American Political Science Association,
Task Force on Inequality and
American Democracy of, 197
America Speaks, 76–77
Anderson, J.E., 27, 86, 88
Anderson, W., 52
Appiah, K. Anthony, 153
Appleby, Paul, 13–14, 25, 32
Arato, 174
Argyris, Chris, 53, 54
Aristotle, 67
Army Corps of Engineers, 36
Arnove, R.F., 182
Assembly line, 41
Athenian model of citizenship, 208
Auburn (Alabama), budget participation
in, 96
Auerbach, C.F., 146

B

Bailey, Stephen, 12
Bailyn, B., 41
Bak, H., 162
Ball, H., 35
Balla, S.J., 37
Barber, B., 74, 76, 77, 136

Barber, B.R., 174
Bardach, E., 31
Barnard, Chester, 46–47, 53–54
Bar-On, B-A., 164
Baumgartner, F.R., 29
Beck, 174
Beito, D.T., 170
Bellah, R.N., 172, 173
Bennett, L.W., 72, 207
Berger, P.L., 174, 175
Berkley, G., 3, 10, 11
Berkshire, M., 72, 78
Berner, M., 90, 93, 96
Bernstein, S.R., 172
Berry, F.S., 57
Bessemer process, 41
Bianchi, A., 185
Bingham, L.B., 97, 127
Blacksburg Manifesto, 200
Blair, L.H., 96
Bland, R.L., 91, 99
Boddie, S.C., 172
Bogason, P., 80
Bologh, R.W., 162
Booher, D.E., 71
Boris, E., 179
Boundaries of Citizenship, The (Spinner), 155
Box, Richard C., vii–xii, 15, 17, 40, 58, 68, 77, 86, 92, 128, 173, 185, 187, 194–210, 202, 207, 208, 213
Boyte, H.C., 174
Brady, H.E., 104, 174
Brainerd, P., 185
Brettschneider, M., 135, 139, 145, 146
Brigham, S., 77, 79
Brilliant, E.L., 182
Brody, E., 176
Buchanan, James, 55
Budget participation
    benefits of, 84, 91–92, 94
    democracy and, 86–89
    effectiveness of, 99–100
    levels of, 85
    mechanisms for, 94–99
    public hearings, 90–91, 96
    purposes of, 84–85

Budget participation *(continued)*
    recommendations for, 101–102
    stakeholders in, 92–94
    traditional process for, 89–91
Bullivant, B.M., 156, 162
Bureau of Land Management, 126
Bureau movement, 42
Burke, C.C., 178
Burlington (Iowa), budget participation in, 95–96, 97
Burrell, G., 51
Bush, George H.W. (Sr.), 170
Bush, George W., 170–171
Byrne, J.A., 185

C

Calculus of Consent, The (Tullock), 55
Callahan, K., 71, 72, 81
Carberry-George, B., 91
Catron, B.L., 200
Chandler, R.C., 15
Chaplin, Charlie, 44
Citizen advisory committees, 93–94, 97
Citizen-initiated performance assessment (CIPA), 113
Citizen participation
    accountability and, 74–75, 87
    arenas for, 72
    call for, 64–65
    dilemmas of, 79–81
    in election process, 65, 86, 87, 202
    in giving circles, 187–188
    history of, 66–71
    inauthentic processes for, 71
    information gathering and, 163–164
    initiatives and referenda, 74
    in local government, x, 72, 73–74
    in performance measurement, 110–116
    in policy implementation, 33, 34, 37
    public administrators' attitude toward, 71–72
    in social change, 202–203, 206–208
    stages of, 77–78, 79
    See also Budget participation; gender equality

Citizenship
  Athenian model of, 208
  defined, 66
  engaged, 76–77
Citizen surveys, 96, 113–114
Civic environmentalism, 125–126
Civic republicanism, 120–121, 122, 129
Civil rights movement, 165
Civil service
  establishment of, 5
  growth of, ix, 42–43, 69
  reform of, 7
Clarke, S.E., 173
Cleveland, Frederick, 108
Cleveland, Harlan, 13, 17
Clinton Administration, 109
Cnann, R.A., 172
Coates, P., 111
Coates, P.M., 79, 111, 113
Cobb, N.K., 185
Cohen, J., 174, 181
Collins, K.J., 128
Commission model of local government, xi
Community boards, 91
Community Development Block Grant
    program, 33
Conflict resolution, democratic practice
    in, 124–127
Congress
  drafting process in, 30–31
  policy implementation and, 33, 34
  tax cuts in, 179
Consciousness, coming to, 77–78
Considine, M., 37
Constitution, U.S., viii, 3, 9–10, 23, 87,
    119, 120–121, 122, 129
Conway, M.M., 134
Cooke, J., 67, 68
Cooper, P.J., 34
Cooper, T.L., 15
Council-manager model of local
    government, xi, 93, 100
Cox, E. Eugene, 182
Crick, Bernard, 64
Critical Social Theory in Public
    Administration (Box), 203–204
Crosby, N., 94

Crowd, The: A Study of the Popular Mind
    (LeBon), 49
Cultural identity, 152, 153–154
Cultural integration, 163
Cultural pluralism, 155, 156, 163
Cultural relativism, 155–156

D

Dahl, R.A., 22, 51
Data analysis, for performance
    measurement, 115–116
Dayton (Ohio), tax referendum in, 91
Deactivation, in network model, 57
Decentralized organizational
    arrangements, 55
Decision agenda, 30
Deep democracy, 136–137, 145–147
Democracy
  administrative law and, 122–128
  basic concepts about, ix–xi
  classical liberalism and, 172–173
  classical republicanism and, 173
  deep, 136–137, 145–147
  defined, vii–viii, 21–22, 40–41, 173
  expansion of, ix
  forms of institutions, 22–23
  Jacksonian, 5, 68–69
  multiculturalism and, 134–136
  multigendered, 143–144, 147
  philanthropy and, 173–185
  public participation and, 86–89
  in revolutionary and republican era,
      viii–ix, 67–68
  workplace, 41, 49
  See also Citizen participation
Democracy, public service and
  vs bureaucratic values, 11
  democratic values for, 9–11
  historical changes in, 4–7, 67–71
  knowledge and skill requirements for,
      11–14
  paradox of, 3, 18
  policymaking, 24–26, 36–38
  pros and cons of, 7–9
  representative bureaucracy, 156–163
  roles and responsibilities, 14–18

Democracy and the Public Service
    (Mosher), 4–5
Democracy in America (Tocqueville), 7,
    67, 174
Democratic network governance,
    57–58
Denhardt, J.V., 10, 15, 16, 70, 187
Denhardt, R.B., 10, 15, 16, 40, 51,
    55, 70, 96, 162, 187
DeShaney v. *Winnebago County*, 119,
    120–121
Diaz, W., 177, 178
Dicke, L.A., 171, 172
Dickson, 45
Dimock, Marshall, 25
Dinnerstein, Dorothy, 135, 139–140,
    141, 146–147
Direct democracy, x
Dispute resolution, democratic practice
    in, 124–127
Distributive justice, 159
Donaldson, L., 55, 56
Donohue, 164
Drafting process, 30–31
Drucker, P., 47
Due process of law, 119
Durkheim, E., 174
Dwivedi, O.P., 171
Dye, T., 21

E

Ebdon, Carol, xii, 72, 84–106, 86,
    91, 92, 93–94, 95, 96, 97, 98,
    99, 100, 102, 213
Economic efficiency, as public
    administration goal, 198
Eggers, W.D., 56–57
Eikenberry, Angela M., xii, 169–193,
    175, 184, 186, 213–214
Elites
  government by, 4–5, 68
  philanthropy of, 182–183
Emery, A., 122
Emery, F., 122
Environmentalism, civic, 125–126

Environmental Protection Agency (EPA),
    123, 124
Environmental protection laws, 33
Epstein, P., 79, 111
Equality
  democratic, 23
  See also Gender equality; Social equity
      in public administration
Equality of opportunity, x
Ethics (Spinoza), 142
Eugene (Oregon), budget participation in, 98
Evans, S.M., 174
Evers, L., 99, 100
Expert advisor role, 201

F

Faith-based organizations, 170–171
Fannin, W.R., 201
Fausto-Sterling, A., 143–144
Federalist Papers, 24, 32, 67
Federal Register, 121, 122
Feedback, worker, 49
Feltey, K.M., 71, 86, 92
Feminine Mystique, The (Friedan), 162
Ferguson, K.E., 162
First Amendment, 26
Fischer, F., 72
Fischer, M., 181
Fisher, D., 182
Fishkin, J.S., 68
Follett, Mary Parker, 47–48, 59, 173
Food programs, emergency, 180–181
Forest Service, U.S., 126
Foundations, elite, 182
Franklin, Aimee, xii, 84–106, 86, 91, 92,
    93–94, 95, 97, 98, 99, 100, 102, 214
Frederickson, H.G., 10, 15, 16, 18, 77,
    157, 199
Frederickson, P., 171, 172
Friedan, B., 162
Friedrich, Carl, 24
Fromm, Eric, 74
Functions of the Executive, The
    (Barnard), 46
Fund for the City of New York, 111

G

Gaebler, T., 108–109
Gatens, Moira, 137, 138, 142, 143–144, 146, 147
Gawthrop, L.C., 6, 13, 15, 16, 17, 65, 77
Gender equality
  deep democracy and, 136–137, 145, 145–147
  mind/body dualism and, 137–138, 142, 143, 147
  minorities and, 161–162
  multicultural approach to, 134–136, 145
  multigendered democracy and, 143–144, 147
  in newly democratizing nations, 132, 143
  oppressive regimes and, 131, 132
  in organizational culture, 162–163
  proportional representation and, 131–132, 146
  psychoanalytic approach to, 139–142
  quotas and, 132, 138–139
General systems theory (GST), 52
Giddens, A., 59n1
Giving circles, 186–188
Glaser, M.A., 96
Glassner, B., 73
Golden age of organization theory, 51
Goldsmith, S., 56–57
Golembiewski, R.T., 54, 163
Goodenough, W., 152
Goodnow, Frank, 24
Gordon, P., 170
Gormley, W.T., Jr., 37
Governing by Network (Goldsmith and Eggers), 56–57
Governmental Standards and Accounting Board (GASB), 111
"Government by gentlemen," 4–5, 68
Government Performance and Results Act, 109
Grace, K.S., 185, 186
Grass Roots Ecosystem Management, 126
Great Depression, 6, 69, 196
Great Society, 77

Grewe, T., 93, 100
Griggs, L.B., 163
Grønbjerg, K.A., 170
Gross, R., 175
Groundwater Rule project, 124
Group identity, 152, 153–154, 161
"Group mind," 49
Guinier, Lani, 146
Gulick, L., 42–43
Gunderman, R.B., 188
Gunew, S., 153
Gurwitt, R., 91
Gutmann, A., 136, 154, 155–156

H

Habermas, Jürgen, 136, 154, 174
Hage, Jerald, 56
Hall, P.D., 170, 182
Halvorsen, K.E., 92
Hamill, Peter, 77
Hamilton, Alexander, 25, 55, 129
Hamilton, Mary R., xi–xii, 3–20, 214
Hammond, B.R., 200
Harding, S., 164
Harmon, M.M., 43, 46, 59n3
Harris, A., 140
Harris, D.A., 162
Hart, D.K., 10, 203
Hartmann, T., 22, 24
Harvard group, 47
Hassard, J., 165
Hatry, H.P., 96
Havens, J.J., 177
Hawkesworth, Mary, 133
Hayes, M., 29
Held, D., 172
Held, W.G., 31
Henderson, G., 163
Henderson, L.J., 45, 53
Herman, A., 177, 184
Heying, C., 79
Heyl, B., 45
Hill, Anita, 141
Hindera, J.J., 158, 159
Hirst, P., 174

Ho, Alfred, xii, 107–118, 108, 110, 111,
    113, 214
Hobbes, Thomas, 137
Hodgkinson, V.A., 177, 178, 179
Hofstadter, R., 41
Holohan, I., 120
hooks, b., 161, 162
Hopson, D.P., 163
Hopson, D.S., 163
Human relations movement, 45–47, 53–54
Human Side of Enterprise, The
    (McGregor), 60n4
Hummel, R., 163
Hutchinson, Janet R., xii, 131–149, 142,
    144, 214
Hutchinson, P., 78

I

Income inequality, 196–197
Independent Sector, 178, 179, 180
Individualism, 172, 175
Industrial democracy, 41
Industrial society, shift to, 41–42
Industrial technology, 41
Information gathering
  in budget participation, 95–96
  for social change, 204–205
Ingraham, P.W., 3, 5, 6
Ingram, H., 37
Initiatives, x, 74
Innes, J.E., 71
Intellectual Crisis in Public
    Administration, The (Ostrom), 55
Interest groups, 27, 122
Internal Revenue Service, 34, 37, 169
International Women's Congress, Eighth,
    142
Internet, 115, 122, 203
Irigiray, Luce, 142
Irvin, R.A., 207

J

Jabbra, J.G., 171
Jacksonian democracy, 5, 68–69
Jefferson, Thomas, ix, 22, 23, 25, 122

John, D., 125
Johnson, G.W., 91, 92, 94, 96
Jones, B., 70
Jones, B.D., 29
Jones, L.R., 99
Jones, M.M., 186
Joulfaian, D., 179
Jun, J.S., 162
Juster, R.J., 91, 92, 94, 96

K

Kahn, J., 91, 108
Kahn, P.W., 127
Kahn, R.L., 52
Kast, F.E., 52
Kathlene, L., 94
Katz, D., 52
Katz, M.B., 183
Kearny, R.J., 69
Kellner, 52
Kelly, J.M., 94
Kemmis, D., 125, 173, 185
Kensen, S., 80
Kernaghan, K., 157
Kerwin, C., 121
Kettl, D., 171
Kimball, R., 67
King, Cheryl Simrell, xii, 14, 64–83,
    71, 86, 92, 187, 203–204, 215
Kingdon, J.W., 29, 30
Kirlin, John, 8
Klein, Melanie, 139
Koenig, H., 33
Krane, Dale, xii, 21–39, 22, 23, 33,
    35, 215
Kravchuk, R.S., 10, 11
Krugman, P., 179, 196
Kweit, M.G., 79, 80, 93
Kweit, R.W., 79, 80, 93
Kymlicka, W., 134

L

Laissez-faire management, 49
Lakoff, S., 120
LaPorte, T.R., 53

Laudicina, E.V., 162
Lauth, T.P., 35
Law. *See* Administrative law
Lawrence, Paul, 52
LeBon, Gustave, 49
Legislative intent, 32
Lerner, R., 184
Leviathan (Hobbes), 137
Levitan, 16
Lewin, Kurt, 48–49, 59
Liberal-capitalist, representative
    democracy, viii, 40
Liberalism, classic, 67, 172–173
Light, P.C., 25
Lilith, 141
Lindblom, C., 94
Lipset, S.M., 16, 18
Listen to the City project, 76–77
Local government
    agency rulemaking/adjudication and,
        123–124, 126–129
    budget process in. *See* Budget
        participation
    citizen participation in, x, 72, 73–74
    institutional forms of, xi, 22–23
Locke, John, 23, 67, 120
Loges, W.E., 203
London, R., 171, 172
Long, Norton, 25
Longo, Christopher, 141
Lorber, J.L., 144
Lorsch, Jay, 52
Louw, L.L., 163
Lowi, T.J., 205–206
Lubove, R., 175
Lukensmeyer, C.J., 77, 79
Lun, N., 96
Lyotard, J.F., 165

M

Madison, James, 24, 25, 32, 55, 67, 129,
    135, 181
Management, defined, 40
Management-by-objectives (MBO), 108
Manager roles, 200–201
Mansbridge, J.J., 136

Marini, F., 77, 157
Markoff, John, 26
Mark up session, 30–31
Marlowe, J., 96
Marshall, Gary S., xii, 22, 23, 40–63, 58,
    187, 215
Marshall, J., 93, 99, 100
Martin, J.A., 94
Maslow, A., 54, 59–60n4
May, W.F., 181, 183
Mayer, R.T., 43, 46, 59n3
Mayo, Elton, 45–46, 53
Mayo, H., 32
Mayor-council model of local
    government, xi
Mazimanian, D., 32, 36
McConnell, G., 41
McCully, G., 185
McFarlane, D.R., 34
McGregor, D., 54, 60n4, 65
McGuire, M., 57
McIver, J.P., 102
McNair, R.H., 70
McSwite, O.C., 51, 77, 173, 187
Mead, Margaret, 49
Medicare Modernization Act of 2003,
    32–33
Meier, K.J., 34, 159
Melkers, J.E., 110
Men, Management and Morality
    (Golembieweski), 54
Menninger, R.W., 183
Methodological individualism, 55
Meyerson, H., 33
Mill, John Stuart, 76, 181
Miller, G.J., 99, 100
Miller, H., 80
Miller, M.A., 96
Miller, T.I., 96
Milward, H.B., 171
Mind/body dualism, 137–138, 142, 143,
    147
Minnowbrook conference, 156–157
Mladenka, K.R., 70
Mobilization, in network theory, 57
Modernity, 59n1, 175
Modern Times, 44

Montesquieu, 67
Moore, M., 74
Moreno, Jacob, 48
Morgan, G., 51
Morone, R., 69
Mosher, F.C., 3, 4–5, 6–7, 8, 11, 12,
    13–14, 17, 42, 68
Multiculturalism
    defined, 151, 152–156
    gender and, 134–136, 145
    organizational, 162
    representative bureaucracy and,
        156–163
Multigendering, 143–144, 147
Musso, J.A., 203

N

Nabatchi, T., 97, 127, 128
Nagai, A., 184
Nagel, T., 134
National Association of Schools of Public
    Affairs and Administration
    (NASPAA), 123
National League of Cities, 124
National Performance Review, 109
National Training Laboratories (NTL), 49
Natural rights theory, 120
Needs, hierarchy of, 54, 59–60n4
Network models of organization, 56–58
Neuhaus, R.J., 174, 175
New Deal, 6, 69
New Public Administration movement,
    53, 77, 78, 156–157, 199–200
Newton, K., 174
New York Bureau of Municipal Research,
    42, 108
Ni, A., 108
Nielsen, W.A., 182
Nienaber, J., 36
Nigro, L.G., 8
Nonprofit organizations
    accountability of, 171–172, 182–183
    defined, 169–170
    modernization of, 175–176
    in policy community, 28

Nonprofit organizations *(continued)*
    resource allocation, 176–177
    revenue of, 178–180
    short-term focus of, 180–181
    social services provided by, 170–171,
        175
    See also Philanthropy
Norman, W., 134
"Notes on the Theory of Organization"
    (Gulick), 43

O

Oakes, Uriah, 141
Odendahl, T., 177, 183
Offe, 174
Okin, S.M., 134
Olasky, M., 170
O'Leary, R., 97, 127, 128
Omaha (Nebraska), budget process in,
    89–91
Organizational America (Scott and Hart),
    203
Organizational culture, 162–163
Organizational multiculturalism, 162
Organizations, defined, 40
Organizations Working Together (Alter
    and Hage), 56
Organization theory
    of Follett, 47–48
    golden age of, 51
    of human relations movement, 45–47,
        53–54
    of Lewin, 48–49
    network model of, 56–58
    organizational humanism, 54
    public choice, 55–56
    rational model of, 50–51, 54
    scientific management, 43–45
    systems approach to, 51–53
    value-neutral approach to, 53
Orosz, J.F., 93
Osborne, D., 78, 108–109
Ostrander, S.A., 177, 181
Ostrom, E., 55, 102
Ostrom, Vincent, 3, 54–55

Ostrower, F., 178
O'Toole, D.E., 93, 99, 100
Ott, S.O., 45
Overhead democracy, 40–41
Oztas, N., 203

P

Paine, Thomas, 67
Pal, L.A., 161, 165
Papers on the Science of Administration
    (Gulick and Urwick), 42–43
Pareto, Vifredo, 45
Parker, M., 165
Parliamentary model, 22
Parsons, T., 51
Passey, A., 173
Passive representation, 158–159, 160–161
Pateman, Carol, 133, 134
Paulson, A., 186
Pendelton Act of 1883, 5
Performance measurement
    accountability and, 75, 109, 110
    benefits of, 109–110
    citizen participation in, 110–116
    clientele for, 107
    defined, 108
    development of, 108–109
Perkins, J., 162
Personality and Organization (Argyris), 54
Philanthropy
    benefits to democracy, 173–175
    decline in, 178–179
    democratization of, 184–185
    elite control and, 182–183
    giving circles, 186–188
    motivation for, 181–182
    new era in, 185–186, 188
    rate of, 178
    resource allocation, 175–178
    short-term focus of, 180–181
    "us versus them" mentality in, 183
    See also Nonprofit organizations
Phronesis, 76
Planning-programming-budgeting system
    (PPBS), 108

Plato, 67
Pluralistic integration, 155, 156
Policy community, 28–29
Policy implementation
    agency personnel choices in, 34–35
    constraints on, 34
    diverse interests in, 31–32
    funding in, 33–34
    policy design and, 32–33
    political context and, 35–36
Policymaking
    agenda-setting in, 28–30
    bureaucratic, 24–26, 36–37
    information-gathering process, 163–164
    policy design and, 30–31
    problem identification in, 26–27
    purposes of, 23–24
Policy tools, 30, 37
Politics-administration relationship, ix,
    65–66, 199, 205
Popovich, M., 78
Poppendieck, J., 170, 180, 181, 182,
    183
Popular sovereignty, 37, 172
Portney, K.E., 74
POSDCORB (Planning, Organizing,
    Staffing, Directing, COrdinating,
    Reporting, and Budgeting), 43
Posner, P.L., 37
Postmodernism, 165, 198
Preble, G., 74
Preuss, 174
Price, D.K., 3
Principles of Scientific Management
    (Taylor), 44
Problem identification, 26–27
Procedural democracy, x
Professional associations, policymaking
    role of, 27
Progressive movement, 69–70
Proportional representation, 131–132,
    146, 160
"Proverbs of Administration, The"
    (Simon), 50
Public Administration Review, 53
Public choice theories, 55–56, 112

Public hearings, in budget process, 90–91, 93, 96
Public interest, 16, 86–87
Public opinion
agenda setting and, 29
policy implementation and, 36
Public organization theory. *See* Organization theory
Public participation. *See* Citizen participation
Putnam, R.D., 71, 174–175, 176, 184, 185

Q

Quotas, women's representation and, 132, 138–139

R

Rational model of organization, 50–51, 54
Rawls, J., 134
Reagan, Ronald, 179
Redford, E.S., 41, 59n2
Reed, B.J., 58, 187
Reed, Christine M., xii, 58, 119–130, 187, 215
Referendums, x, 74
Rehnquist, William, 119
Reich, R.B., 136
Reinventing Government (Osborne and Gaebler), 108–109
Reinventing Government movement, 170
Reitan, T.C., 56
Representative bureaucracy, 156–163
Representative democracy, x, 21
Republicanism
civic, 120–121, 122, 129
classical, 173
Response cards, 113–114
Results-oriented government, 109
Results That Matter (Epstein, Coates, and Wray), 111
Rich, A., 162–163
Richardson, W.D., 8

Riggs, F., 157–158, 160
Rimmerman, C.A., 70, 74
Robbins, M.D., 92, 94, 98
Roberts, N., 79, 80, 92, 97, 101
Roelofs, J., 182
Roethlisberger, 45, 53–54
Rogers, J., 174, 181
Rohr, J.A., 3
Rom, M.C., 170
Roosevelt administration, 6, 69
Rosemount (Minnesota), budget participation in, 96–97
Rosenbloom, D., 205, 206
Rosenbloom, D.H., 3, 5, 6, 9–11, 120, 121
Rosener, J.B., 94
Rosenzweig, J.E., 52
Rothman, S., 184
Rouse, J., 3, 10, 11
Rousseau, Jean Jacques, 23, 181
Rubin, I.S., 91, 99, 103
Rulemaking, democratic practice in, 122–124
Russell, E.W., 10, 24

S

Sabatier, P., 32
Said, Edward, 152, 156
Salamon, L.M., 170, 171, 175, 178, 179, 180
Salée, Daniel, 154–155
Sandel, M.J., 173, 174, 185
Sargentich, T.O., 124
Sartori, G., 22
Schacter, H.L., 86, 163
Schaefer, P., 94
Schattschneider, E.E., 28, 89
Schervish, P.G., 177, 184
Schlesinger, Arthur, 194
Schlozman, K.L., 104, 174
Schneider, A.L., 37
Schweitzer, C., 186
Scientific management, 5, 6, 43–45
SCOPe project, 124, 128
Scott, W.G., 203

Seidenfeld, M., 121, 125, 127
Separation of powers, x–xi, 22, 87, 120
Service effort and accomplishments (SEA), 111
Sex education programs, 34
Shafritz, J.M., 10, 24, 45
Shohat, E., 156, 165
Siegel, D., 157
Silverman, D., 44
Silverstein, L.B., 146
Simon, Herbert A., 50–51, 52
Simonsen, W., 92, 94, 98
Sinha, C., 69
Sinipoli, R.C., 195
Skocpol, T., 174, 175, 176, 180
Skowronek, S., 68
Small Business Regulatory Enforcement Fairness Act (SBREFA), 123
Smith, S., 90, 93, 96
Smith, S.R., 37, 179
Snitow, A., 140
Social Contract (Rousseau), 181
Social equity in public administration, 194–196
  categories of actions, 203–208
  role typology and, 199–201
  societal constraints on, 202–203
  societal context for, 196–199
Social inequality, measures of, 196–197
Social process, in organization theory, 47–48
Social Psychology of Organizations, The (Katz and Kahn), 52
Sociometric methods, 48
Sørensen, E., 57–58
Spinner, Jeff, 155, 156, 161
Spinoza, Benjamin de, 142, 147
Spivak, G.C., 153
Spoils system, 5
Staeheli, L.A., 185
Stam, R., 156, 165
Standpoint epistemology, 164
Stansbury, J., 207
Steuerle, C.E., 178, 179
Steuernagel, G.A., 134
Stewart, T.R., 70

Stillman, R.J. II, 3, 5, 25, 36, 129
Stivers, C., 14, 66, 70, 86, 92, 138, 187
Stoller, Robert, 143
Streisand, B., 185
"Study of Administration, The" (Wilson), 69
Substantive democracy, x
Suleiman, Ezra, 8-9
Surveys, citizen, 96, 113–114
Susel, B.O., 71, 86, 92
Sustainable Seattle Group, 111
Swain, D., 79

T

Tabarrok, A., 170
Taft Commission on Economy and Efficiency, 42
Tax policy
  budget participation and, 88–89, 103
  charitable giving and, 179
Tax referendum, 91
Taylor, Frederick, 43–44, 48
T-Groups, 49
Theory X and Theory Y, 54, 60–61n4
Thomas, Clarence, 160
Thomas, J.C., 70, 77, 86, 94, 96, 97, 99
Thompson, D., 136
Thompson, F., 99
Thompson, J.D., 52
Thompson, V.A., 157, 158, 205
Thoreau, Henry David, 181
Timney, M., 70
Title IX, 134
Tocqueville, Alexis de, 7, 67, 68, 76, 173–174, 176
Tonkiss, F., 173
Topeka (Kansas), budget participation in, 93
Torfing, J., 57–58
Toubia, Nahid, 147
Town meeting model of local government, xi
Transformational Public Service (King and Zanetti), 203–204
Tullock, Gordon, 55

U

Uganda, women's rights in, 132, 135, 139
United Way, 179
Urwick, L., 42–43

V

Van Horn, C.E., 35
Van Meter, D.S., 35
Van Til, J., 176
Verba, S., 104, 174
Voluntary organizations, 170, 174–175, 176
  See also Nonprofit organizations

W

Wagner, D., 183
Waldo, Dwight, 9, 10, 51, 65
Wamsley, G.L., 200
Wang, X., 72, 91, 93, 100
Warren, M.E., 174, 181
Washington, George, 7
Washington State, citizen participation in, 74–75
Watergate scandal, 6
Water safety standards, 84
Watson, D.J., 91, 92, 94, 96
Wayne, S.J., 22
Wealth inequality, 196–197
Weare, C., 203
Webb, K.W., 96
Weber, E.P., 125, 126
Weber, M., 43
Weeks, E.C., 136
Weisberg, J., 33
Weisbord, M., 49, 60n4
Weitzman, M.S., 179
Welfare reform, "charitable choice"
  amendment in, 170

Wendroff, A.L., 185, 186
West, C., 154
White, Orion, 52n2
Whittington, K.E., 182
Wichita (Kansas), budget participation in, 98
Wiebe, R., 68
Wiebe, R.H., 41
Williamson, Oliver, 56
Willoughby, K.G., 110
Wilson, Woodrow, 24, 55, 69, 199
Wolch, J.R., 172
Woll, P., 41, 42
Wolpert, J., 177, 178, 179, 180
Women's Business Ownership Assistance
  (WBOA) program, 30
Women's rights. *See* Gender equality
Women's suffrage movement, 134
Wood, G.S., 195
Woodhouse, E., 94
Work, organization of, 43–44
Workplace democracy, 41, 49
World Conference on Women, Fourth, 138
Wray, L.D., 79, 111

Y

Yang, K., 72, 81
Yates, Andrea, 141
Yates, D., 24
Yeatman, A., 162, 164, 165
Young, C.D., 158, 159
Young, I.M., 136, 139, 145–146, 154, 159, 160

Z

Zanetti, L.A., 203–204
Zero-base budgeting (ZBB), 108